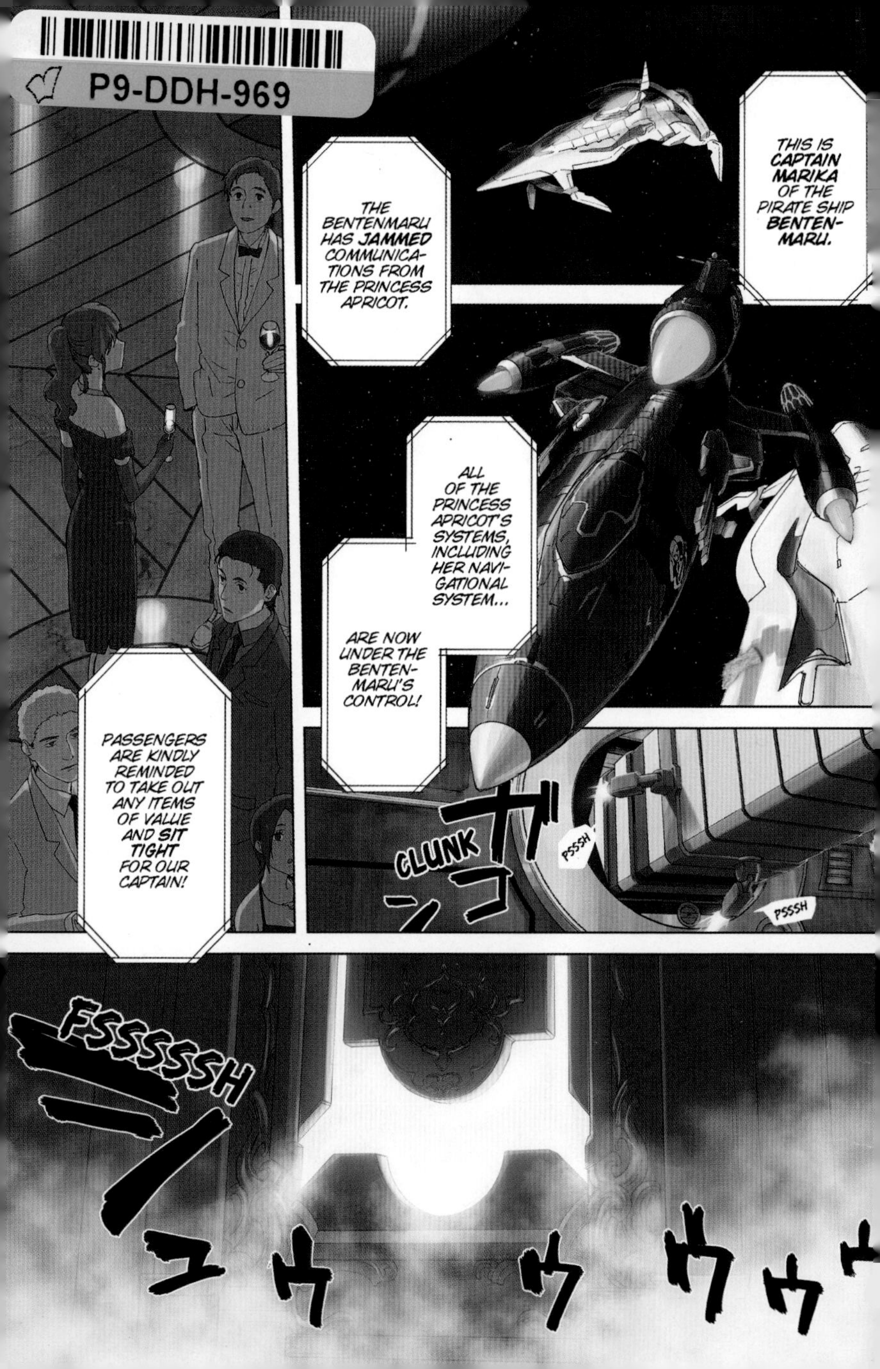
THIS IS CAPTAIN MARIKA OF THE PIRATE SHIP BENTEN-MARU.
THE BENTENMARU HAS JAMMED COMMUNICA-TIONS FROM THE PRINCESS APRICOT.
ALL OF THE PRINCESS APRICOT'S SYSTEMS, INCLUDING HER NAVI-GATIONAL SYSTEM...
ARE NOW UNDER THE BENTEN-MARU'S CONTROL!
CLUNK
PSSSH
PSSSH
PASSENGERS ARE KINDLY REMINDED TO TAKE OUT ANY ITEMS OF VALUE AND SIT TIGHT FOR OUR CAPTAIN!
FSSSSSSH

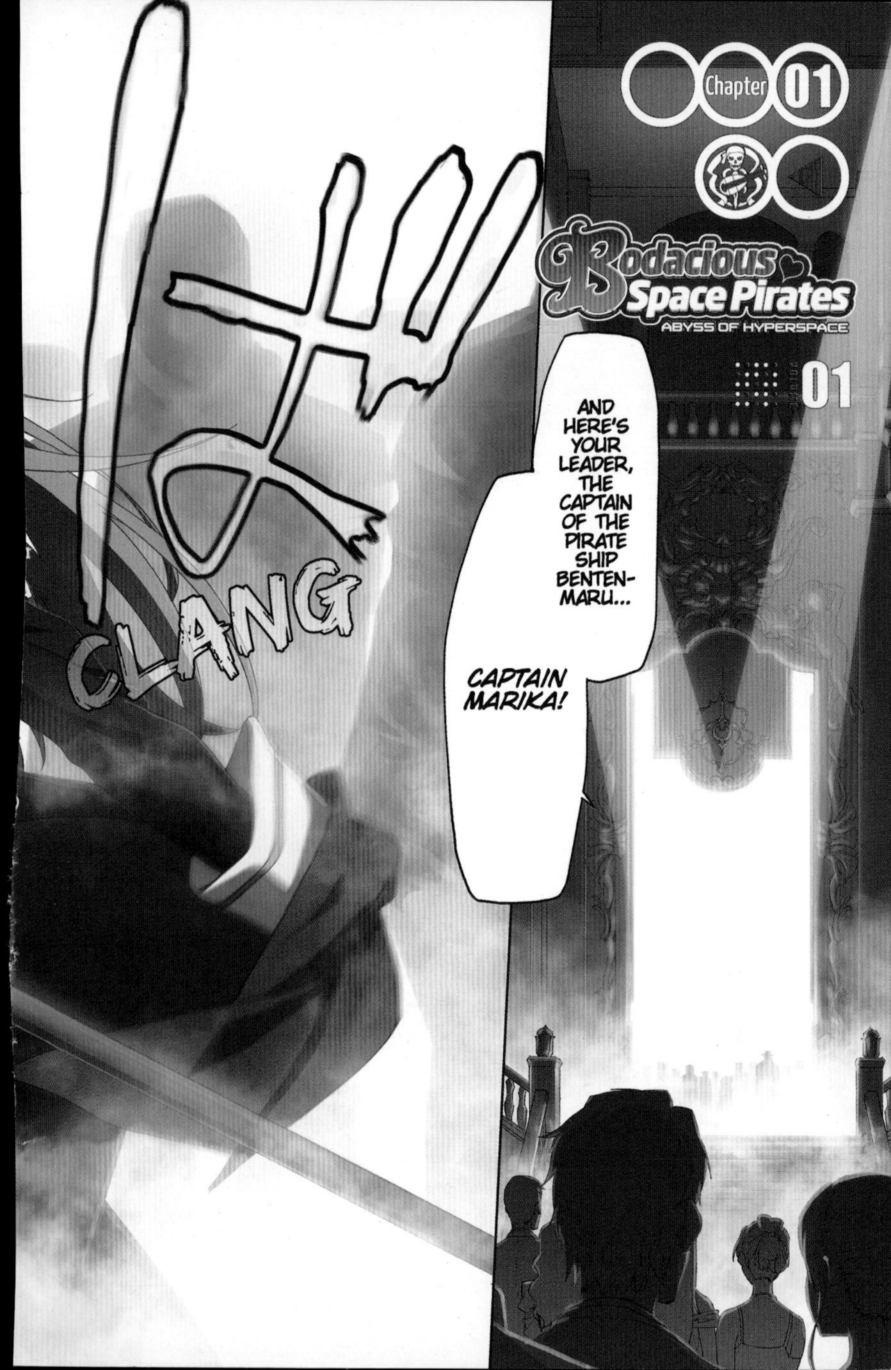
Chapter 01
Bodacious Space Pirates
ABYSS OF HYPERSPACE
01
AND HERE'S YOUR LEADER, THE CAPTAIN OF THE PIRATE SHIP BENTEN-MARU...
CAPTAIN MARIKA!
CLANG

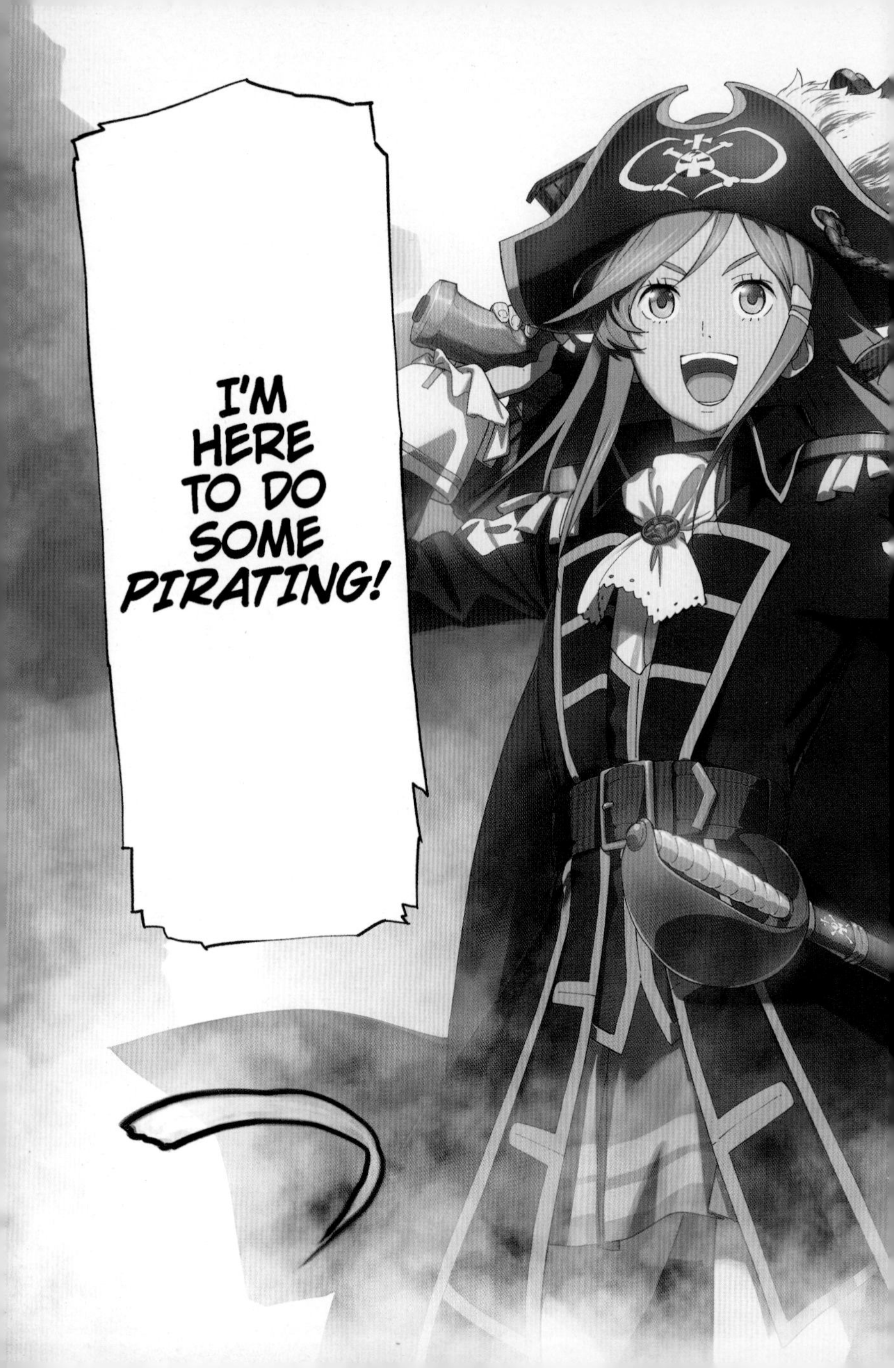
I'M HERE TO DO SOME *PIRATING!*

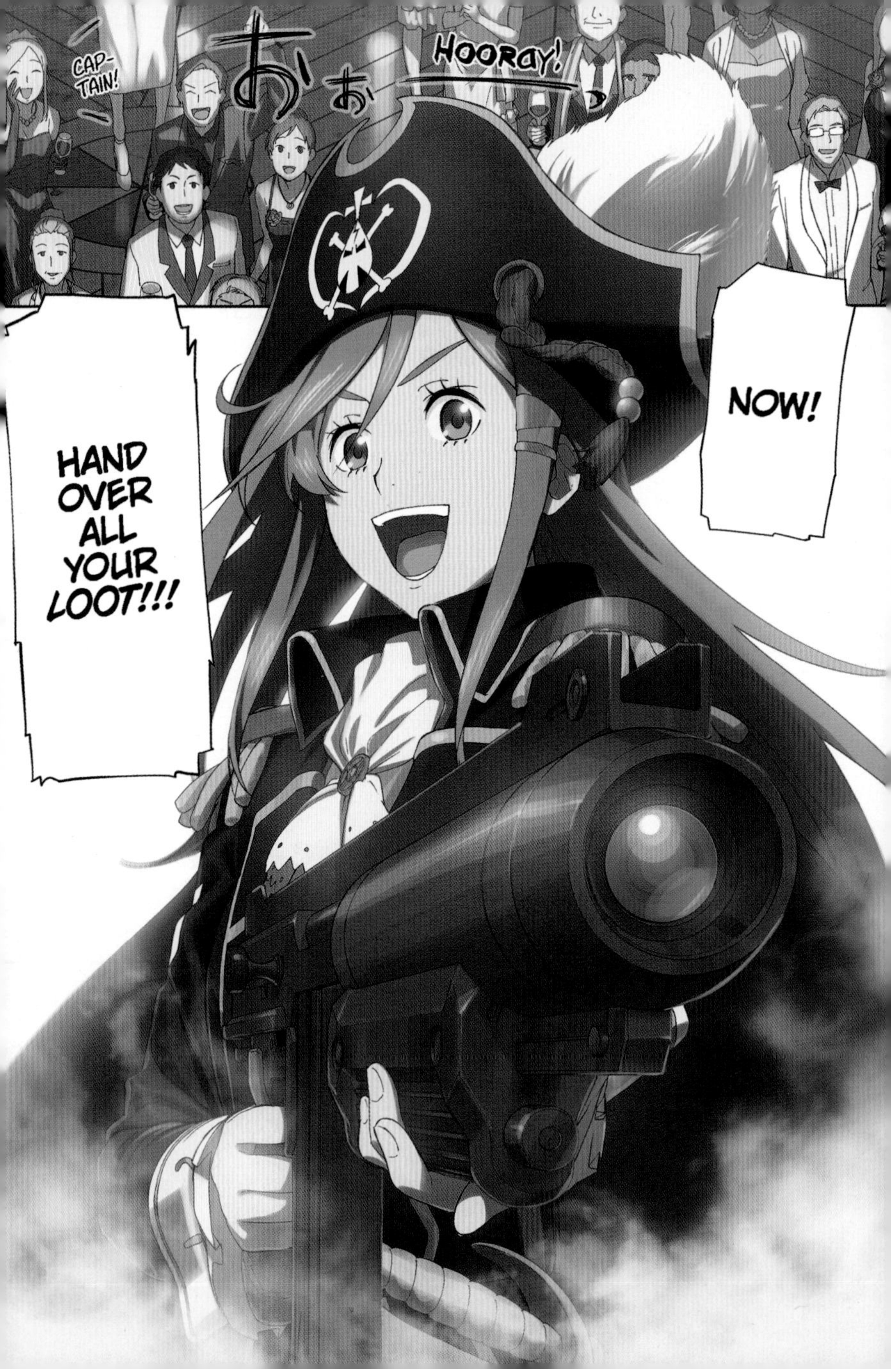
HOORAY!
おぉ
CAP-TAIN!
NOW!
HAND OVER ALL YOUR LOOT!!!

VOLUME 01

BODACIOUS SPACE PIRATES

[THE MOVIE]

ABYSS OF HYPERSPACE

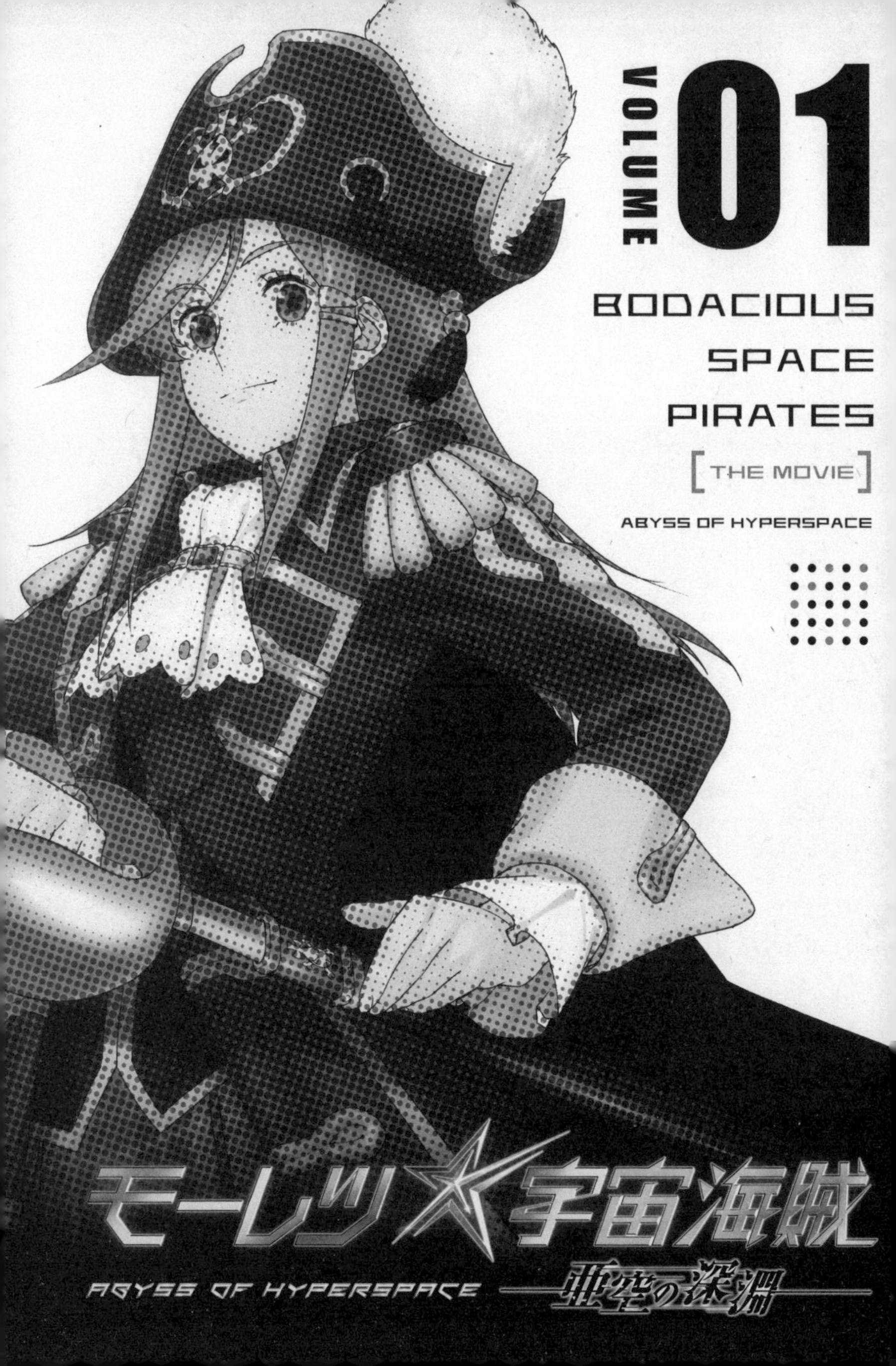
モーレツ★宇宙海賊
ABYSS OF HYPERSPACE
亜空の深淵

SEVEN SEAS ENTERTAINMENT PRESENTS

Bodacious Space Pirates
ABYSS OF HYPERSPACE   VOL. 1

art: CHIBIMARU / script: TATSUO SATO / plot: BODACIOUS SPACE PIRATES MOVIE
PRODUCTION COMMITTEE / original concept: YUICHI SASAMOTO / character design: AKIMAN

TRANSLATION
Ryan Peterson

ADAPTATION
Janet Houck

LETTERING AND LAYOUT
Alexandra Gunawan

COVER DESIGN
Nicky Lim

PROOFREADER
Danielle King

ASSISTANT EDITOR
Lissa Pattillo

MANAGING EDITOR
Adam Arnold

PUBLISHER
Jason DeAngelis

ISBN: 978-1-626921-95-5
Printed in Canada
First Printing: August 2015
10 9 8 7 6 5 4 3 2 1

FOLLOW US ONLINE: *www.gomanga.com*

READING DIRECTIONS

The manga prelude and epilogue sections that
bookend this light novel read from right to left,
Japanese style. If this is your first time reading
manga, you start reading from the top right panel on
each page and take it from there. If you get lost, just
follow the numbered diagram here. Enjoy!!

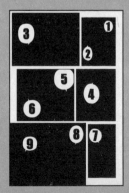

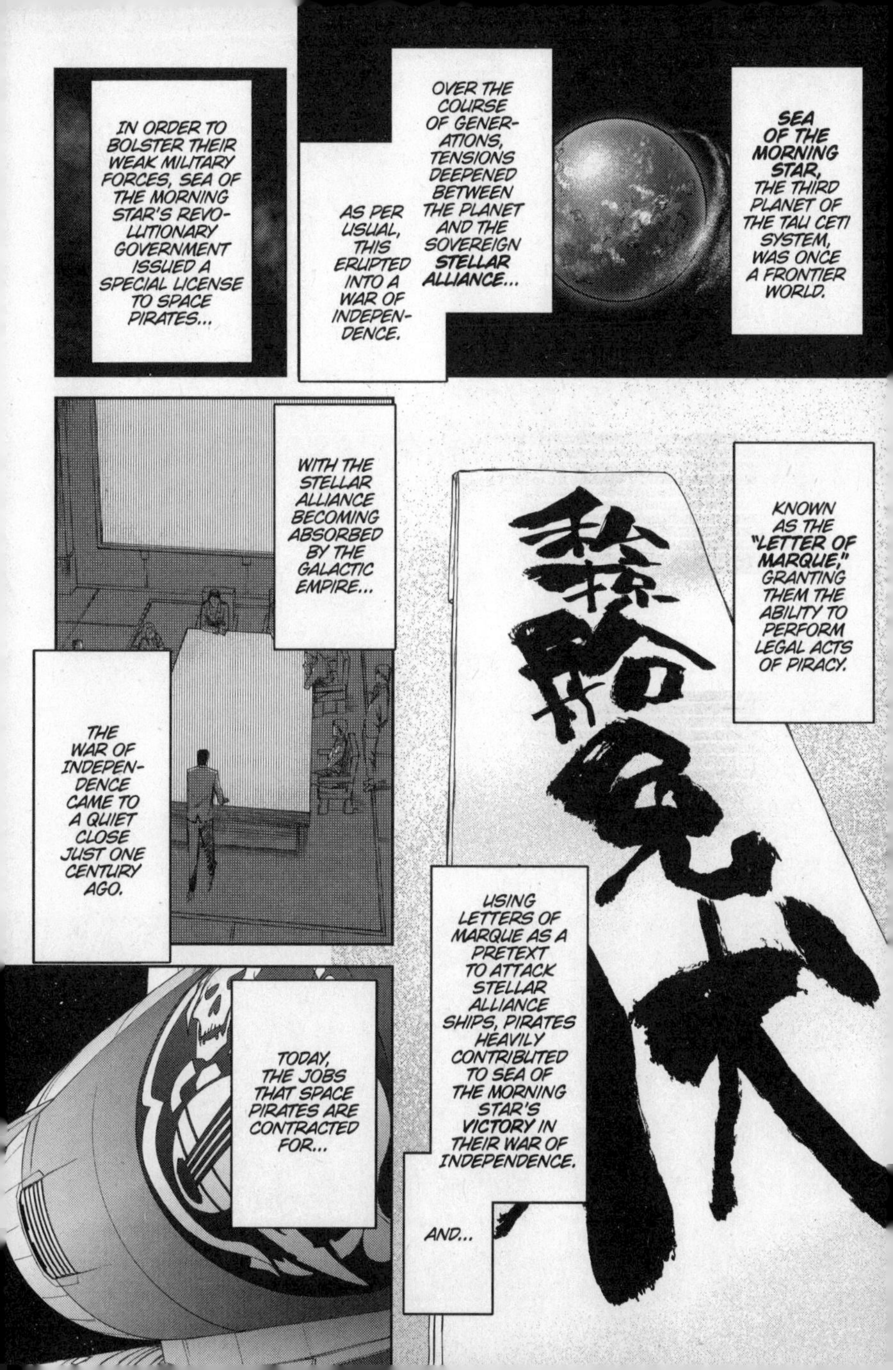
SEA OF THE MORNING STAR, THE THIRD PLANET OF THE TAU CETI SYSTEM, WAS ONCE A FRONTIER WORLD.
OVER THE COURSE OF GENERATIONS, TENSIONS DEEPENED BETWEEN THE PLANET AND THE SOVEREIGN STELLAR ALLIANCE...
AS PER USUAL, THIS ERUPTED INTO A WAR OF INDEPENDENCE.
IN ORDER TO BOLSTER THEIR WEAK MILITARY FORCES, SEA OF THE MORNING STAR'S REVOLUTIONARY GOVERNMENT ISSUED A SPECIAL LICENSE TO SPACE PIRATES...
KNOWN AS THE "LETTER OF MARQUE," GRANTING THEM THE ABILITY TO PERFORM LEGAL ACTS OF PIRACY.
USING LETTERS OF MARQUE AS A PRETEXT TO ATTACK STELLAR ALLIANCE SHIPS, PIRATES HEAVILY CONTRIBUTED TO SEA OF THE MORNING STAR'S VICTORY IN THEIR WAR OF INDEPENDENCE.
WITH THE STELLAR ALLIANCE BECOMING ABSORBED BY THE GALACTIC EMPIRE...
THE WAR OF INDEPENDENCE CAME TO A QUIET CLOSE JUST ONE CENTURY AGO.
TODAY, THE JOBS THAT SPACE PIRATES ARE CONTRACTED FOR...
AND...

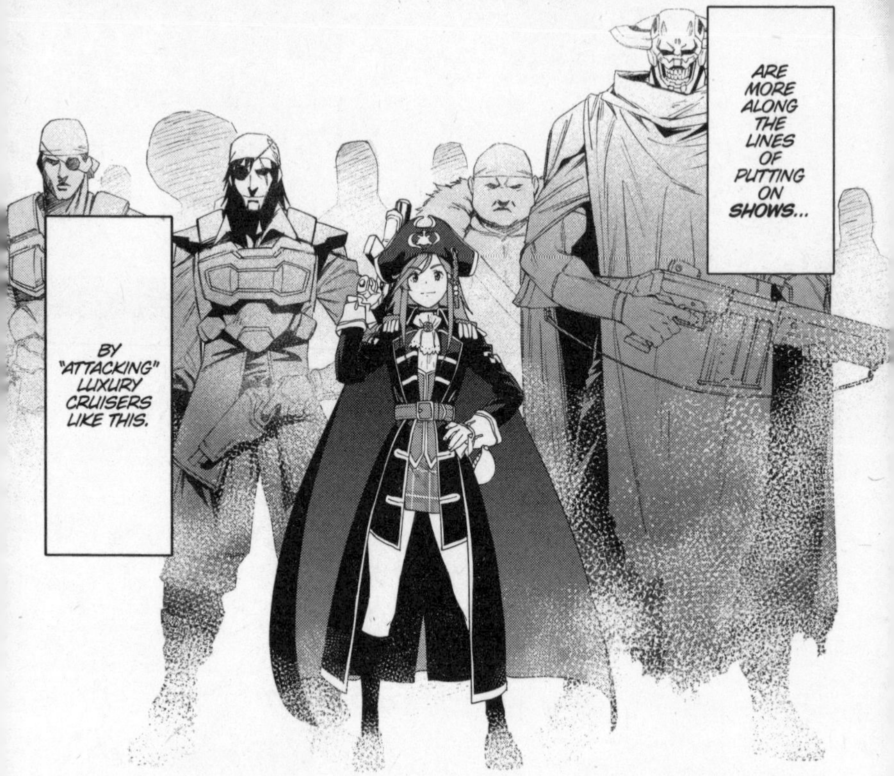
ARE MORE ALONG THE LINES OF PUTTING ON SHOWS...
BY "ATTACKING" LUXURY CRUISERS LIKE THIS.
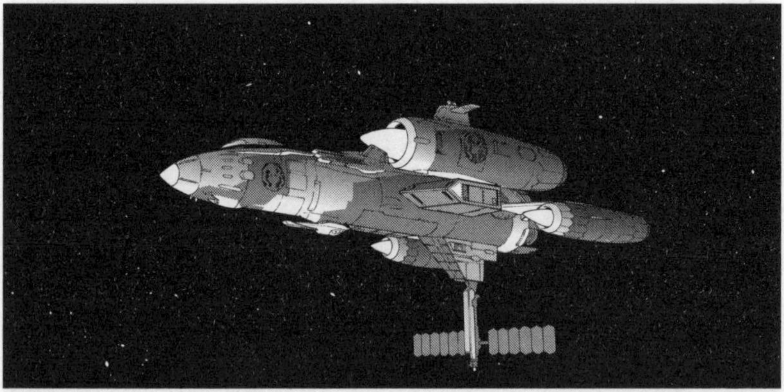

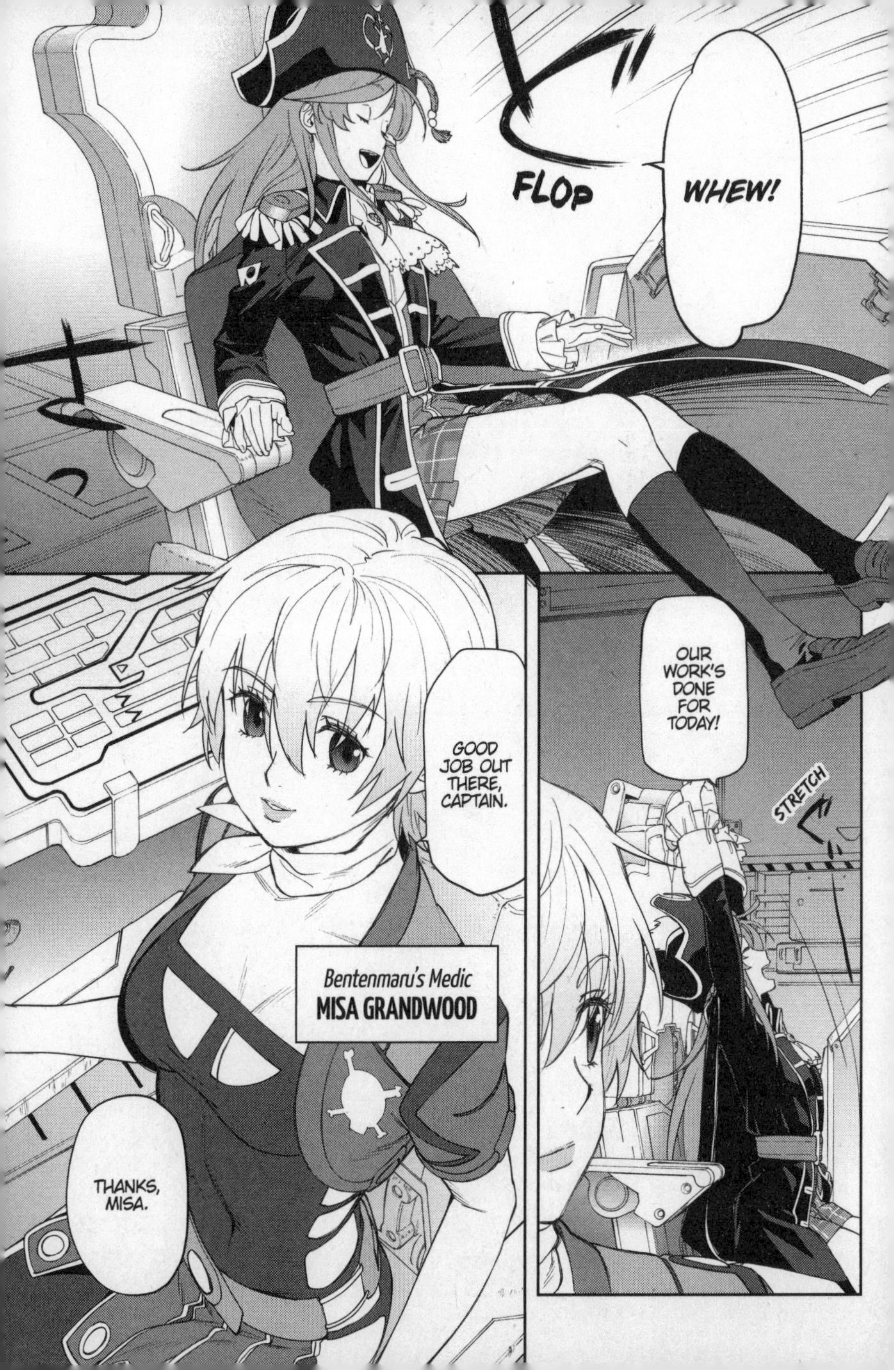
WHEW!
FLOP
OUR WORK'S DONE FOR TODAY!
STRETCH
GOOD JOB OUT THERE, CAPTAIN.
Bentenmaru's Medic
MISA GRANDWOOD
THANKS, MISA.

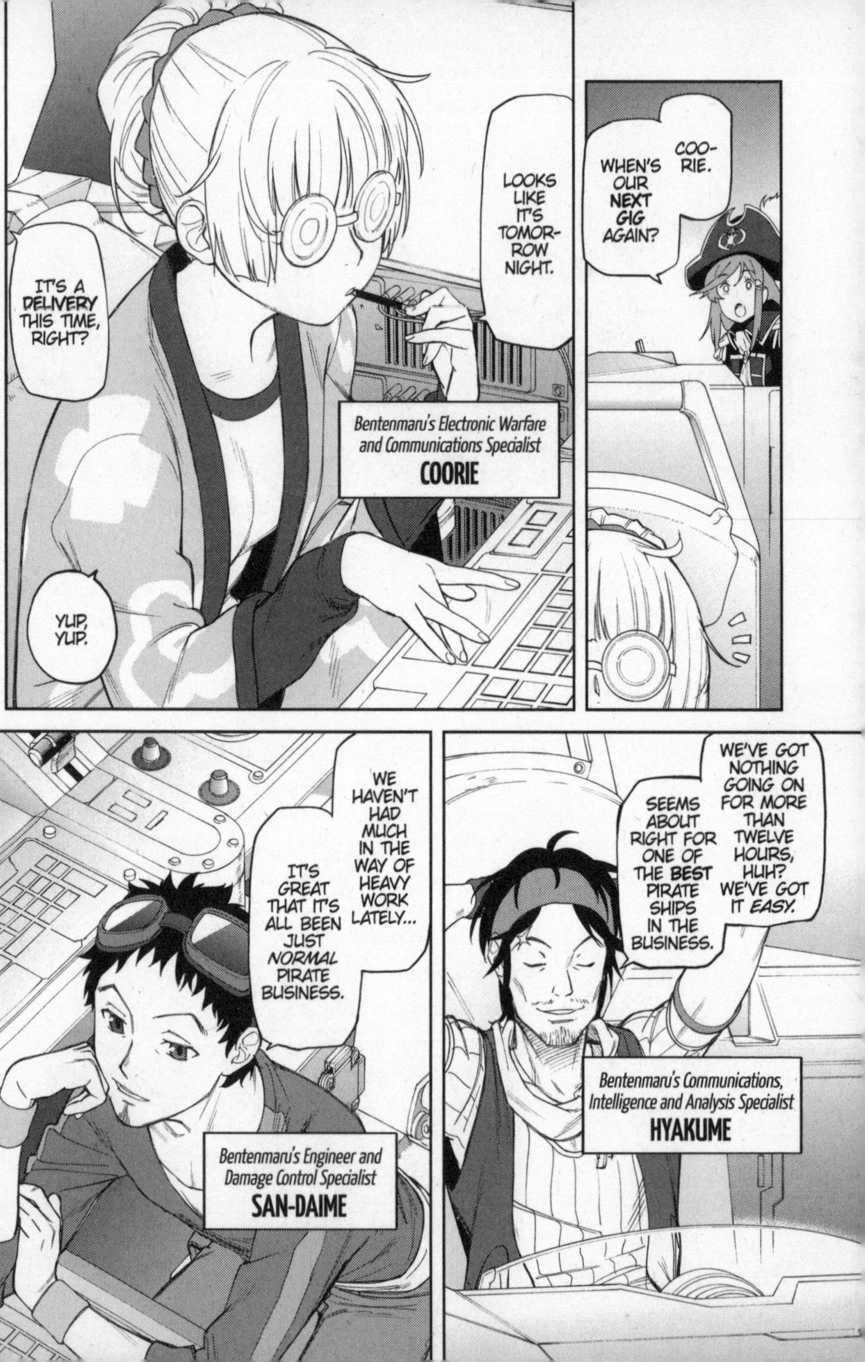
COO-RIE.
WHEN'S OUR **NEXT GIG** AGAIN?
LOOKS LIKE IT'S TOMORROW NIGHT.
IT'S A **DELIVERY** THIS TIME, RIGHT?
Bentenmaru's Electronic Warfare and Communications Specialist
COORIE
YUP, YUP.
WE'VE GOT NOTHING GOING ON FOR MORE THAN TWELVE HOURS, HUH? WE'VE GOT IT *EASY.*
SEEMS ABOUT RIGHT FOR ONE OF THE **BEST** PIRATE SHIPS IN THE BUSINESS.
Bentenmaru's Communications, Intelligence and Analysis Specialist
HYAKUME
WE HAVEN'T HAD MUCH IN THE WAY OF HEAVY WORK LATELY...
IT'S GREAT THAT IT'S ALL BEEN JUST *NORMAL* PIRATE BUSINESS.
Bentenmaru's Engineer and Damage Control Specialist
SAN-DAIME

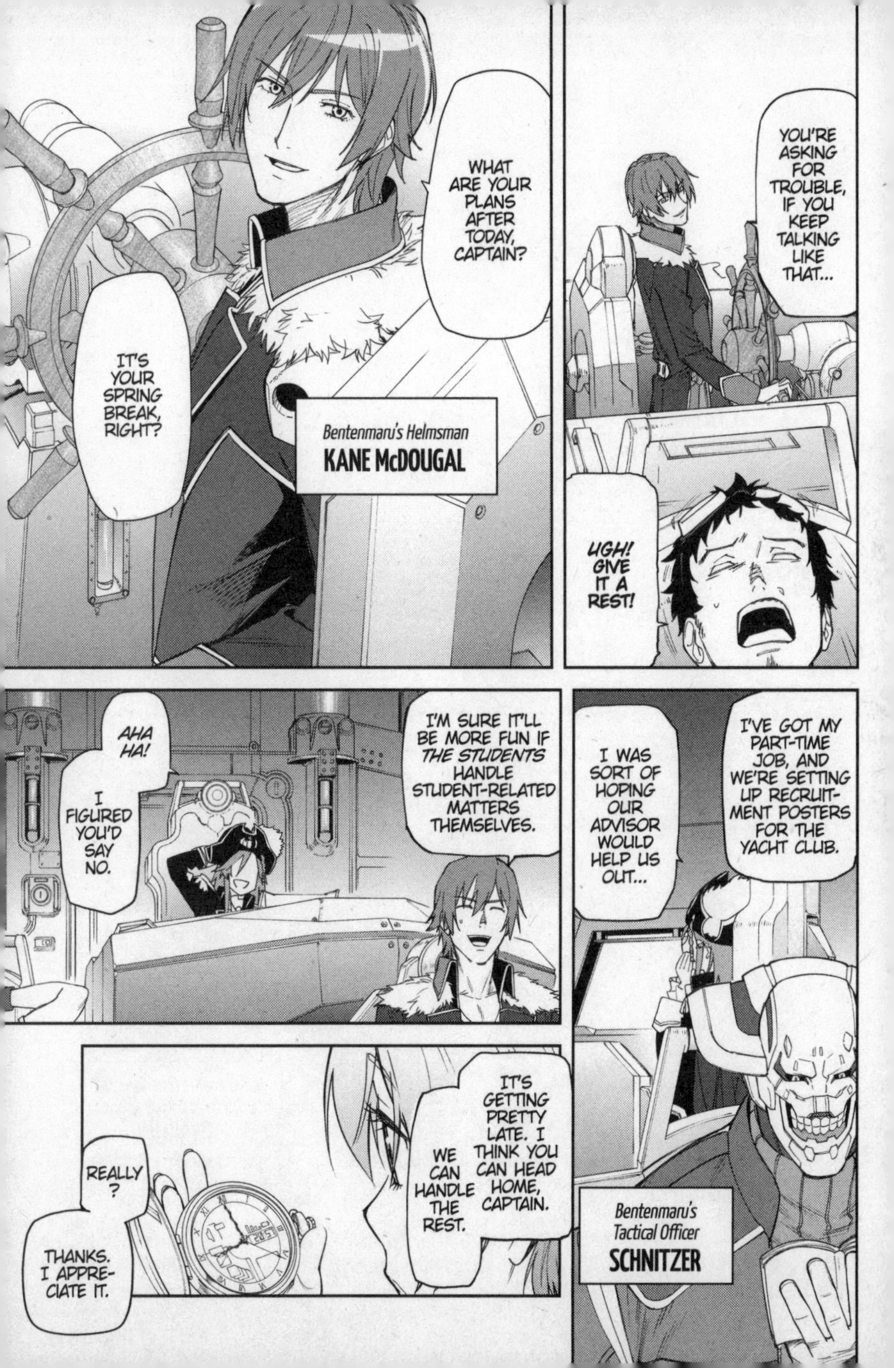

YOU'RE ASKING FOR TROUBLE, IF YOU KEEP TALKING LIKE THAT...
UGH! GIVE IT A REST!
WHAT ARE YOUR PLANS AFTER TODAY, CAPTAIN?
IT'S YOUR SPRING BREAK, RIGHT?
Bentenmaru's Helmsman
KANE McDOUGAL
I'VE GOT MY PART-TIME JOB, AND WE'RE SETTING UP RECRUIT-MENT POSTERS FOR THE YACHT CLUB.
I WAS SORT OF HOPING OUR ADVISOR WOULD HELP US OUT...
Bentenmaru's Tactical Officer
SCHNITZER
I'M SURE IT'LL BE MORE FUN IF *THE STUDENTS* HANDLE STUDENT-RELATED MATTERS THEMSELVES.
AHA HA!
I FIGURED YOU'D SAY NO.
IT'S GETTING PRETTY LATE. I THINK YOU CAN HEAD HOME, CAPTAIN.
WE CAN HANDLE THE REST.
REALLY?
THANKS. I APPRECIATE IT.

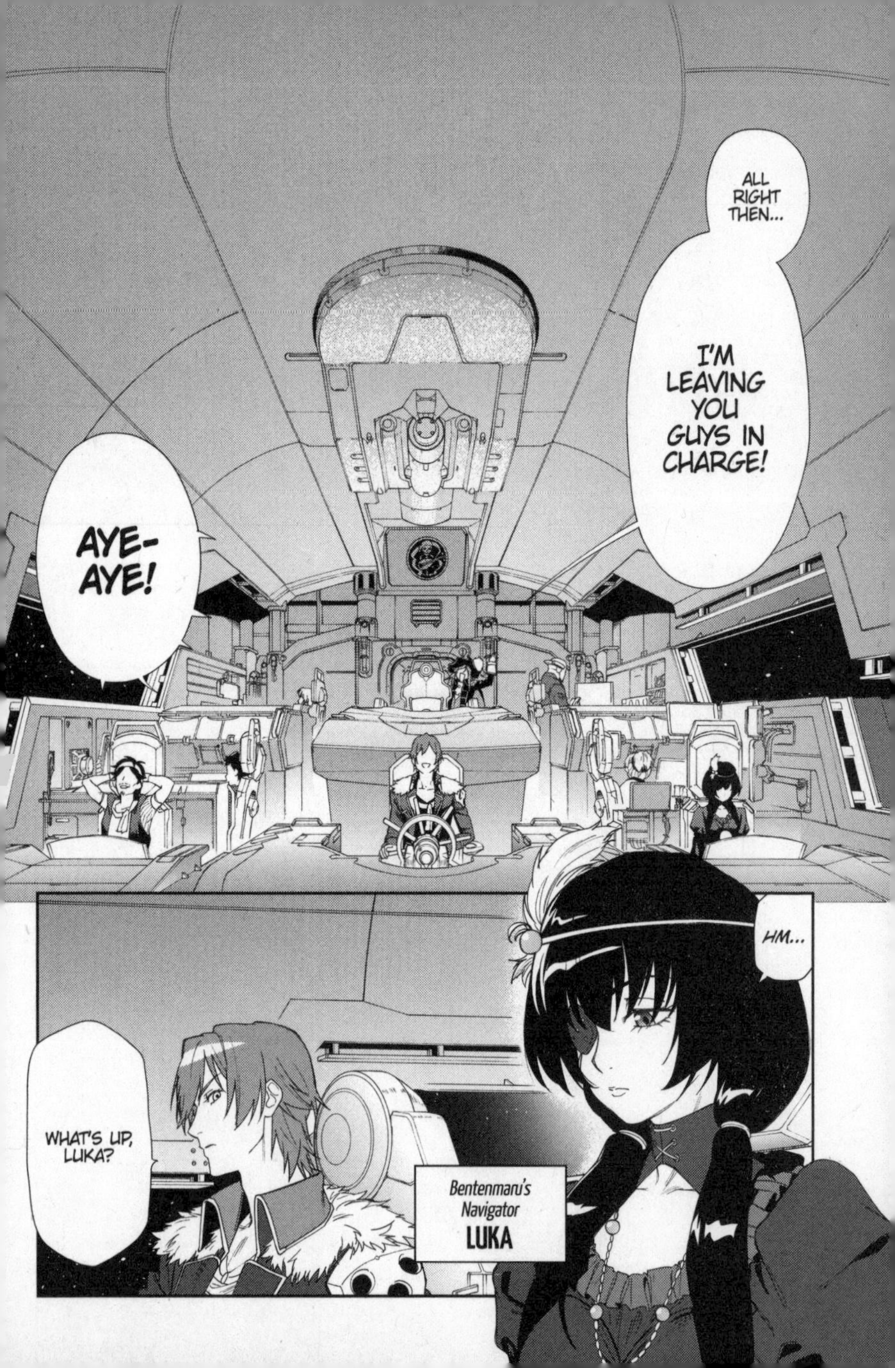
ALL RIGHT THEN...
I'M LEAVING YOU GUYS IN CHARGE!
AYE-AYE!
HM...
Bentenmaru's Navigator LUKA
WHAT'S UP, LUKA?

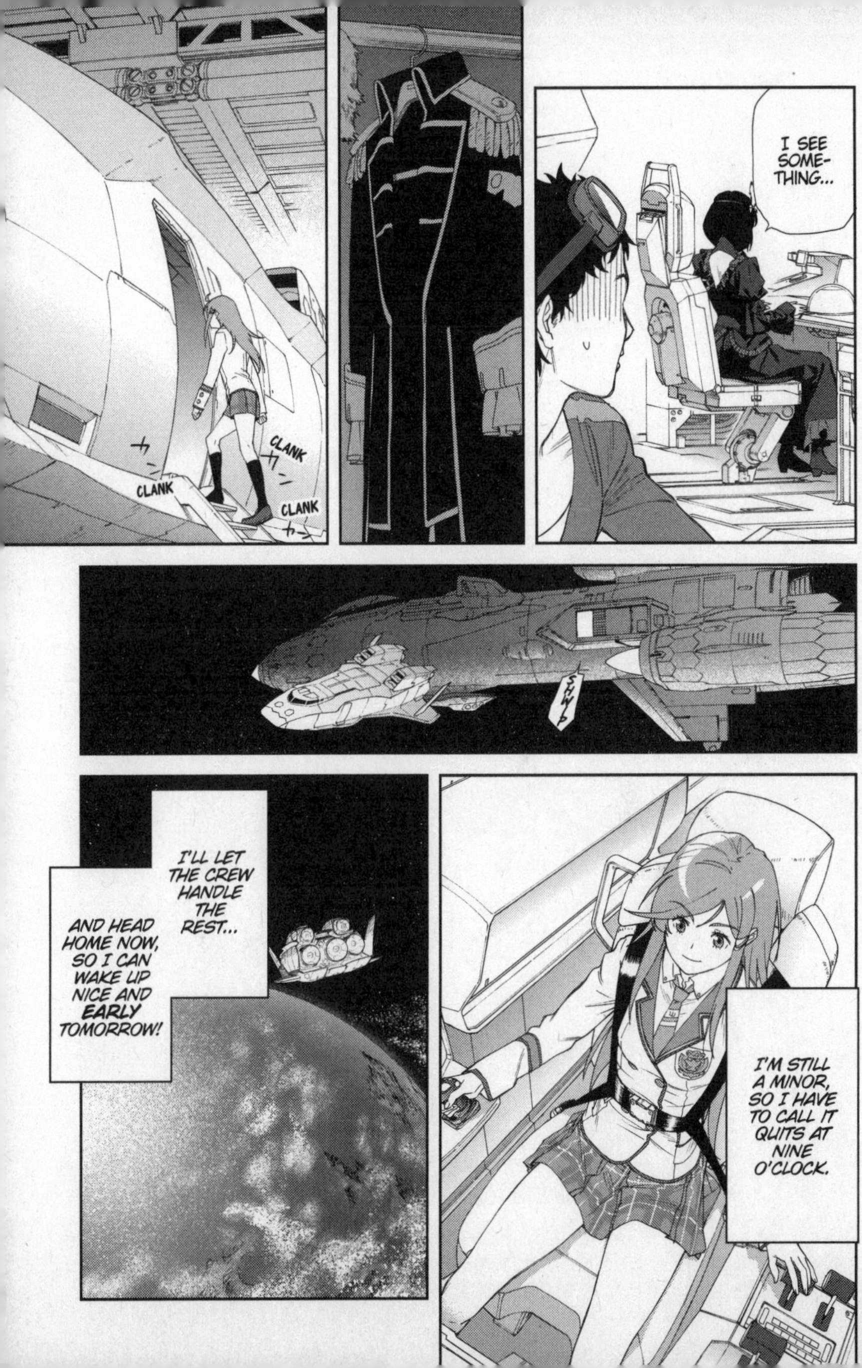
I SEE SOMETHING...
CLANK
CLANK
CLANK
SHWIP
I'M STILL A MINOR, SO I HAVE TO CALL IT QUITS AT NINE O'CLOCK.
I'LL LET THE CREW HANDLE THE REST...
AND HEAD HOME NOW, SO I CAN WAKE UP NICE AND EARLY TOMORROW!

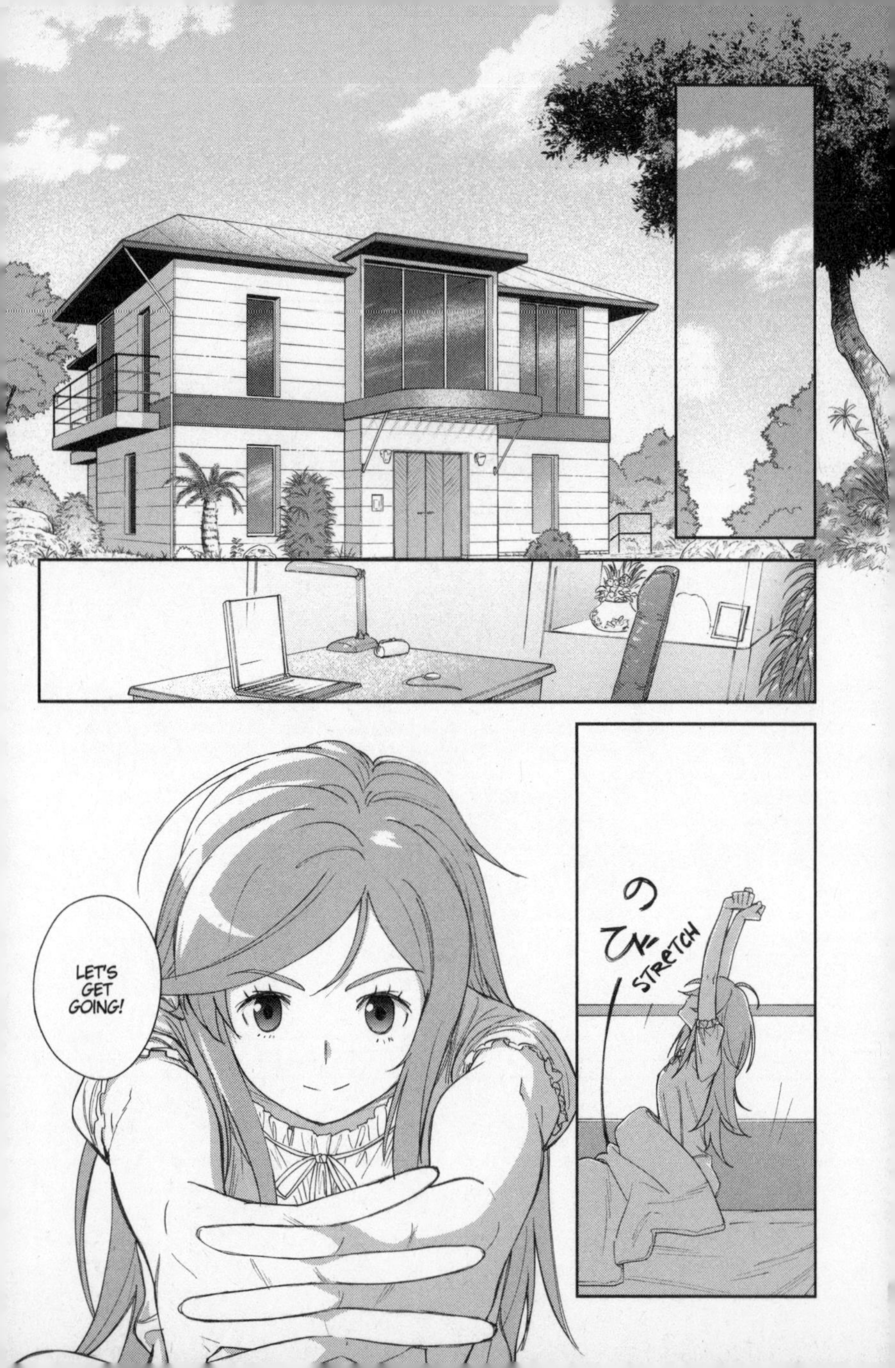
のび
STRETCH
LET'S GET GOING!

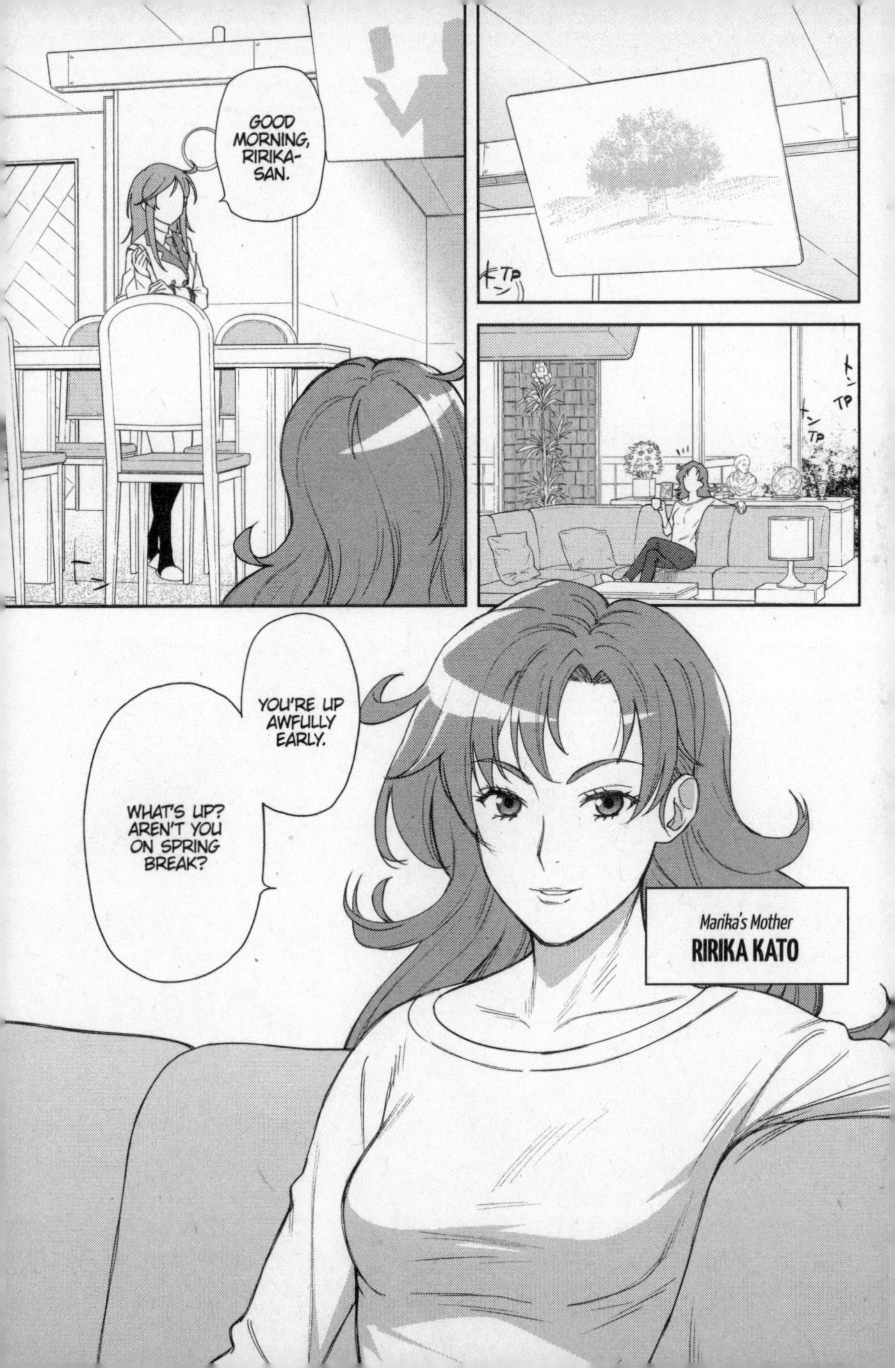
TP
TP
TP
GOOD MORNING, RIRIKA-SAN.
YOU'RE UP AWFULLY EARLY.
WHAT'S UP? AREN'T YOU ON SPRING BREAK?
Marika's Mother
RIRIKA KATO

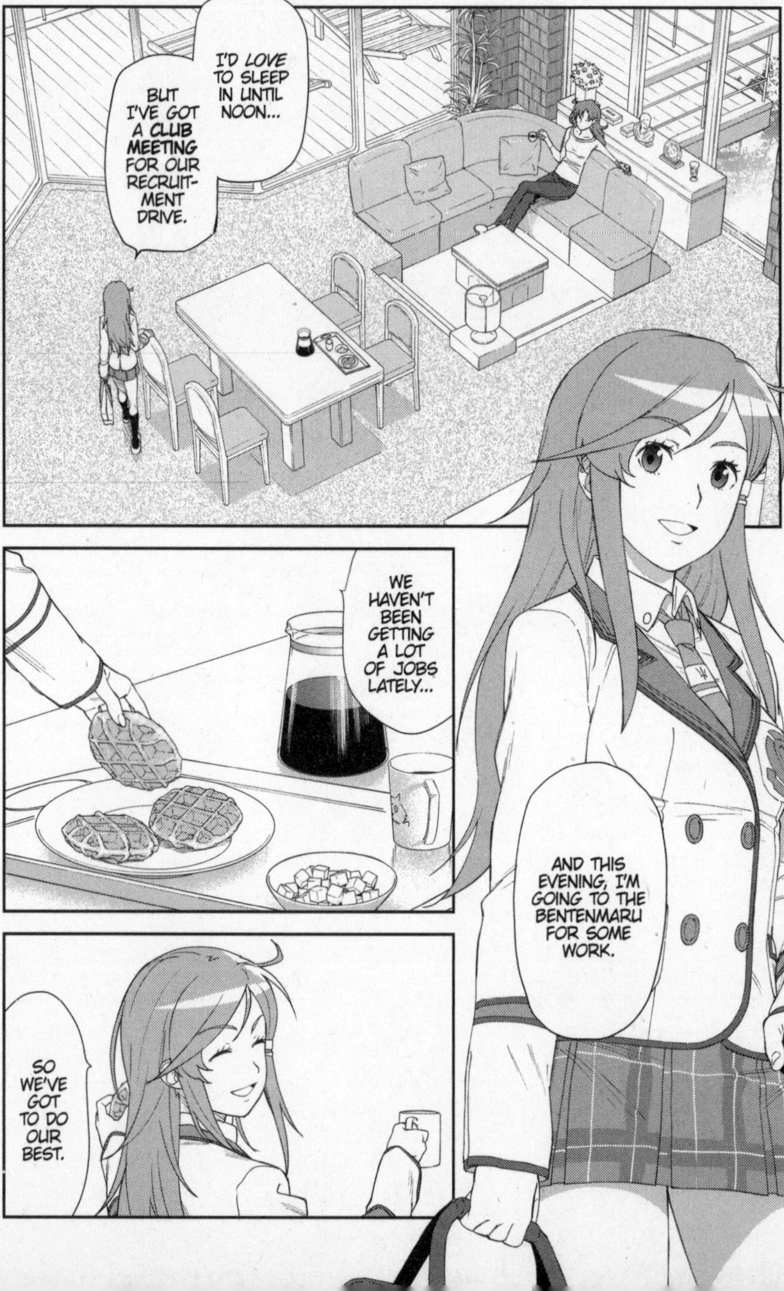
I'D LOVE TO SLEEP IN UNTIL NOON...
BUT I'VE GOT A CLUB MEETING FOR OUR RECRUIT-MENT DRIVE.
AND THIS EVENING, I'M GOING TO THE BENTENMARU FOR SOME WORK.
WE HAVEN'T BEEN GETTING A LOT OF JOBS LATELY...
SO WE'VE GOT TO DO OUR BEST.

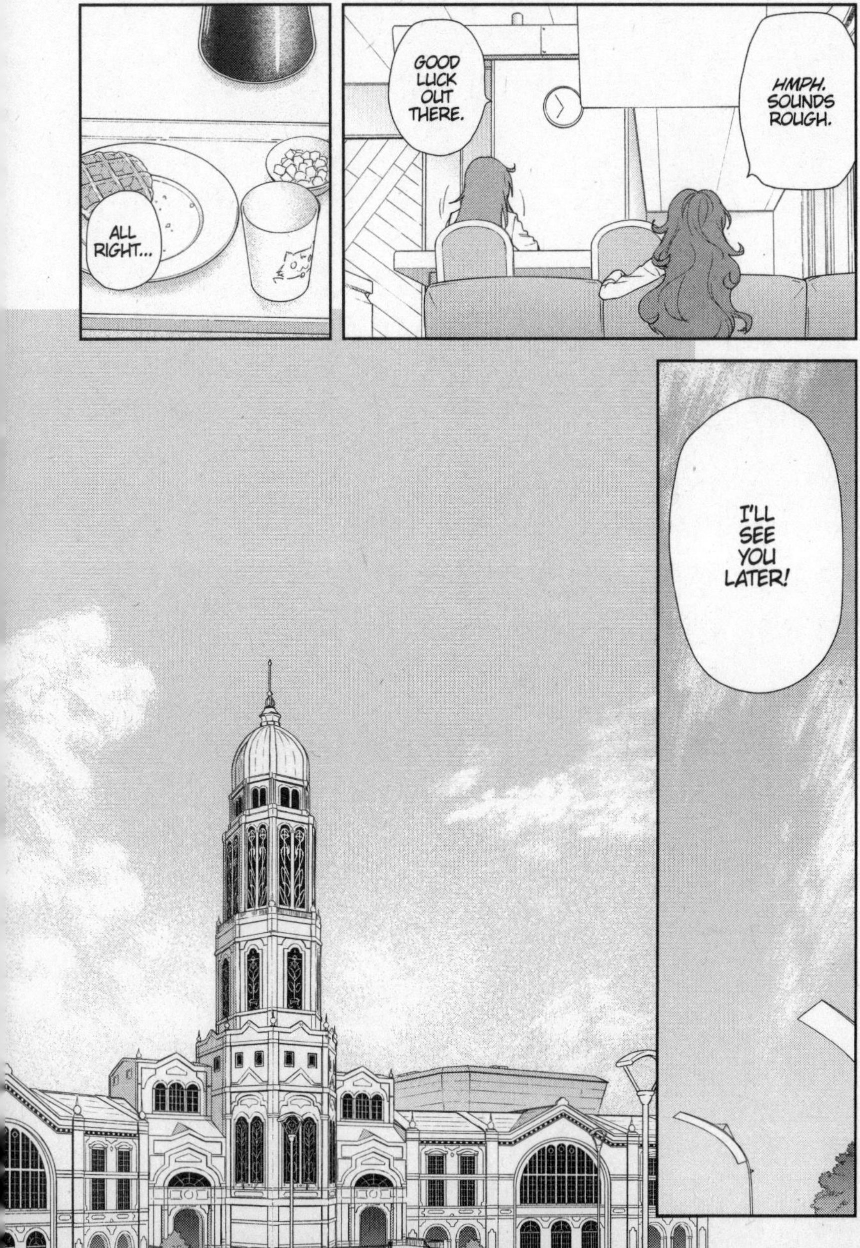
HMPH. SOUNDS ROUGH.
GOOD LUCK OUT THERE.
ALL RIGHT...
I'LL SEE YOU LATER!

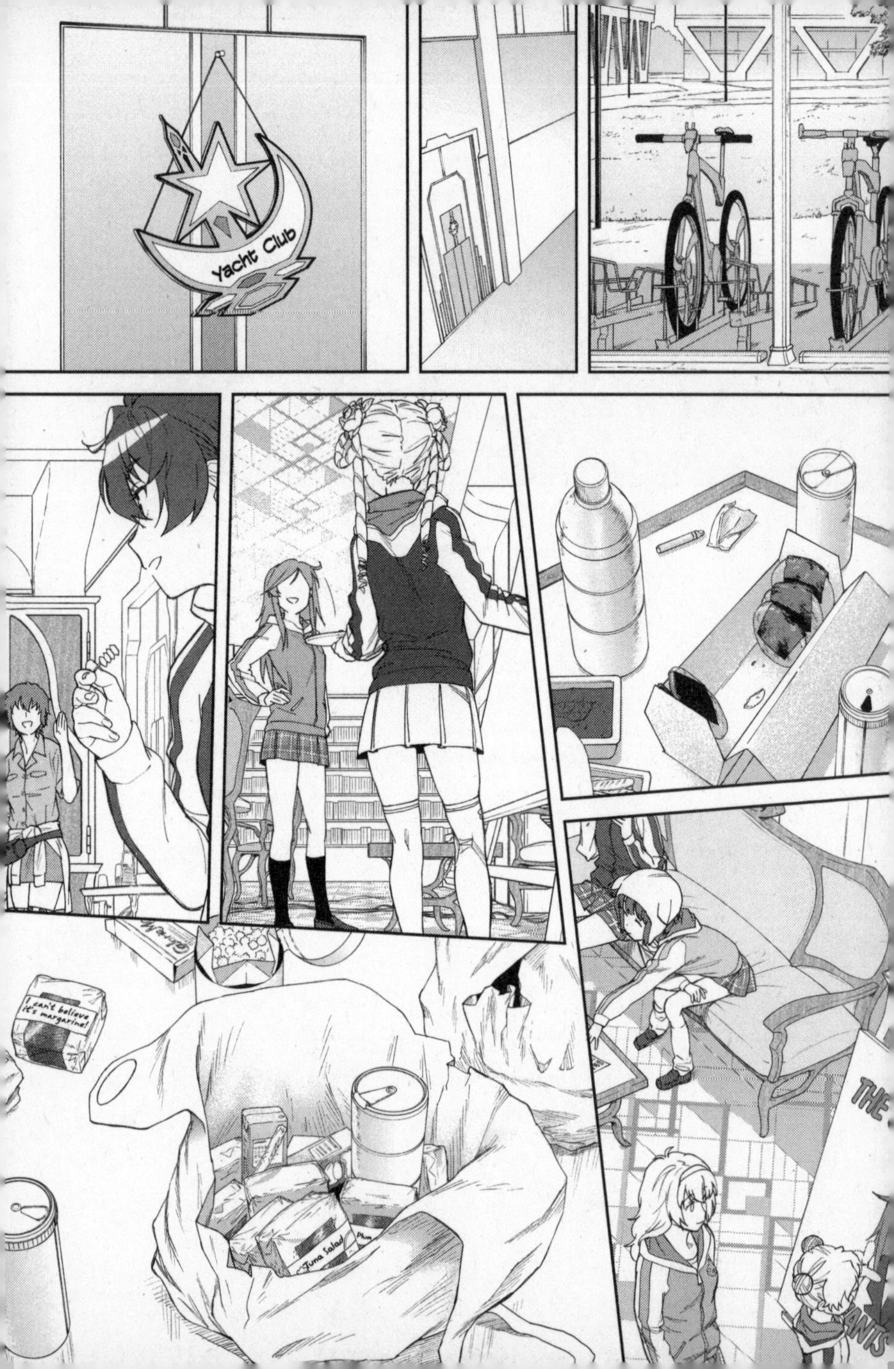
Yacht Club
THE
I can't believe it's margarine!
Tuna Salad
Plum

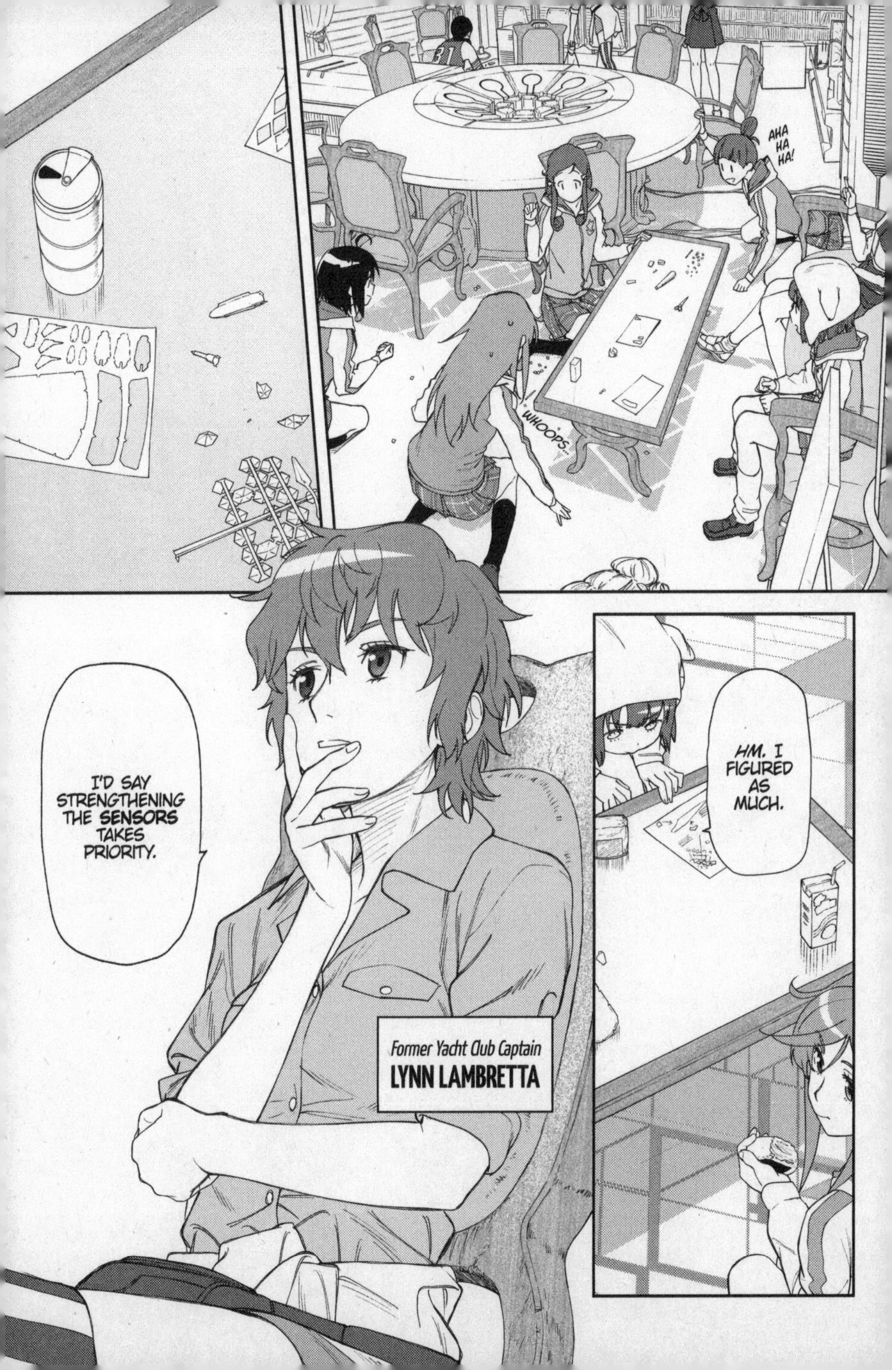
AHA HA HA!
WHOOPS...
HM. I FIGURED AS MUCH.
I'D SAY STRENGTHENING THE SENSORS TAKES PRIORITY.
Former Yacht Club Captain
LYNN LAMBRETTA

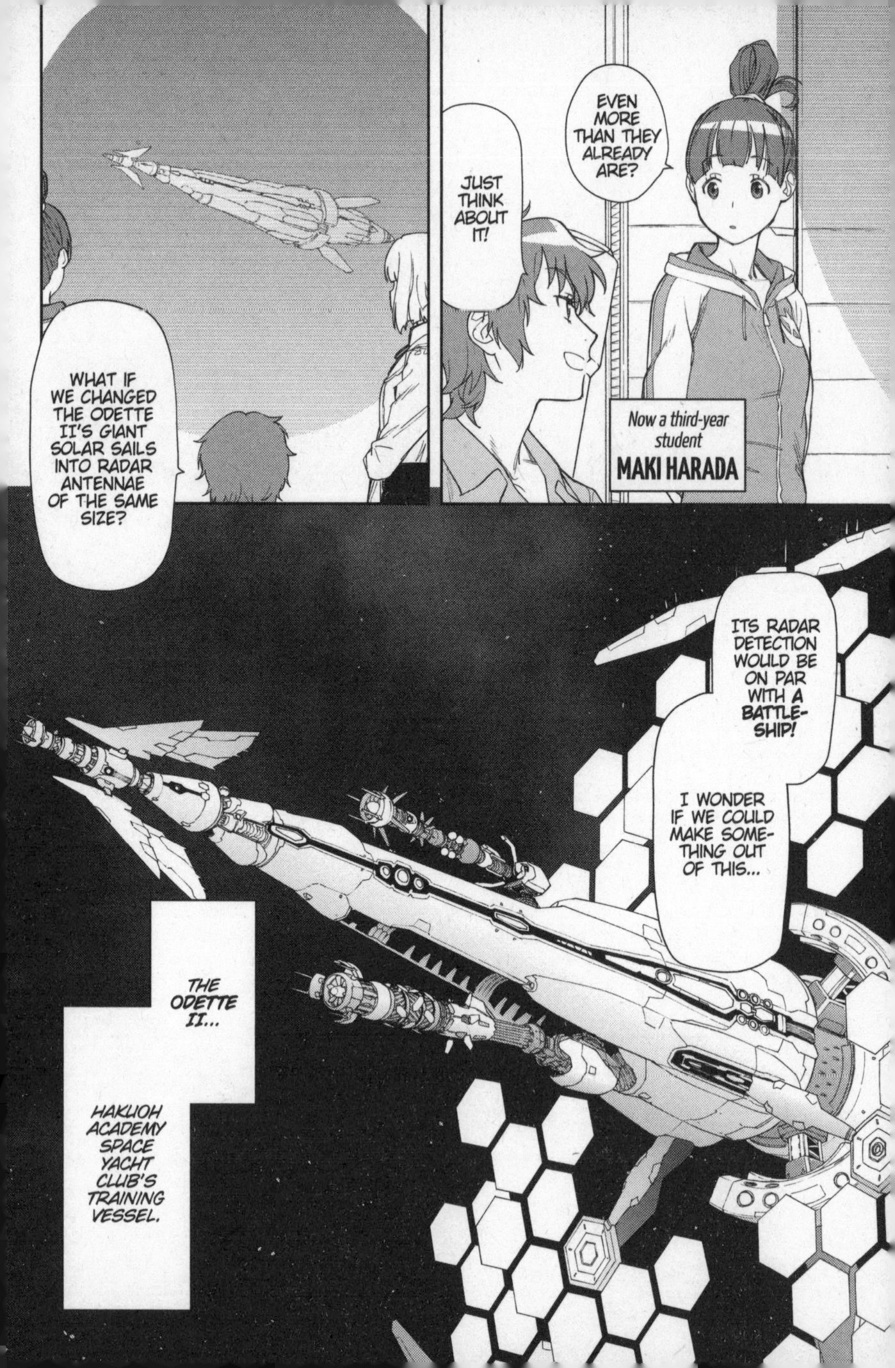
EVEN MORE THAN THEY ALREADY ARE?
JUST THINK ABOUT IT!
Now a third-year student
MAKI HARADA
WHAT IF WE CHANGED THE ODETTE II'S GIANT SOLAR SAILS INTO RADAR ANTENNAE OF THE SAME SIZE?
ITS RADAR DETECTION WOULD BE ON PAR WITH A BATTLE-SHIP!
I WONDER IF WE COULD MAKE SOME-THING OUT OF THIS...
THE ODETTE II...
HAKUOH ACADEMY SPACE YACHT CLUB'S TRAINING VESSEL.

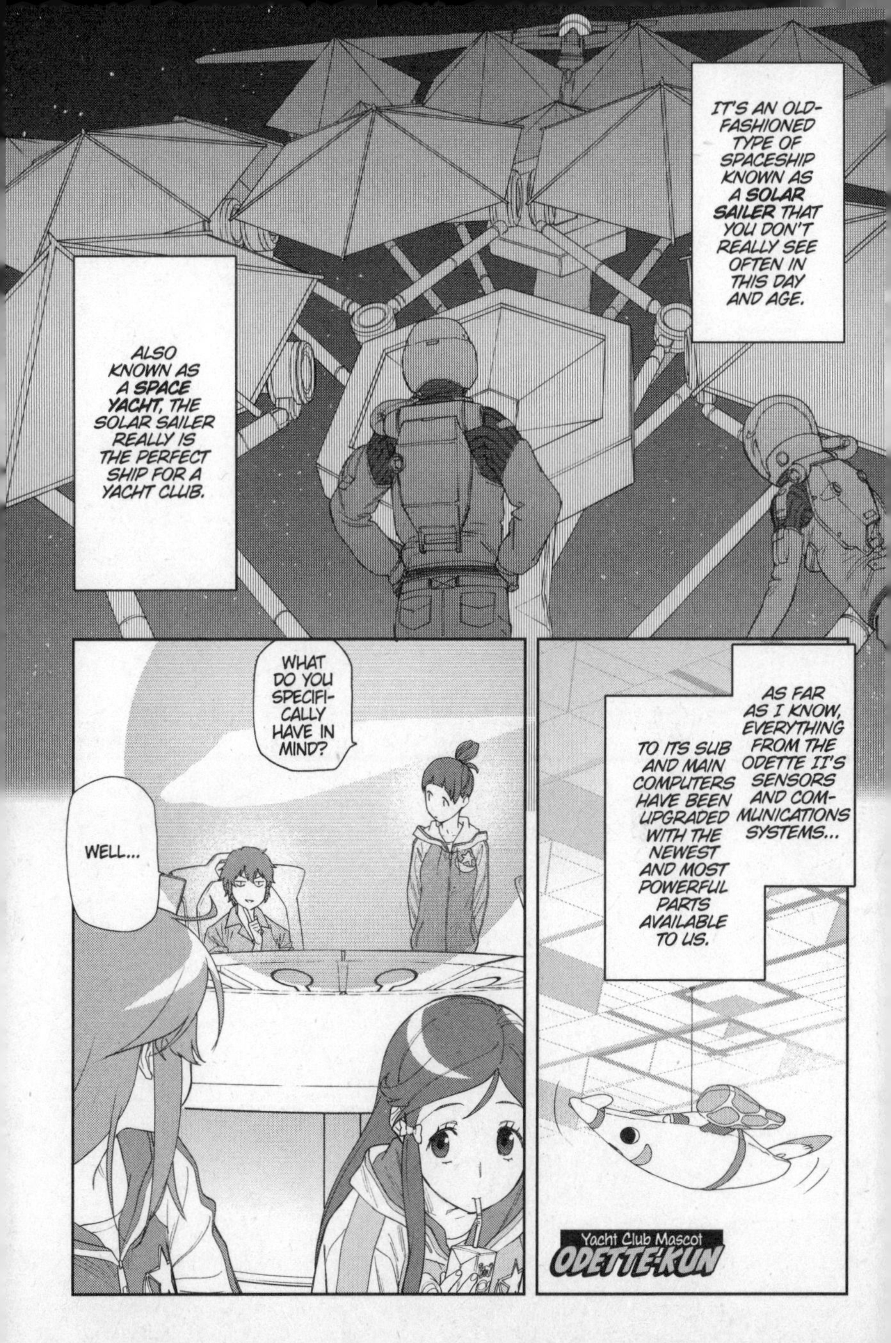
IT'S AN OLD-FASHIONED TYPE OF SPACESHIP KNOWN AS A SOLAR SAILER THAT YOU DON'T REALLY SEE OFTEN IN THIS DAY AND AGE.
ALSO KNOWN AS A SPACE YACHT, THE SOLAR SAILER REALLY IS THE PERFECT SHIP FOR A YACHT CLUB.
AS FAR AS I KNOW, EVERYTHING FROM THE ODETTE II'S SENSORS AND COMMUNICATIONS SYSTEMS...
TO ITS SUB AND MAIN COMPUTERS HAVE BEEN UPGRADED WITH THE NEWEST AND MOST POWERFUL PARTS AVAILABLE TO US.
Yacht Club Mascot
ODETTE-KUN
WHAT DO YOU SPECIFICALLY HAVE IN MIND?
WELL...

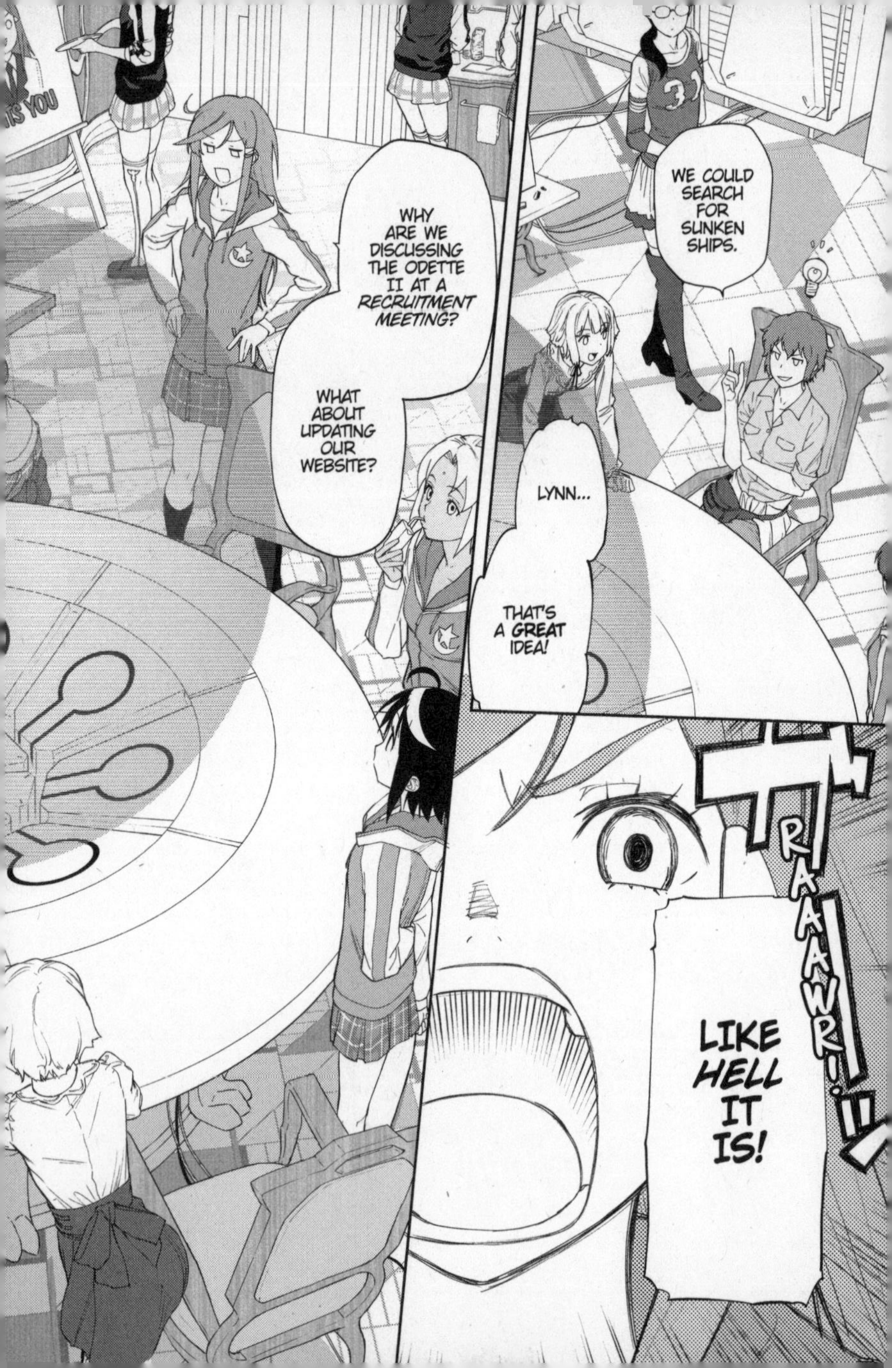
WE COULD SEARCH FOR SUNKEN SHIPS.
LYNN...
THAT'S A GREAT IDEA!
RAAAWR!!!
LIKE HELL IT IS!
WHY ARE WE DISCUSSING THE ODETTE II AT A RECRUITMENT MEETING?
WHAT ABOUT UPDATING OUR WEBSITE?

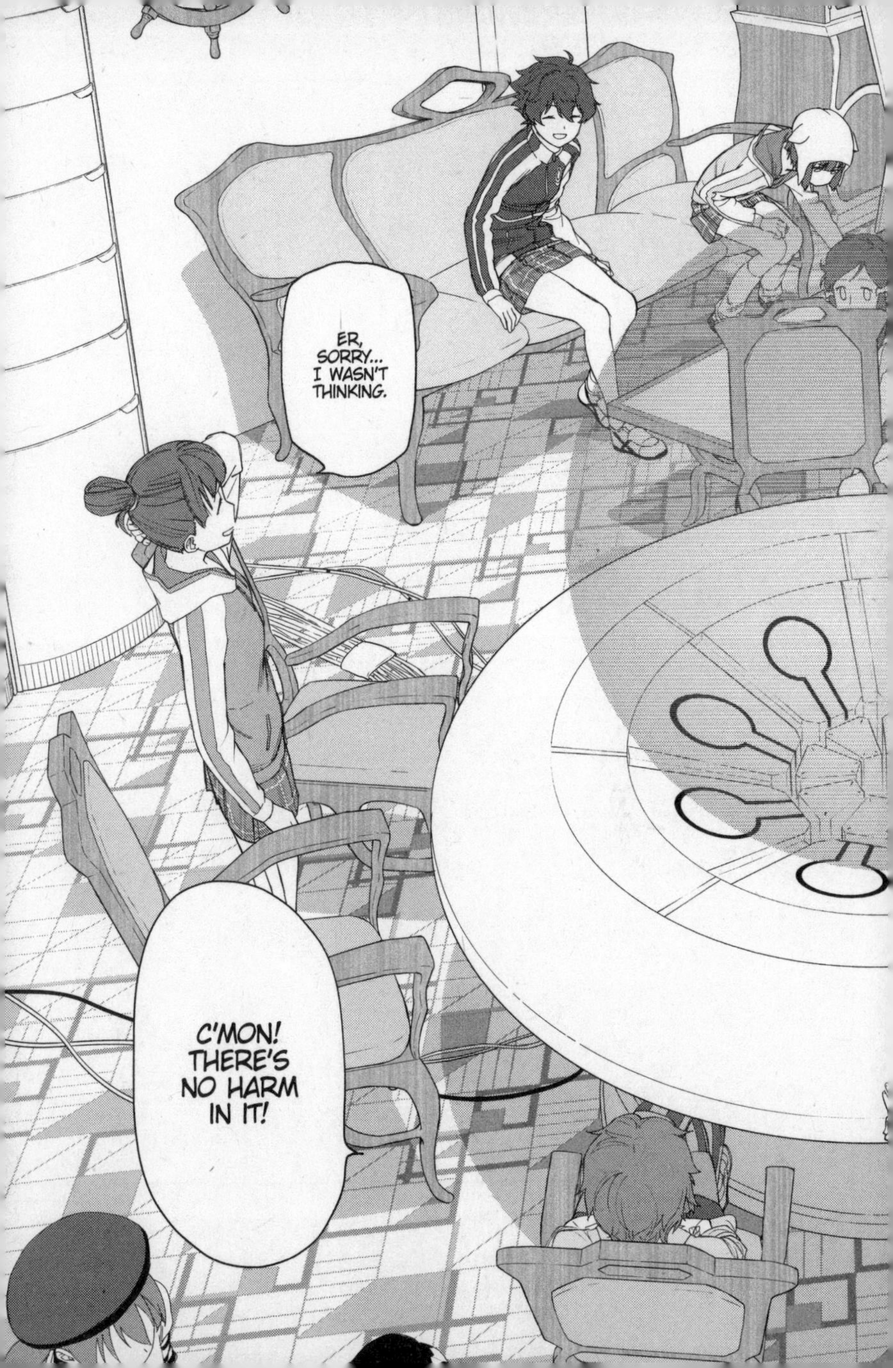
ER, SORRY... I WASN'T THINKING.
C'MON! THERE'S NO HARM IN IT!

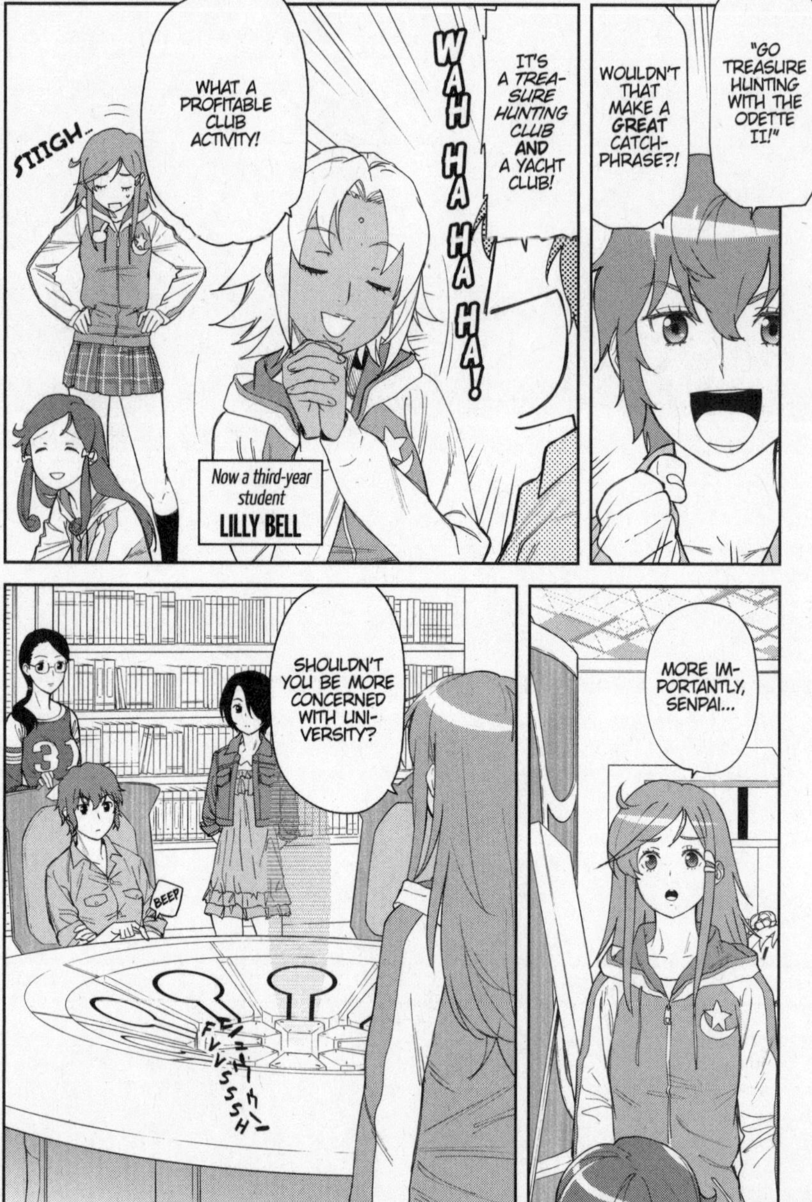
"GO TREASURE HUNTING WITH THE ODETTE II!"
WOULDN'T THAT MAKE A GREAT CATCH-PHRASE?!
IT'S A TREASURE HUNTING CLUB AND A YACHT CLUB!
WAH HA HA HA!
WHAT A PROFITABLE CLUB ACTIVITY!
SIIIGH..
Now a third-year student
LILLY BELL
MORE IMPORTANTLY, SENPAI...
SHOULDN'T YOU BE MORE CONCERNED WITH UNIVERSITY?
BEEP
FVVSSSH

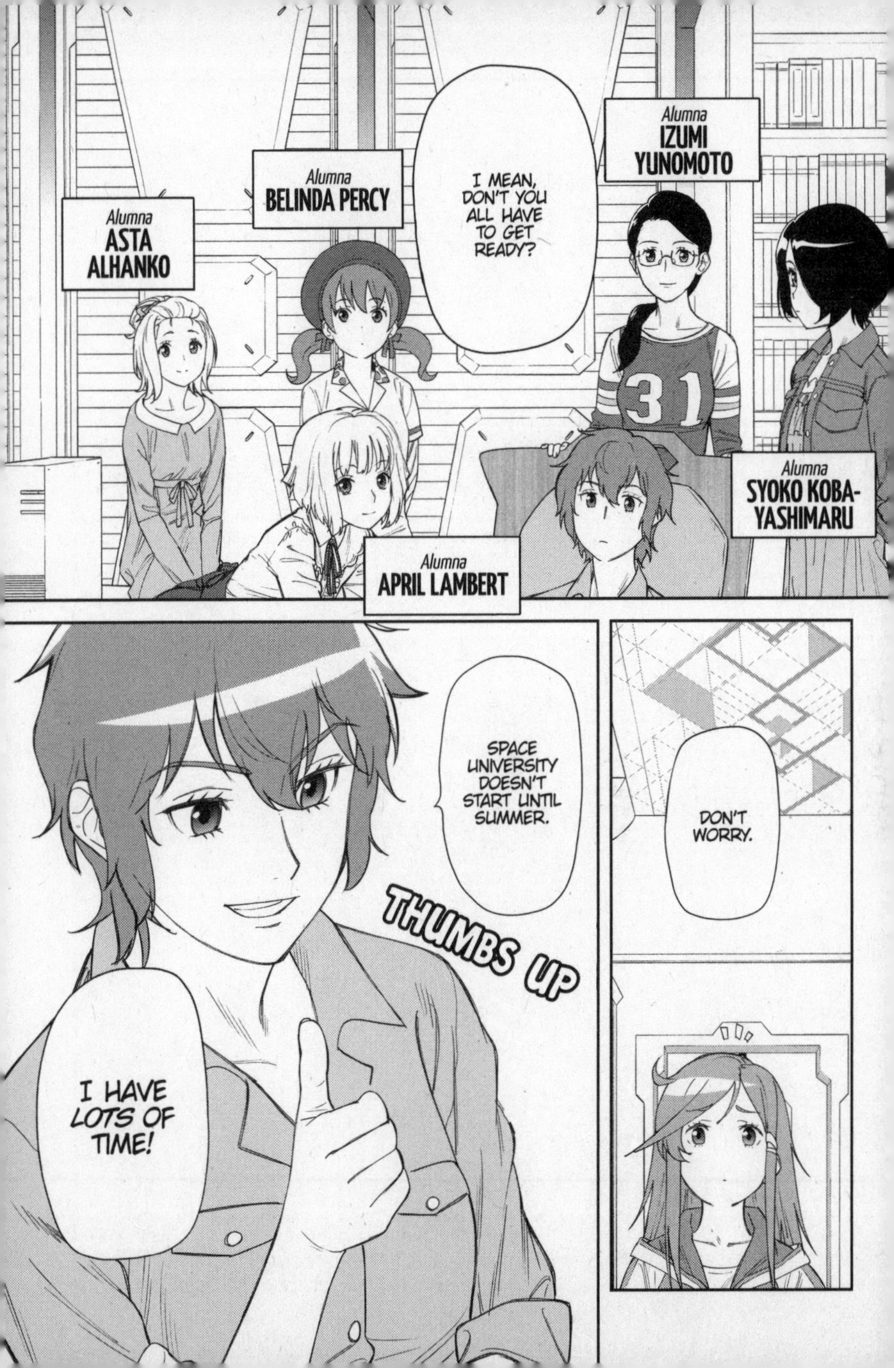
Alumna IZUMI YUNOMOTO
I MEAN, DON'T YOU ALL HAVE TO GET READY?
Alumna BELINDA PERCY
Alumna ASTA ALHANKO
Alumna SYOKO KOBA-YASHIMARU
Alumna APRIL LAMBERT
DON'T WORRY.
SPACE UNIVERSITY DOESN'T START UNTIL SUMMER.
THUMBS UP
I HAVE LOTS OF TIME!

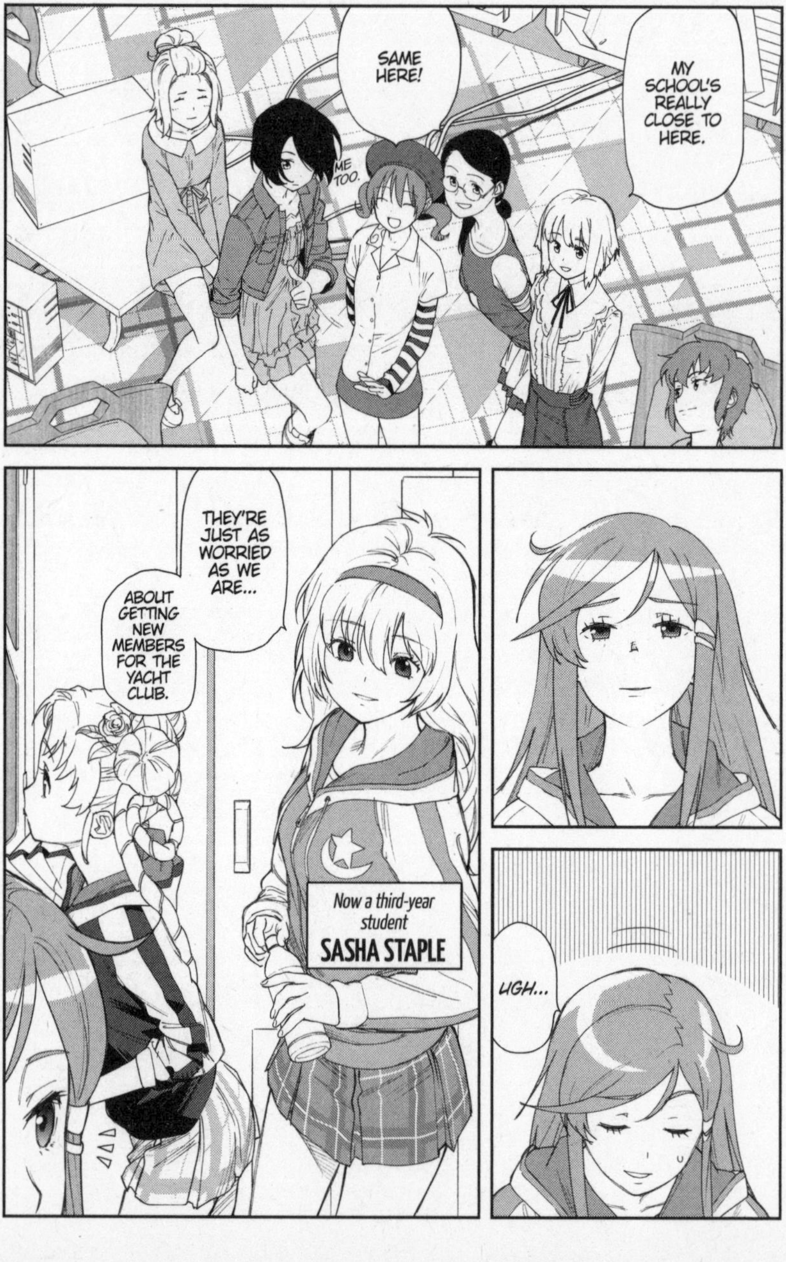
MY SCHOOL'S REALLY CLOSE TO HERE.
SAME HERE!
ME TOO.
UGH...
THEY'RE JUST AS WORRIED AS WE ARE...
ABOUT GETTING NEW MEMBERS FOR THE YACHT CLUB.
Now a third-year student
SASHA STAPLE

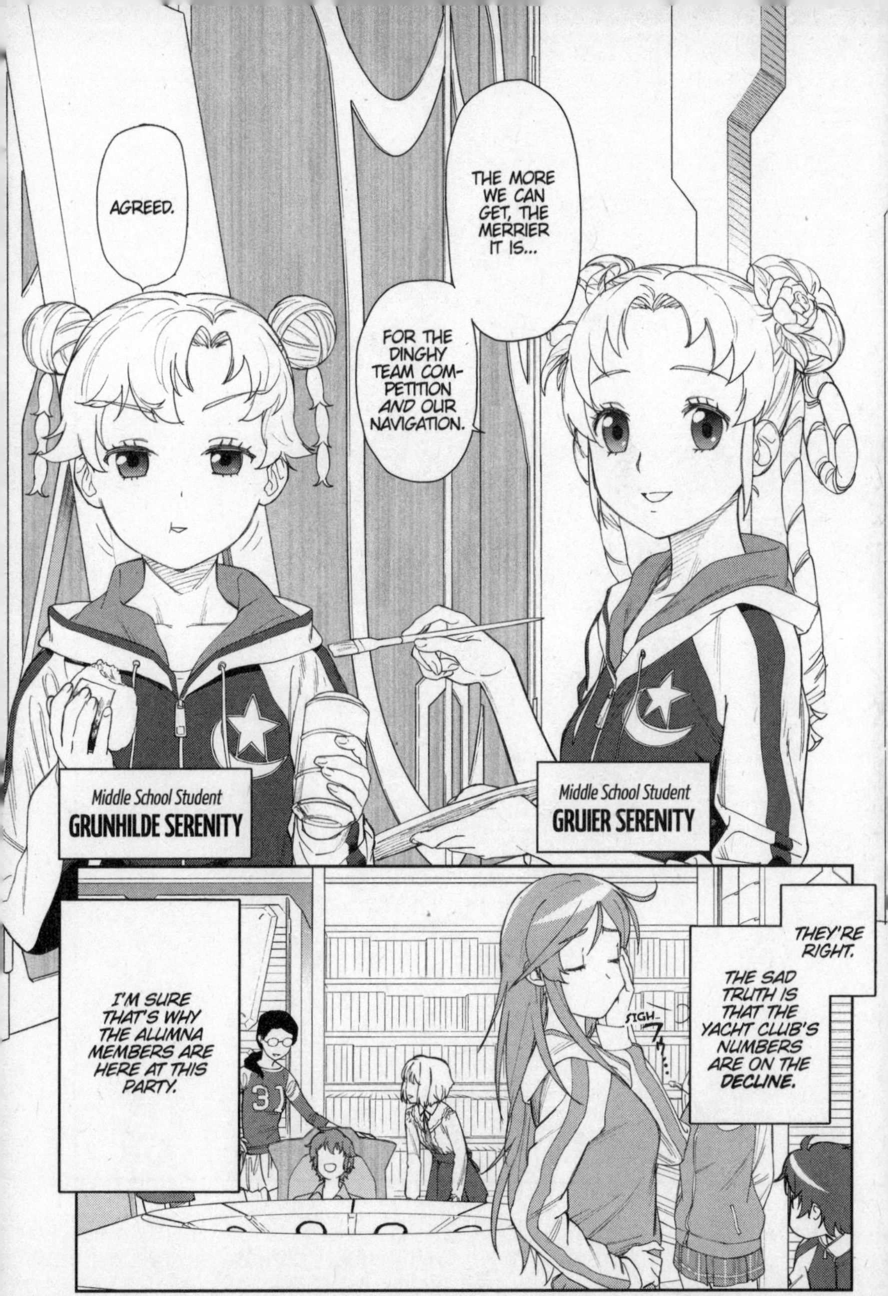
THE MORE WE CAN GET, THE MERRIER IT IS...
FOR THE DINGHY TEAM COMPETITION AND OUR NAVIGATION.
AGREED.
Middle School Student
GRUIER SERENITY
Middle School Student
GRUNHILDE SERENITY
THEY'RE RIGHT.
THE SAD TRUTH IS THAT THE YACHT CLUB'S NUMBERS ARE ON THE DECLINE.
SIGH...
I'M SURE THAT'S WHY THE ALUMNA MEMBERS ARE HERE AT THIS PARTY.

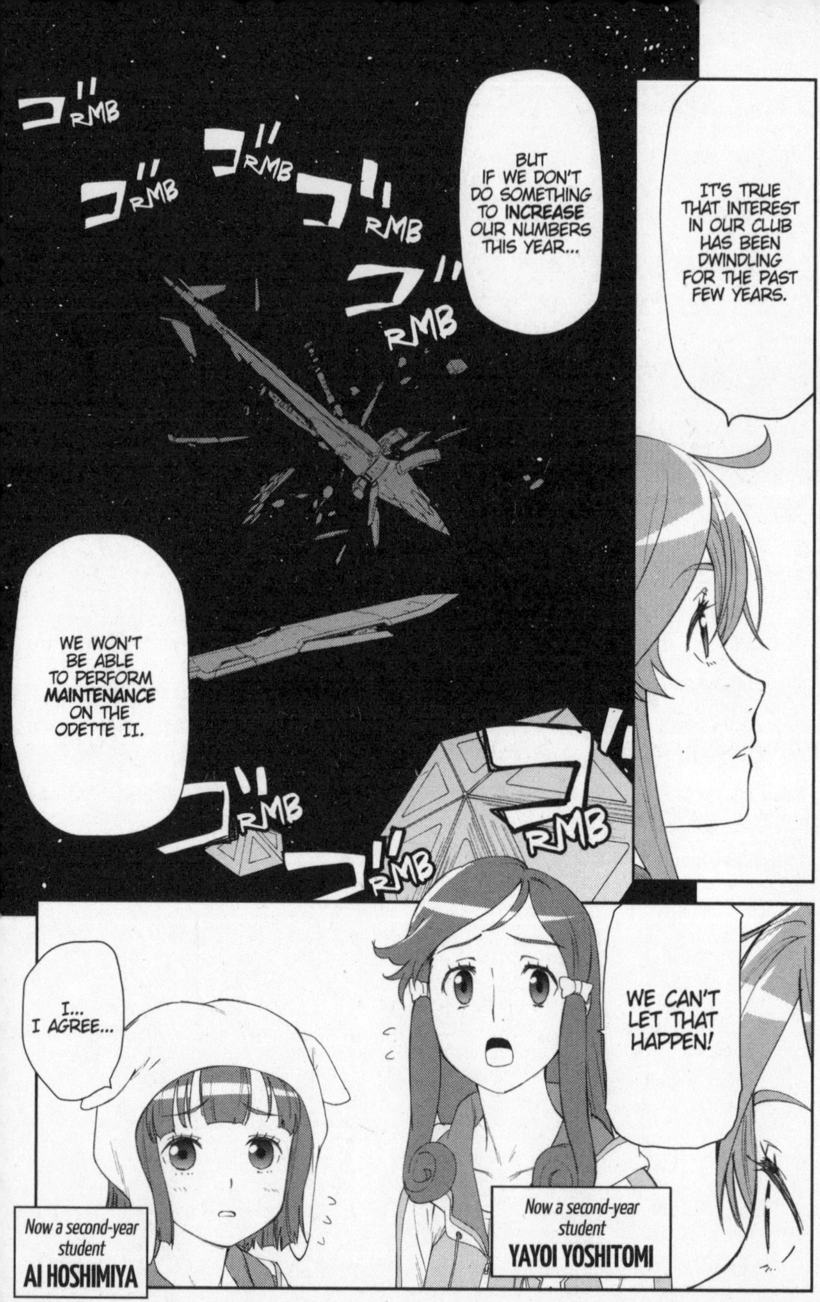
IT'S TRUE THAT INTEREST IN OUR CLUB HAS BEEN DWINDLING FOR THE PAST FEW YEARS.
BUT IF WE DON'T DO SOMETHING TO INCREASE OUR NUMBERS THIS YEAR...
ゴ RMB
ゴ RMB
ゴ RMB
ゴ RMB
ゴ RMB
ゴ RMB
WE WON'T BE ABLE TO PERFORM MAINTENANCE ON THE ODETTE II.
ゴ RMB
ゴ RMB
ゴ RMB
WE CAN'T LET THAT HAPPEN!
Now a second-year student YAYOI YOSHITOMI
I... I AGREE...
Now a second-year student AI HOSHIMIYA

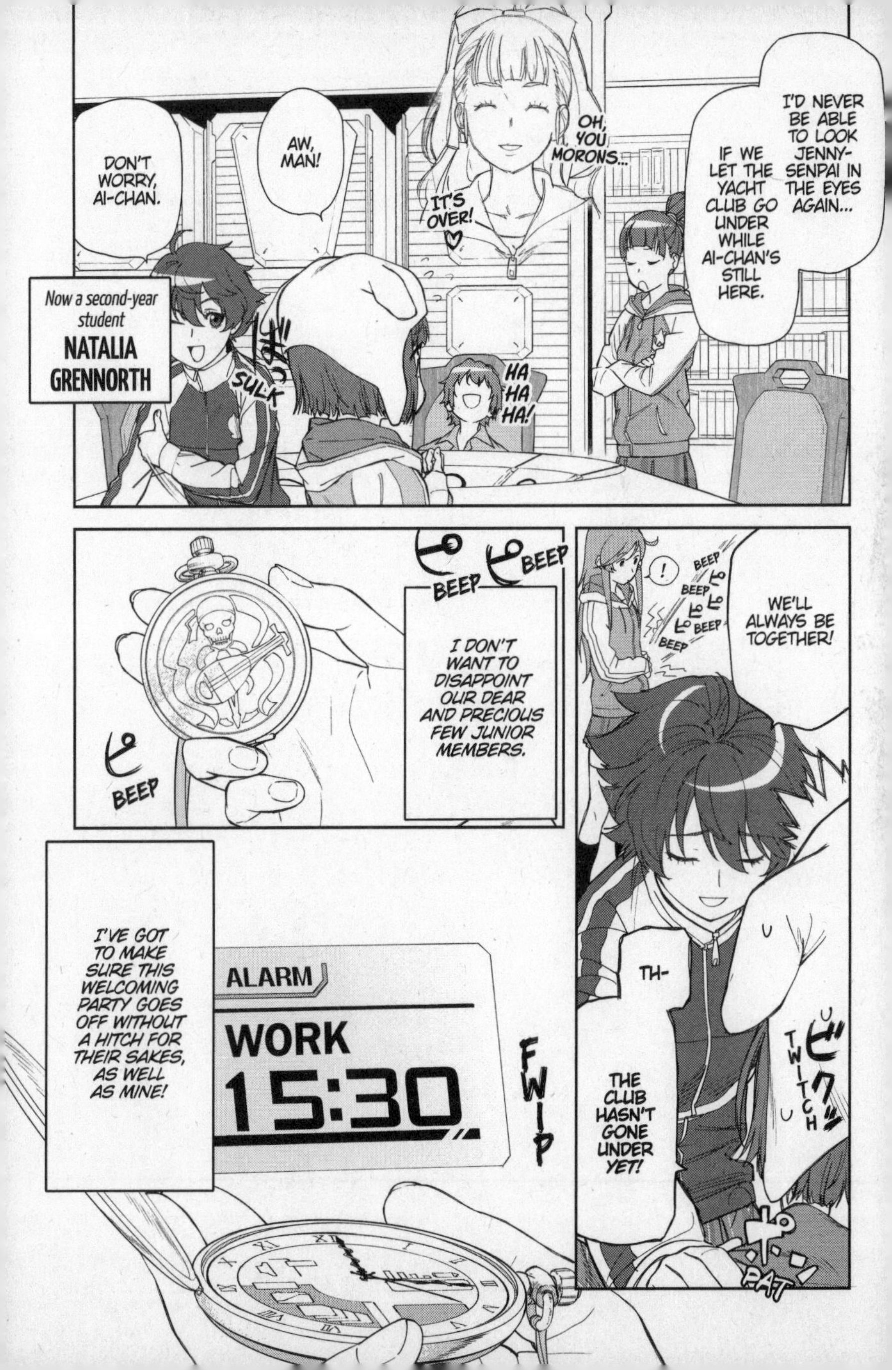
IF WE LET THE YACHT CLUB GO UNDER WHILE AI-CHAN'S STILL HERE.
I'D NEVER BE ABLE TO LOOK JENNY-SENPAI IN THE EYES AGAIN...
OH, YOU MORONS...
IT'S OVER! ♡
AW, MAN!
DON'T WORRY, AI-CHAN.
Now a second-year student
NATALIA GRENNORTH
SULK
HA HA HA!
WE'LL ALWAYS BE TOGETHER!
!
BEEP BEEP BEEP BEEP
TH-
THE CLUB HASN'T GONE UNDER YET!
TWITCH
PAT
BEEP
BEEP
I DON'T WANT TO DISAPPOINT OUR DEAR AND PRECIOUS FEW JUNIOR MEMBERS.
BEEP
FWIP
ALARM
WORK
15:30
I'VE GOT TO MAKE SURE THIS WELCOMING PARTY GOES OFF WITHOUT A HITCH FOR THEIR SAKES, AS WELL AS MINE!

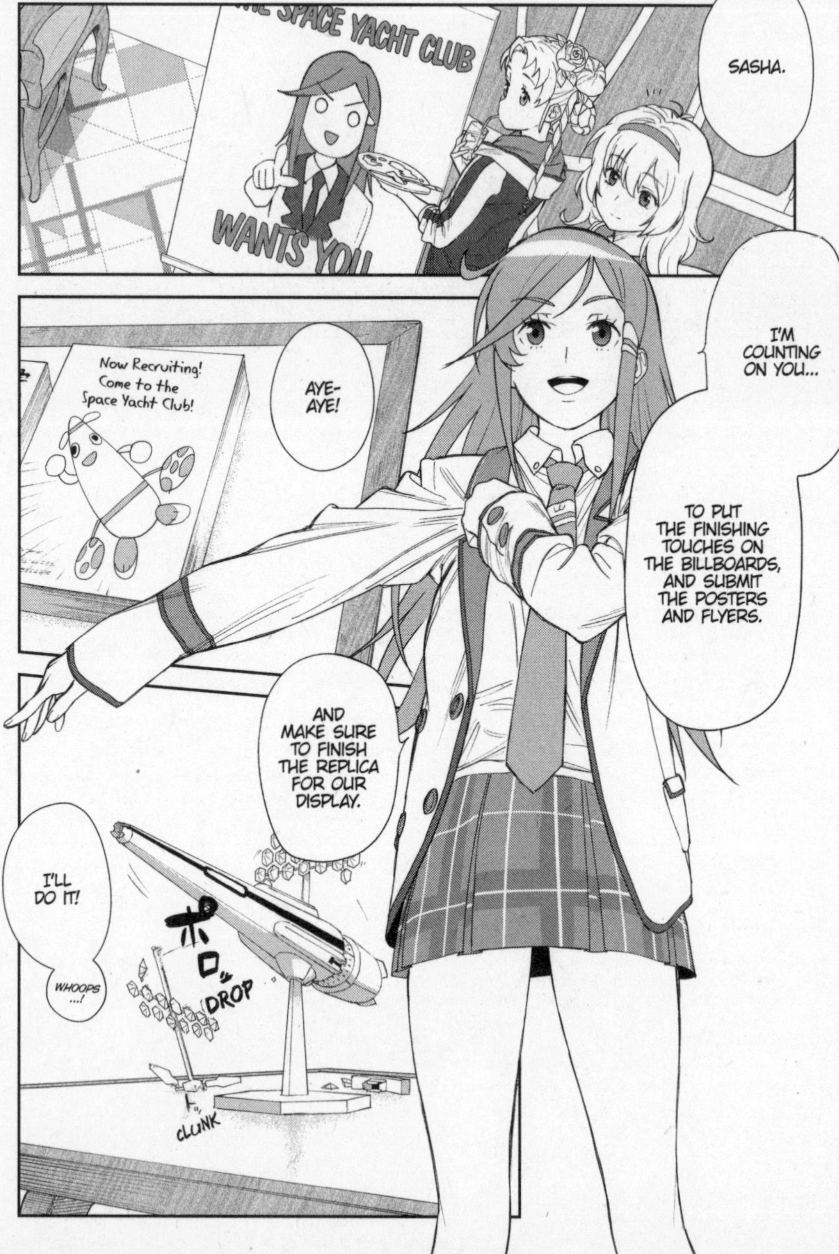
SASHA.
SPACE YACHT CLUB
WANTS YOU
I'M COUNTING ON YOU...
TO PUT THE FINISHING TOUCHES ON THE BILLBOARDS, AND SUBMIT THE POSTERS AND FLYERS.
AYE-AYE!
Now Recruiting! Come to the Space Yacht Club!
AND MAKE SURE TO FINISH THE REPLICA FOR OUR DISPLAY.
I'LL DO IT!
ポロッ
DROP
WHOOPS ...!
CLUNK

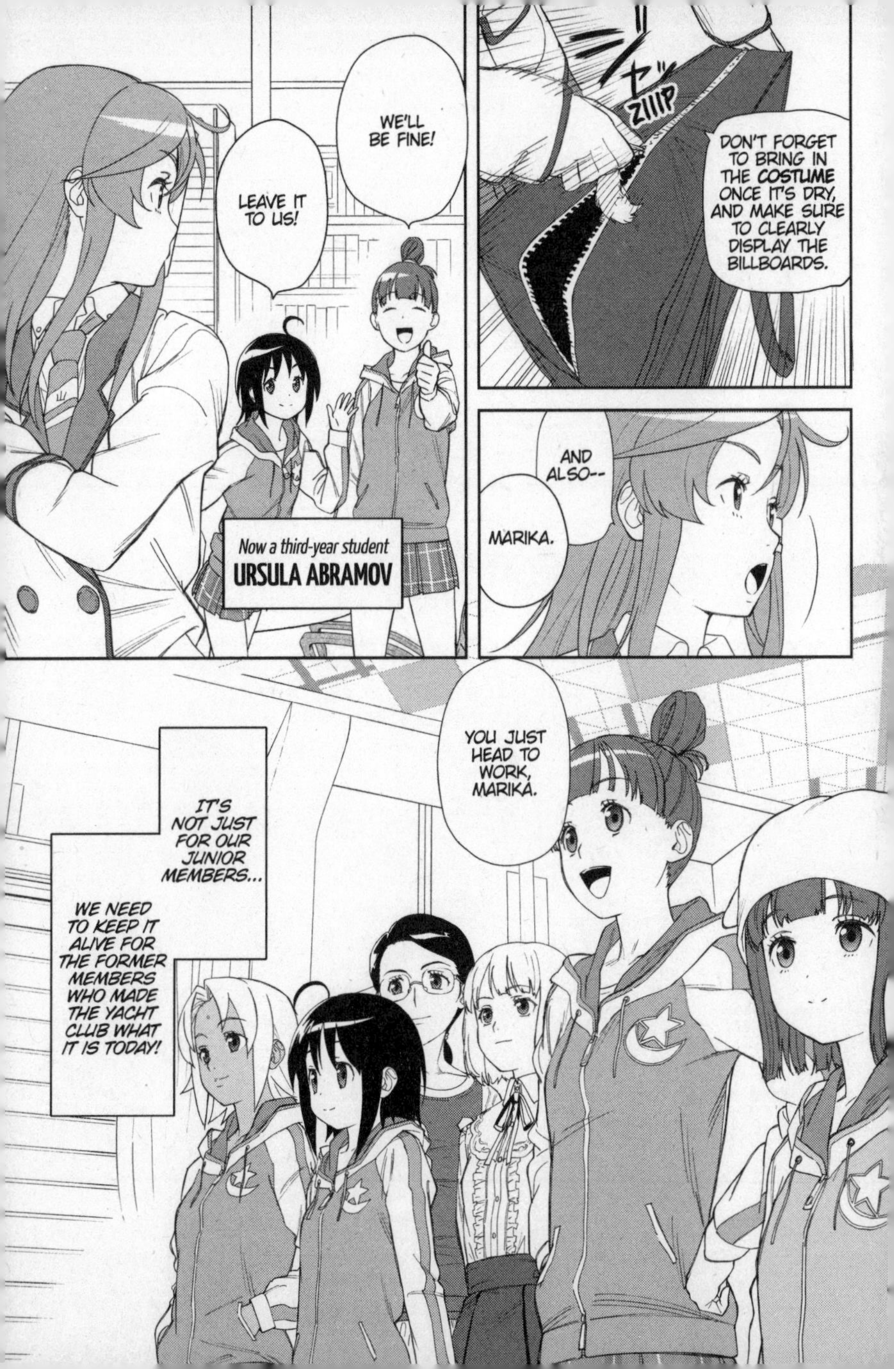
ZIIIP
DON'T FORGET TO BRING IN THE COSTUME ONCE IT'S DRY, AND MAKE SURE TO CLEARLY DISPLAY THE BILLBOARDS.
AND ALSO--
MARIKA.
WE'LL BE FINE!
LEAVE IT TO US!
Now a third-year student URSULA ABRAMOV
YOU JUST HEAD TO WORK, MARIKA.
IT'S NOT JUST FOR OUR JUNIOR MEMBERS...
WE NEED TO KEEP IT ALIVE FOR THE FORMER MEMBERS WHO MADE THE YACHT CLUB WHAT IT IS TODAY!

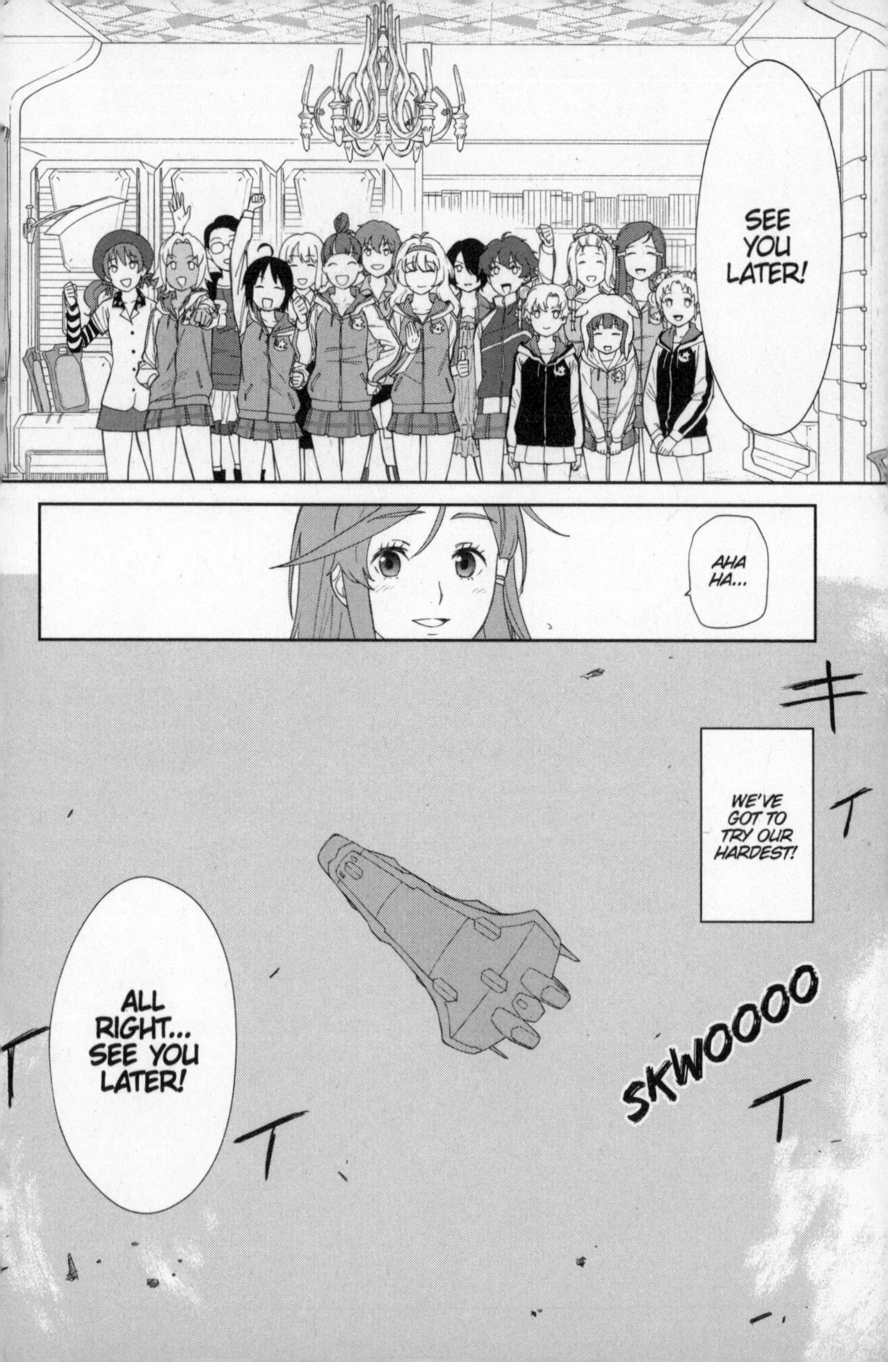
SEE YOU LATER!
AHA HA...
WE'VE GOT TO TRY OUR HARDEST!
SKWOOOO
ALL RIGHT... SEE YOU LATER!

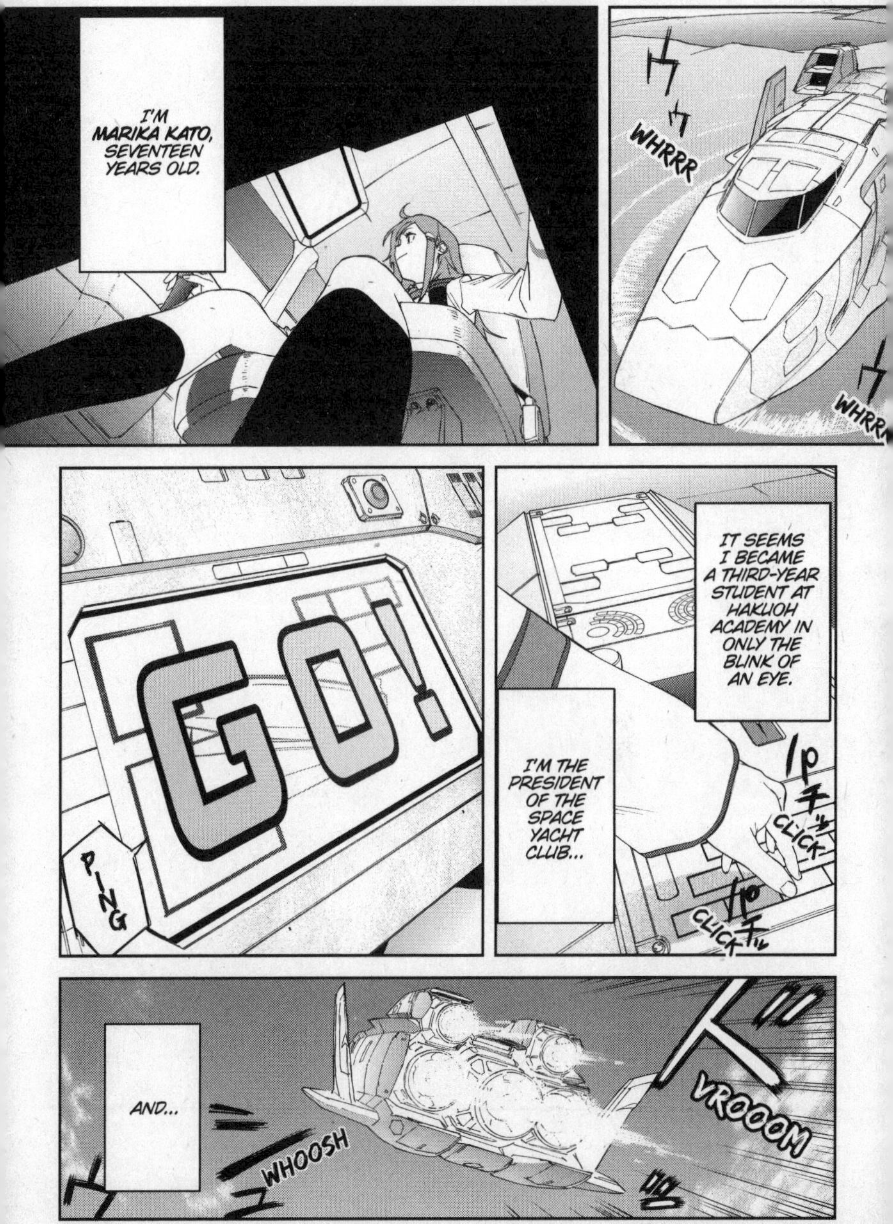

WHRRR
WHRRR
I'M MARIKA KATO, SEVENTEEN YEARS OLD.
IT SEEMS I BECAME A THIRD-YEAR STUDENT AT HAKUOH ACADEMY IN ONLY THE BLINK OF AN EYE.
I'M THE PRESIDENT OF THE SPACE YACHT CLUB...
CLICK
CLICK
GO!
PING
VROOOM
WHOOSH
AND...

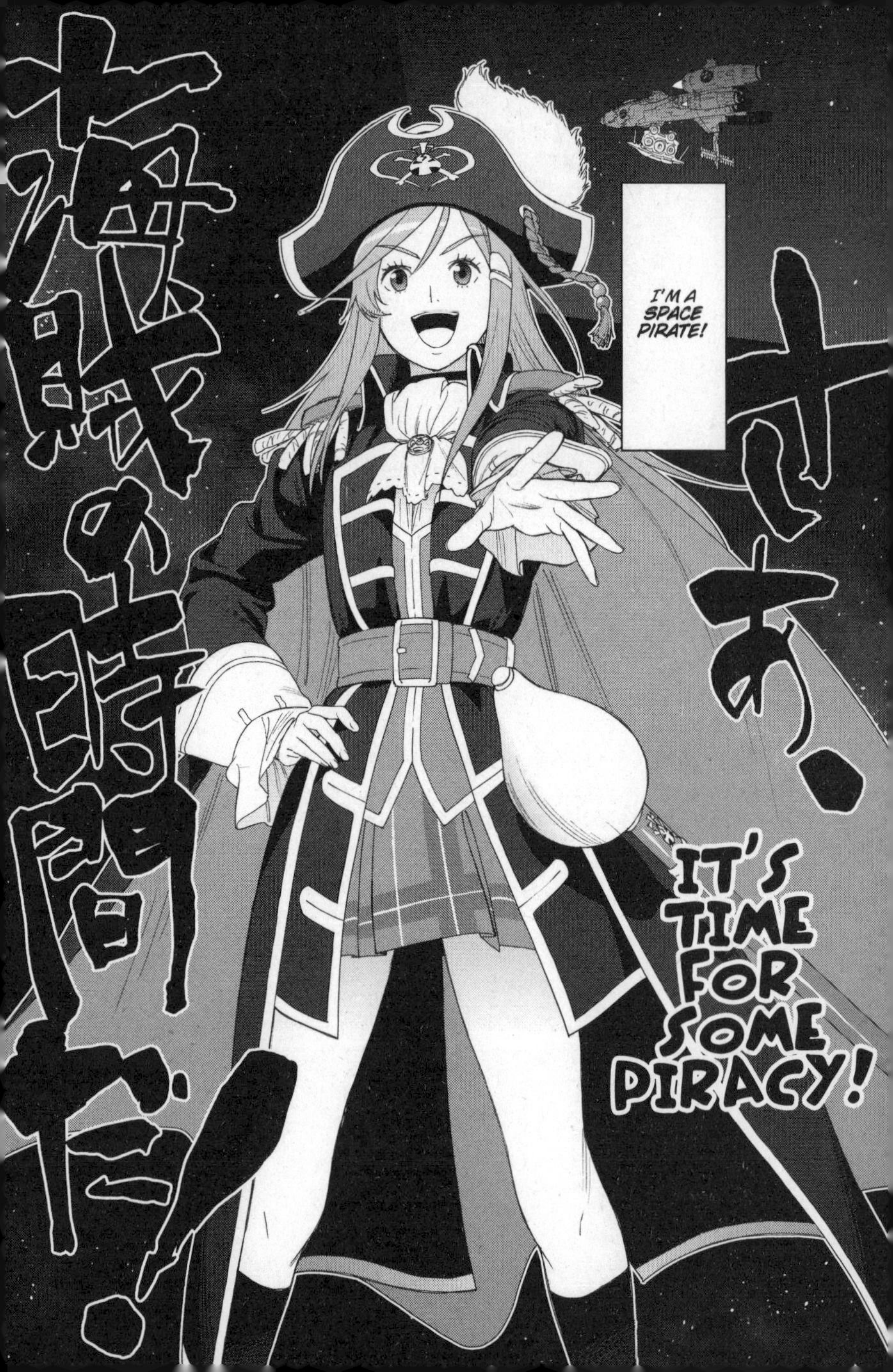
I'M A SPACE PIRATE!
さあ、海賊の時間だ!
IT'S TIME FOR SOME PIRACY!

BODACIOUS
SPACE
PIRATES
[THE MOVIE]
ABYSS OF HYPERSPACE

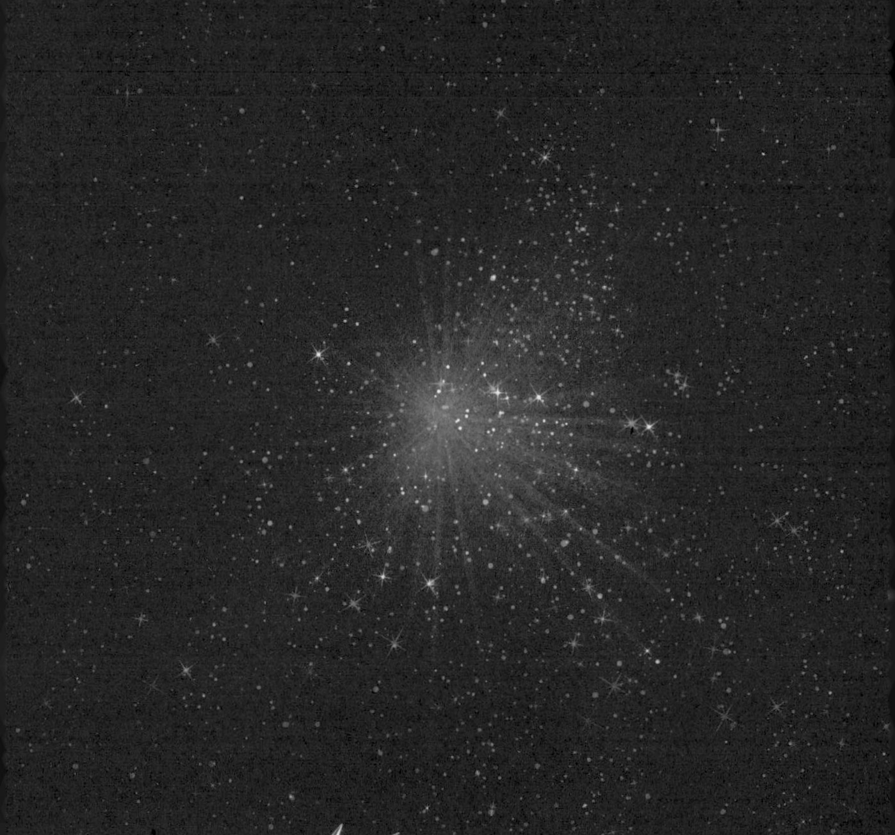

モーレツ★宇宙海賊
ABYSS OF HYPERSPACE 亜空の深淵

VOLUME 01 Chapter 01 end

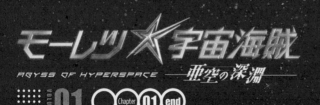

BODACIOUS SPACE PIRATES

[THE MOVIE]

ABYSS OF HYPERSPACE

VOLUME 01

Chapter 02

[START]

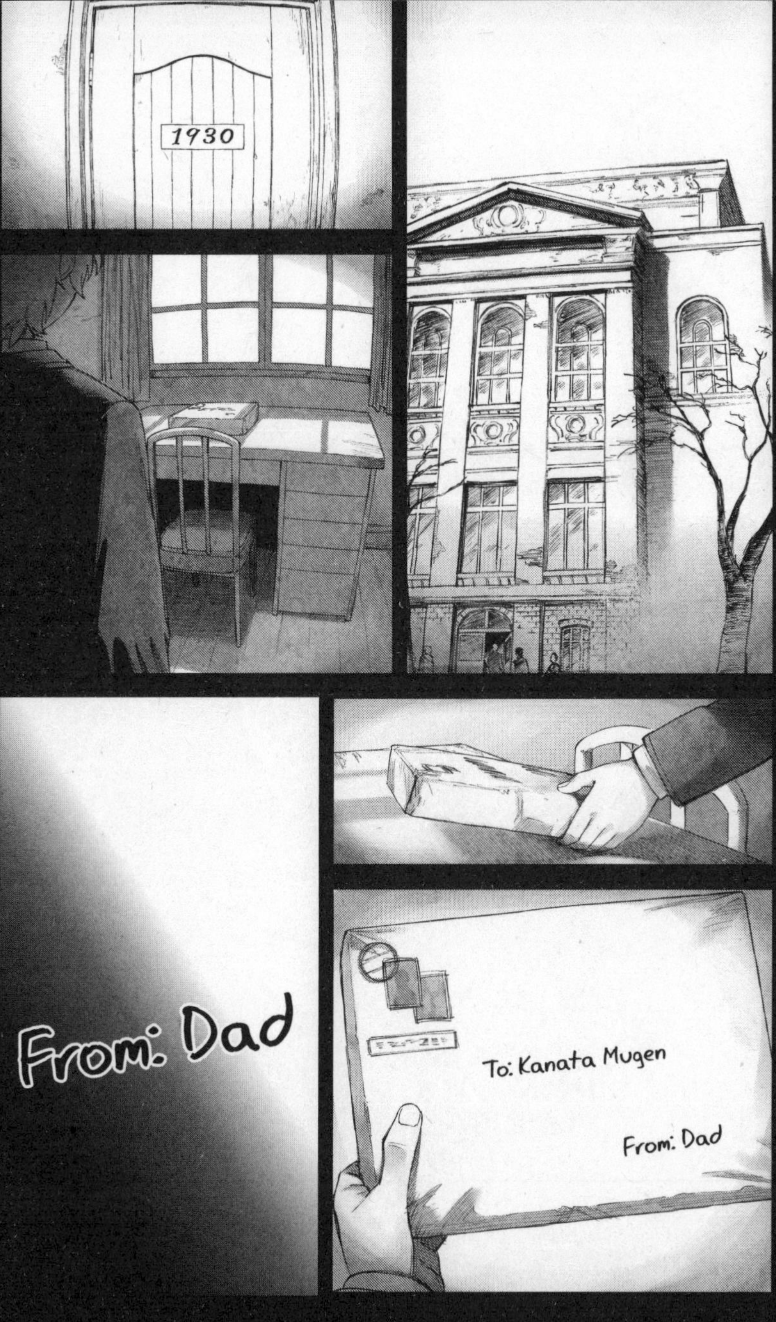
1930
To: Kanata Mugen
From: Dad
From: Dad

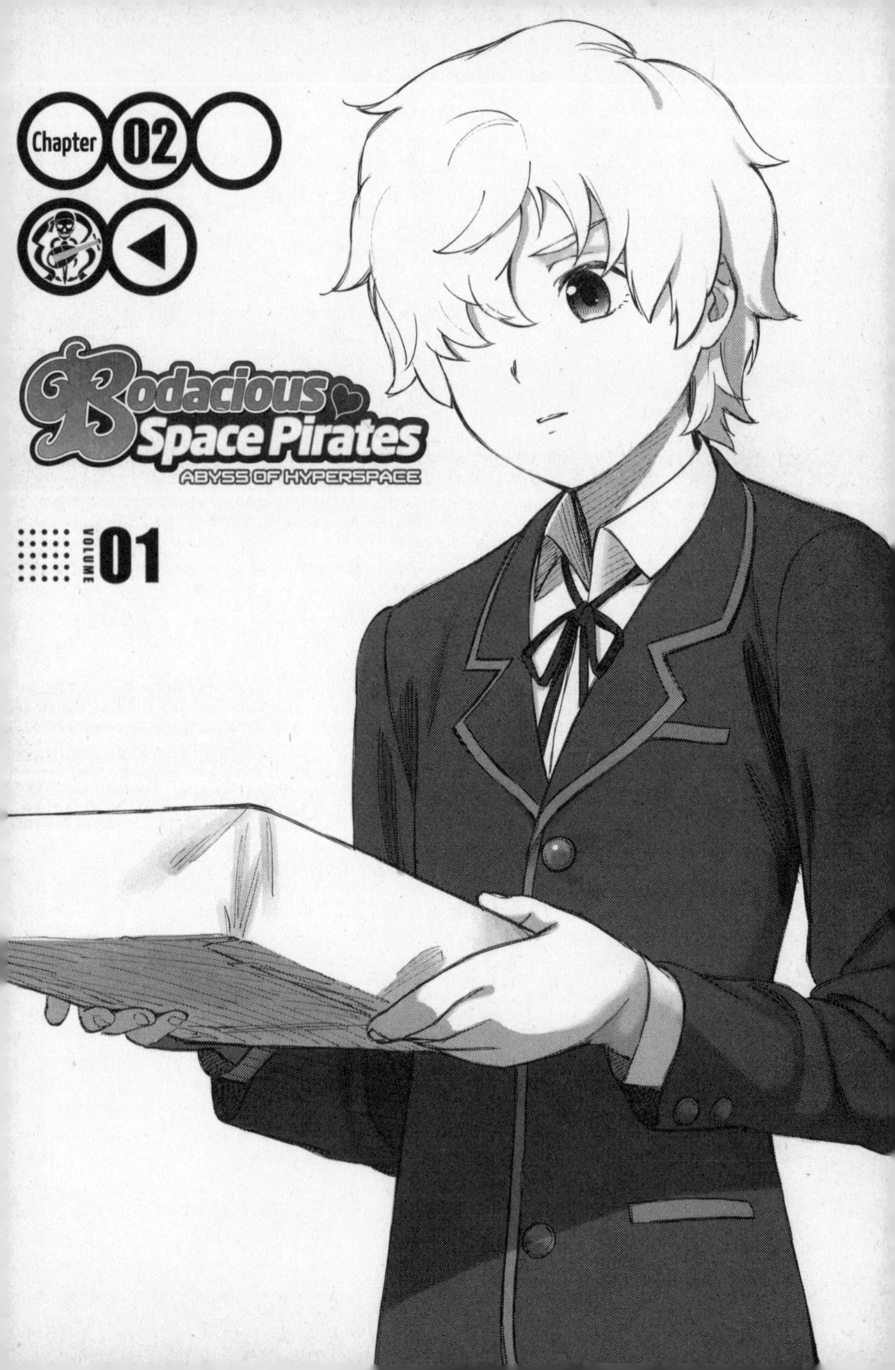
Chapter 02
Bodacious Space Pirates
ABYSS OF HYPERSPACE
VOLUME 01

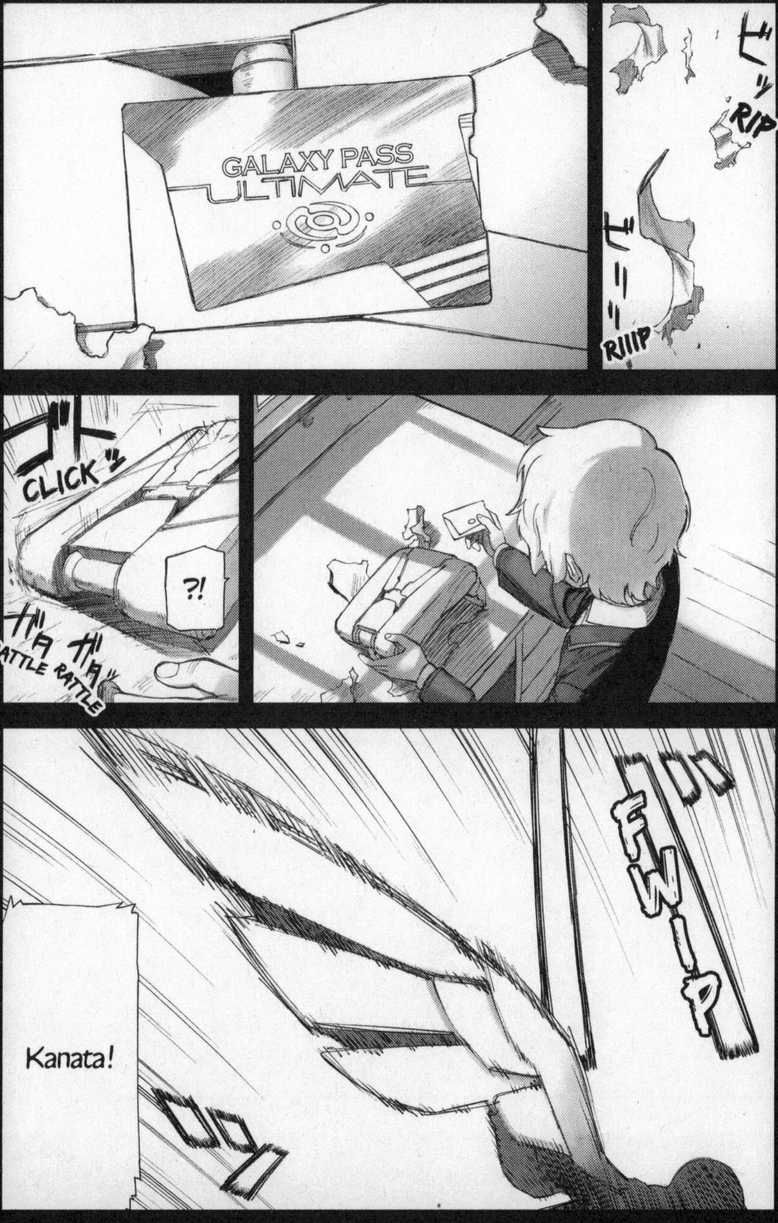
ビッ
RIP
RIIIP
GALAXY PASS ULTIMATE
CLICK
?!
ガタ ガタ
RATTLE RATTLE
FWIP
Kanata!

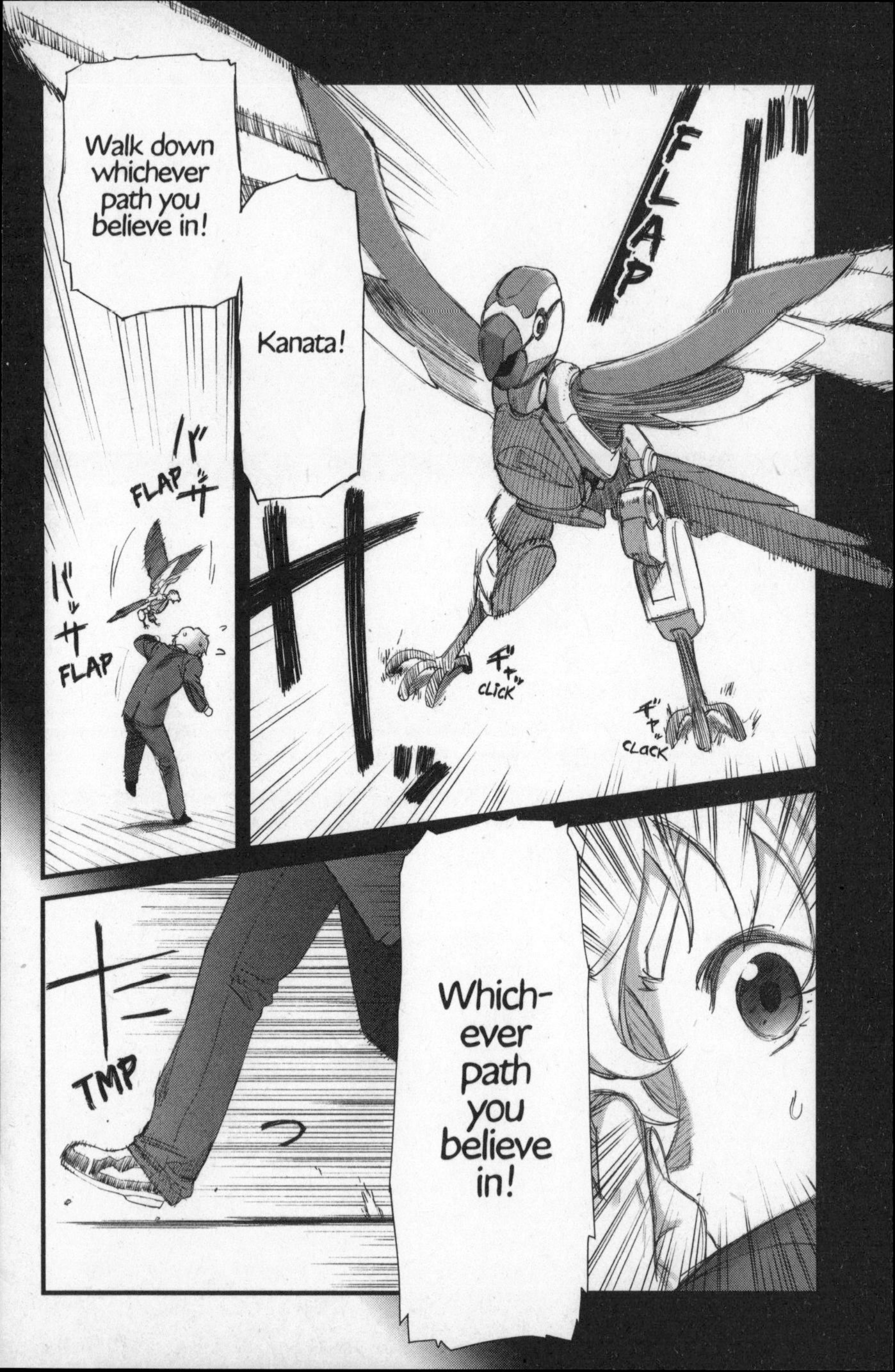
FLAP
Kanata!
CLICK
CLACK
Walk down whichever path you believe in!
FLAP
FLAP
Which-ever path you believe in!
TMP

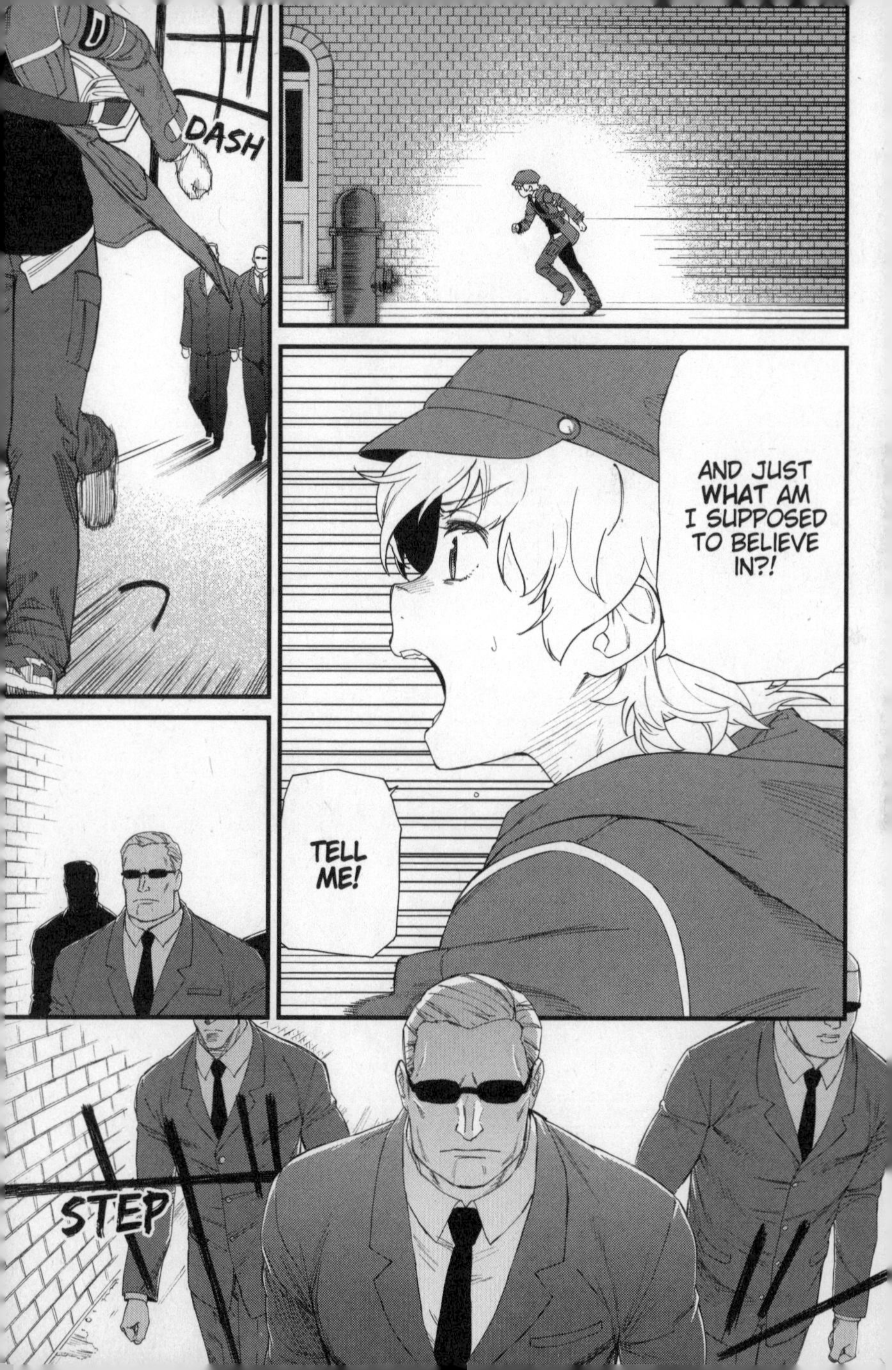
AND JUST WHAT AM I SUPPOSED TO BELIEVE IN?!
TELL ME!
DASH
STEP

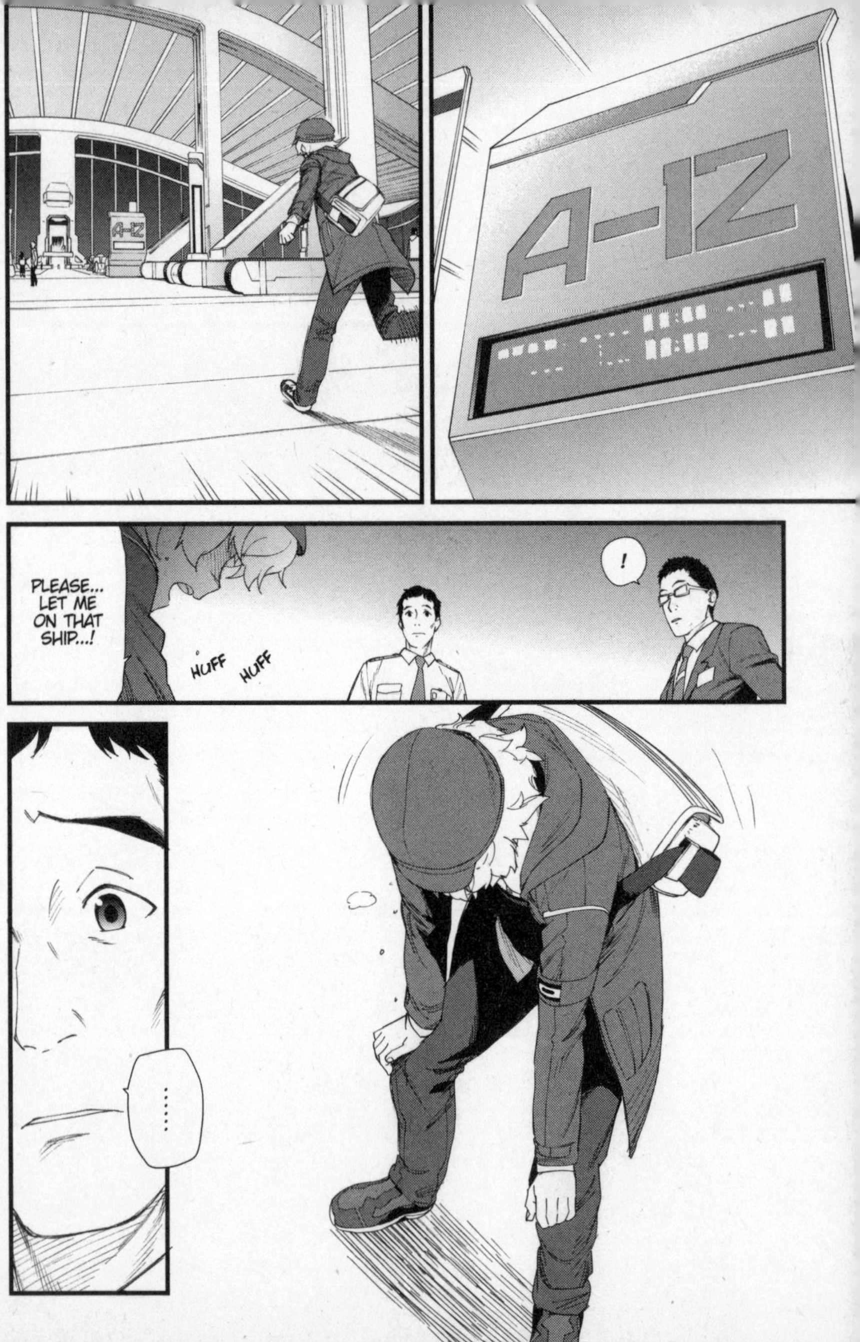
A-12
!
HUFF HUFF
PLEASE... LET ME ON THAT SHIP...!
......

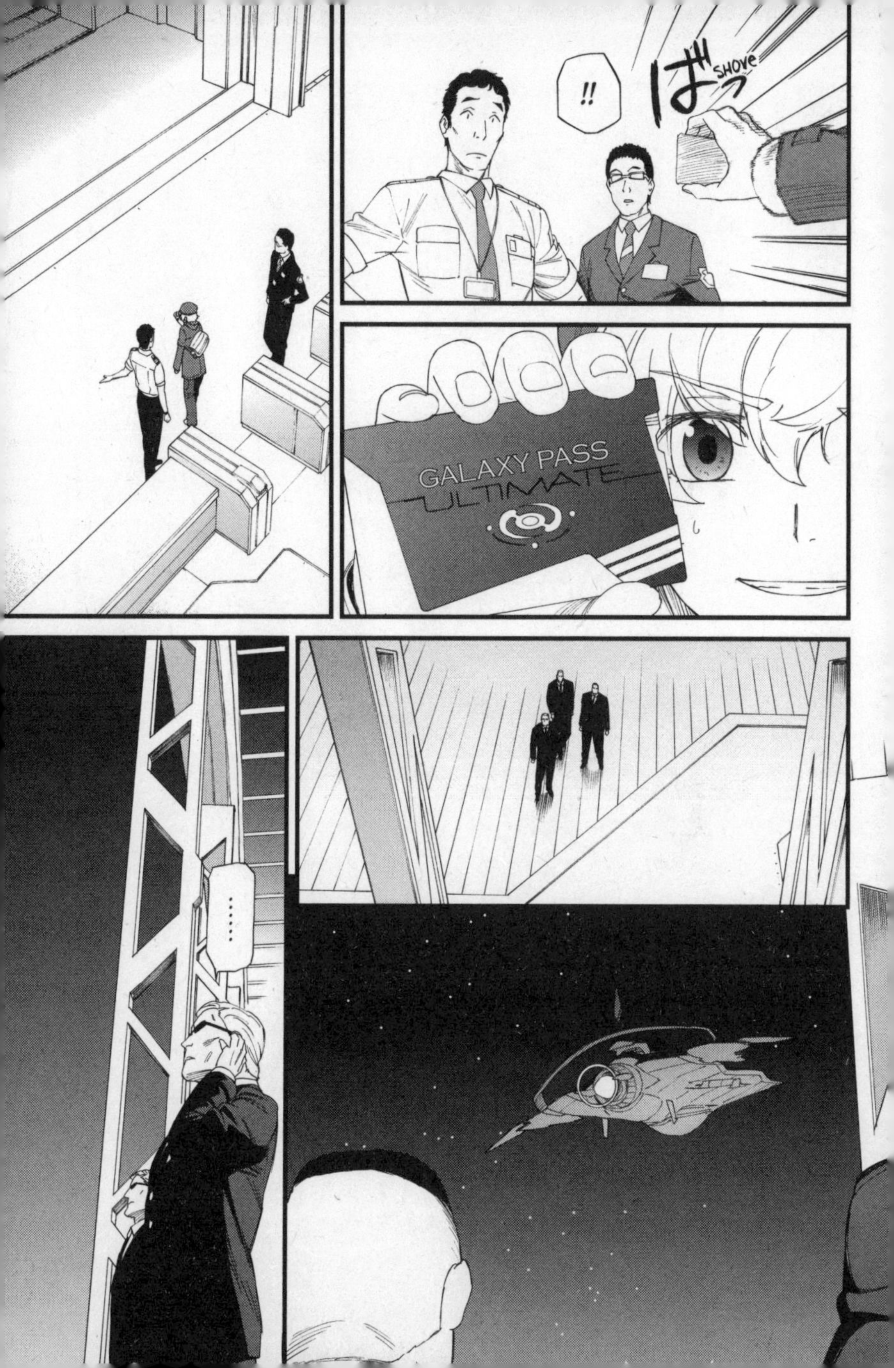
!!
ば
SHOVE
GALAXY PASS
ULTIMATE
......

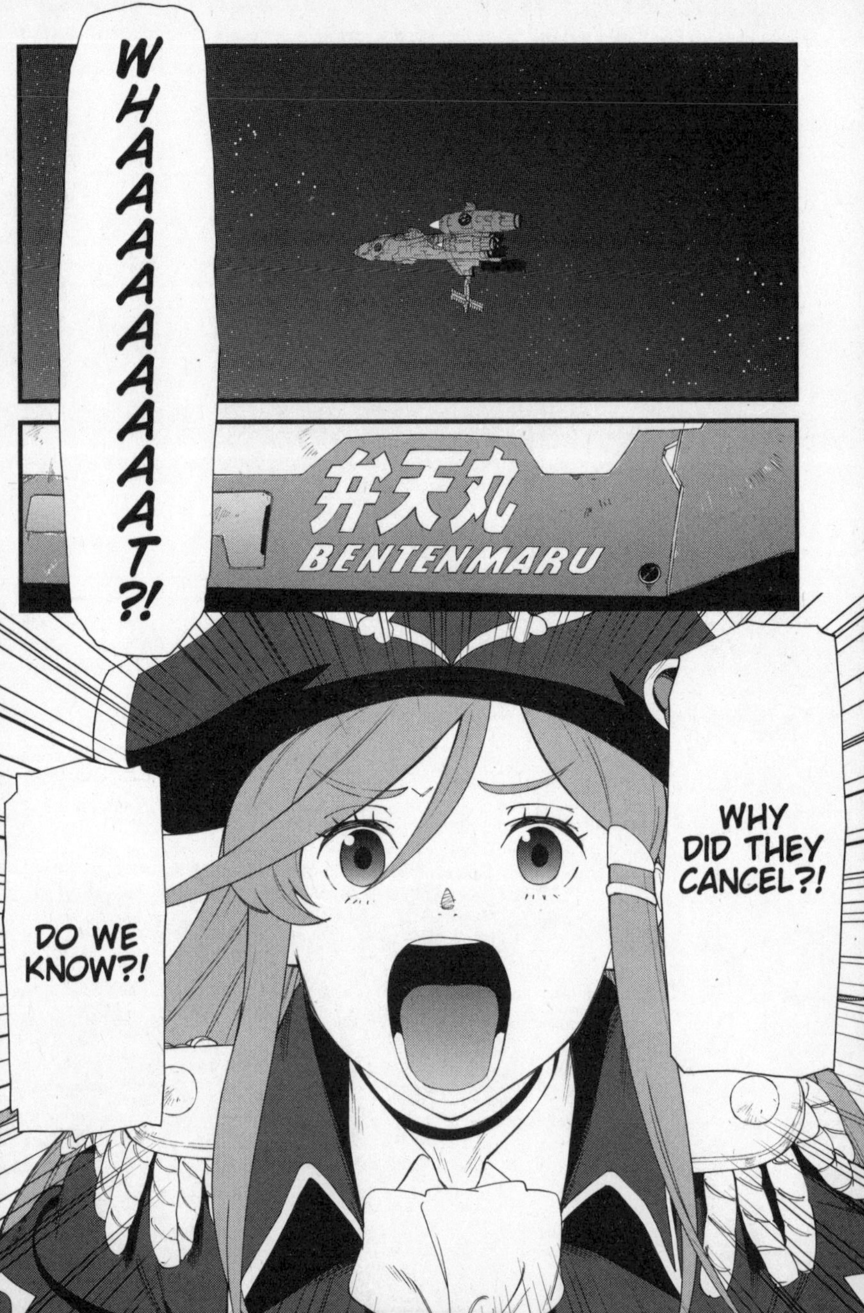
弁天丸
BENTENMARU
WHAAAAAAAAAT?!
WHY DID THEY CANCEL?!
DO WE KNOW?!

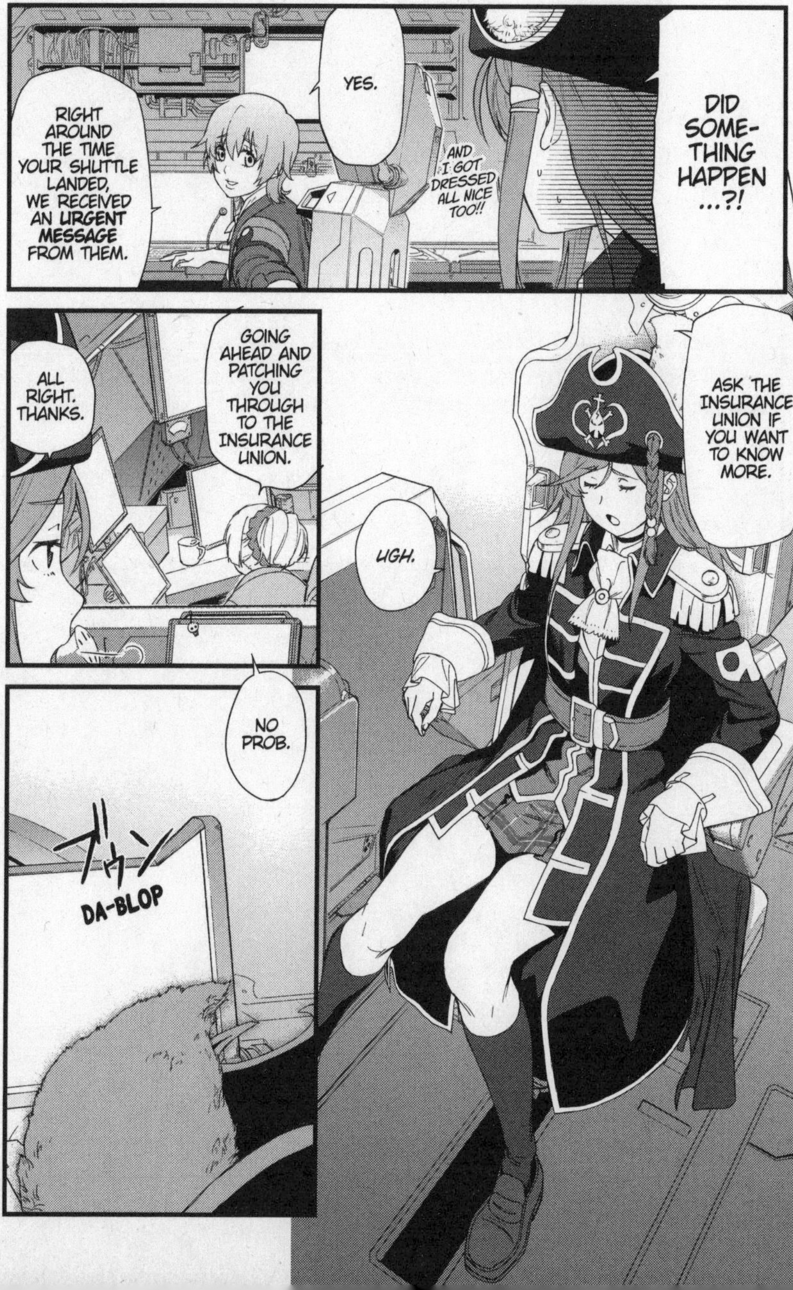
DID SOMETHING HAPPEN ...?!
AND I GOT DRESSED ALL NICE TOO!!
YES.
RIGHT AROUND THE TIME YOUR SHUTTLE LANDED, WE RECEIVED AN URGENT MESSAGE FROM THEM.
ASK THE INSURANCE UNION IF YOU WANT TO KNOW MORE.
UGH.
GOING AHEAD AND PATCHING YOU THROUGH TO THE INSURANCE UNION.
ALL RIGHT. THANKS.
NO PROB.
ブゥン
DA-BLOP

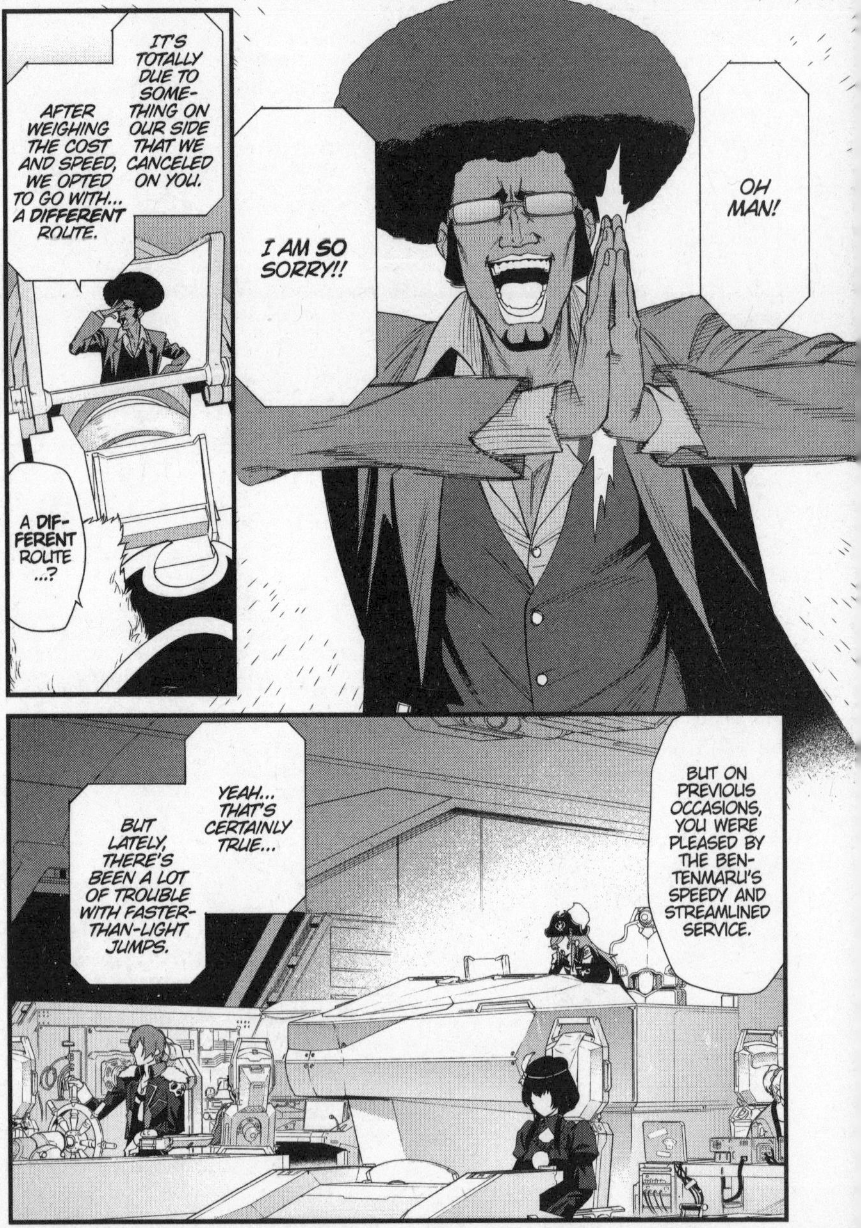
OH MAN!
I AM SO SORRY!!
IT'S TOTALLY DUE TO SOME-THING ON OUR SIDE THAT WE CANCELED ON YOU.
AFTER WEIGHING THE COST AND SPEED, WE OPTED TO GO WITH... A DIFFERENT ROUTE.
A DIF-FERENT ROUTE ...?
BUT ON PREVIOUS OCCASIONS, YOU WERE PLEASED BY THE BEN-TENMARU'S SPEEDY AND STREAMLINED SERVICE.
YEAH... THAT'S CERTAINLY TRUE...
BUT LATELY, THERE'S BEEN A LOT OF TROUBLE WITH FASTER-THAN-LIGHT JUMPS.

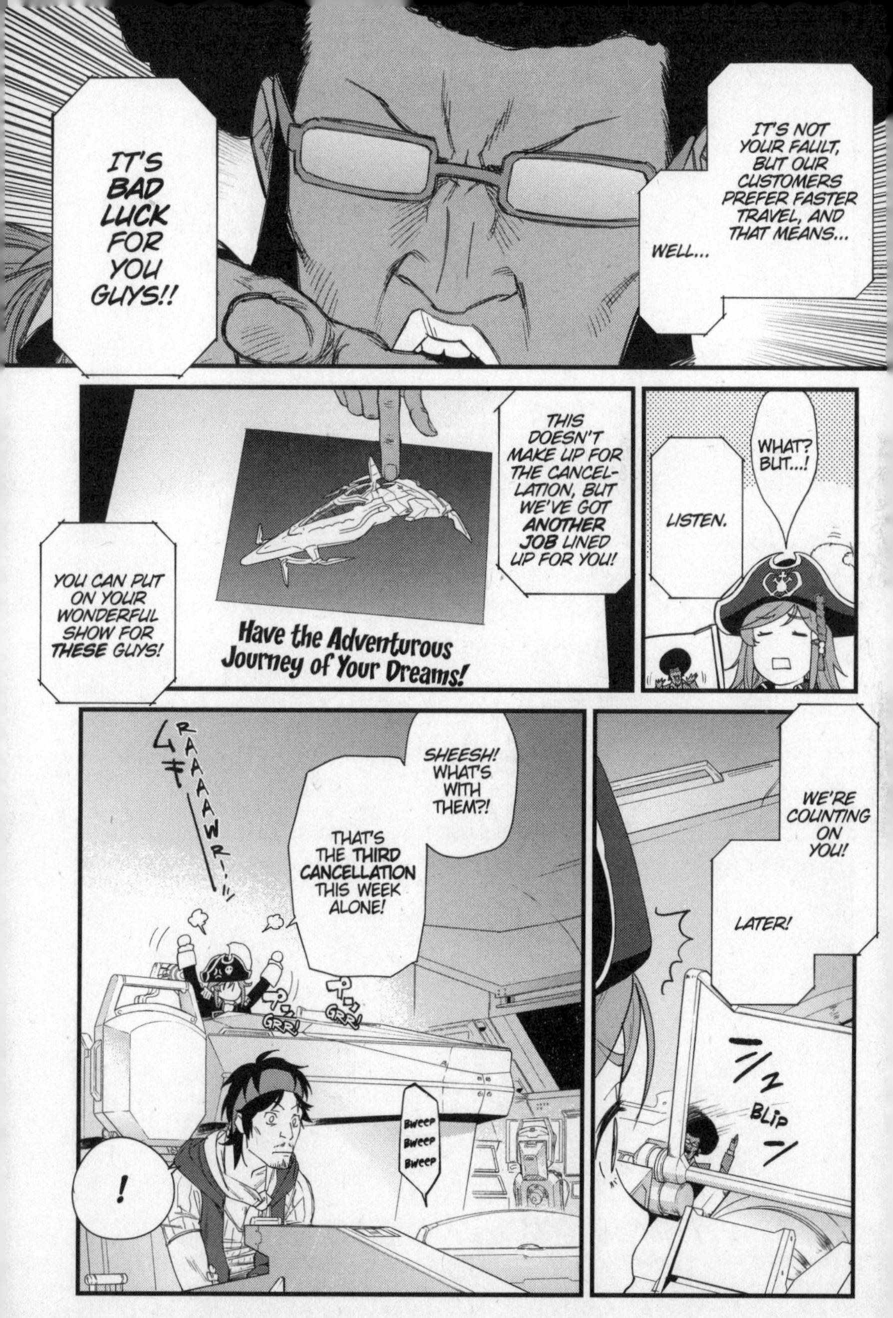

IT'S NOT YOUR FAULT, BUT OUR CUSTOMERS PREFER FASTER TRAVEL, AND THAT MEANS...
WELL...
IT'S BAD LUCK FOR YOU GUYS!!
WHAT? BUT...!
LISTEN.
THIS DOESN'T MAKE UP FOR THE CANCEL-LATION, BUT WE'VE GOT ANOTHER JOB LINED UP FOR YOU!
Have the Adventurous Journey of Your Dreams!
YOU CAN PUT ON YOUR WONDERFUL SHOW FOR THESE GUYS!
WE'RE COUNTING ON YOU!
LATER!
BLIP
SHEESH! WHAT'S WITH THEM?!
THAT'S THE THIRD CANCELLATION THIS WEEK ALONE!
RAAAAAWR...
GRR!
GRR!
BWEEP BWEEP BWEEP
!

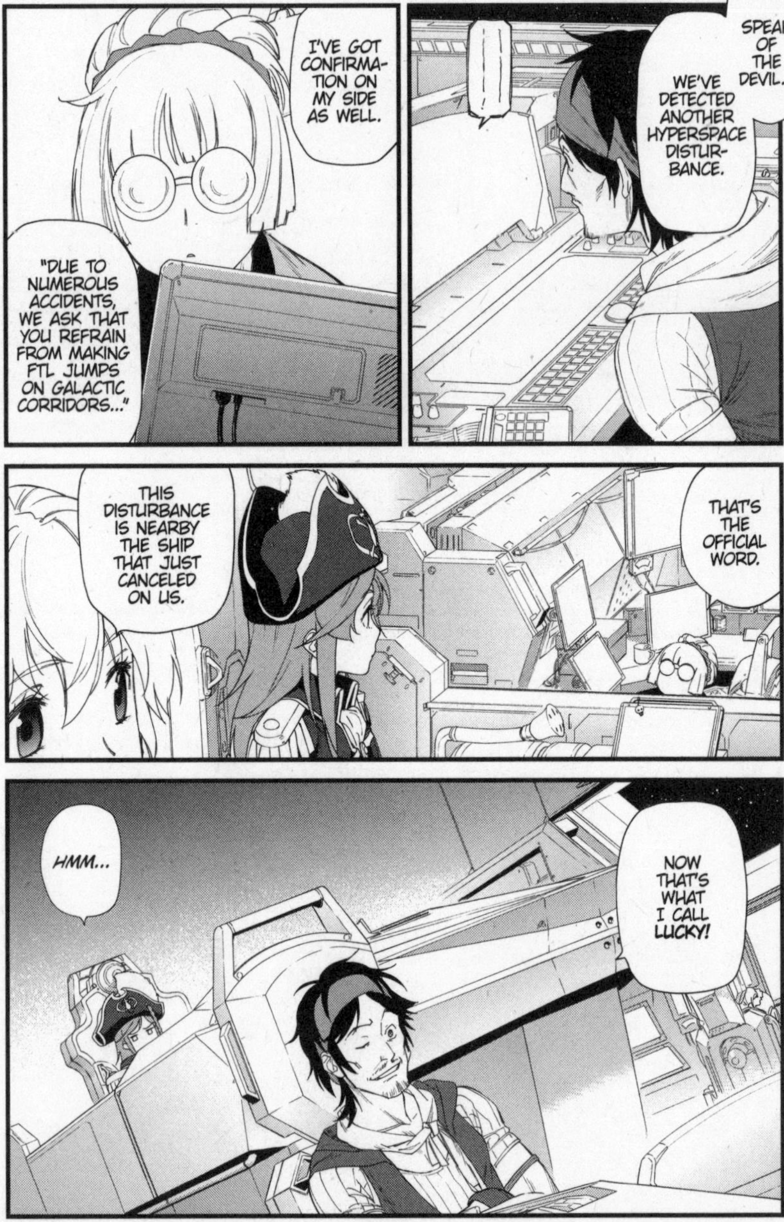

SPEAK OF THE DEVIL...
WE'VE DETECTED ANOTHER HYPERSPACE DISTURBANCE.
...!
I'VE GOT CONFIRMATION ON MY SIDE AS WELL.
"DUE TO NUMEROUS ACCIDENTS, WE ASK THAT YOU REFRAIN FROM MAKING FTL JUMPS ON GALACTIC CORRIDORS..."
THAT'S THE OFFICIAL WORD.
THIS DISTURBANCE IS NEARBY THE SHIP THAT JUST CANCELED ON US.
NOW THAT'S WHAT I CALL LUCKY!
HMM...

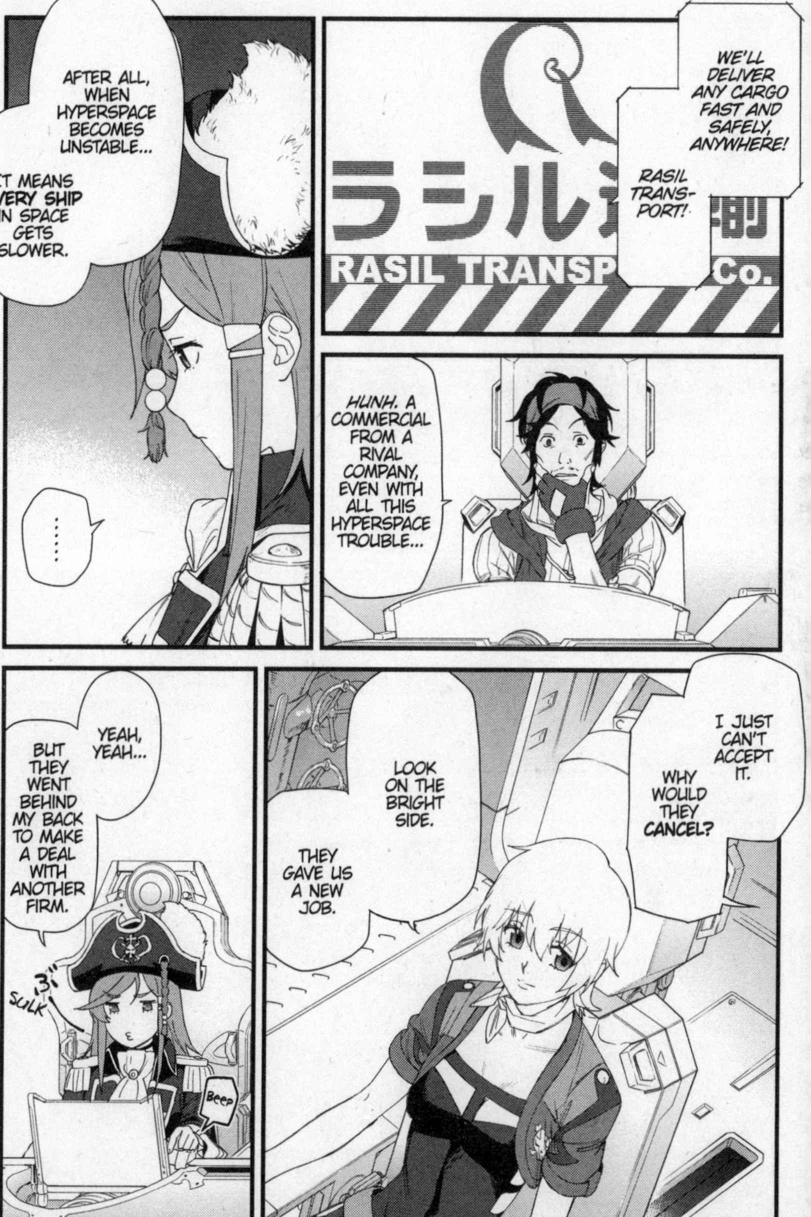
WE'LL DELIVER ANY CARGO FAST AND SAFELY, ANYWHERE!
RASIL TRANS-PORT!
HUNH. A COMMERCIAL FROM A RIVAL COMPANY, EVEN WITH ALL THIS HYPERSPACE TROUBLE...
AFTER ALL, WHEN HYPERSPACE BECOMES UNSTABLE...
IT MEANS **EVERY SHIP** IN SPACE GETS SLOWER.
......
I JUST CAN'T ACCEPT IT.
WHY WOULD THEY **CANCEL?**
LOOK ON THE BRIGHT SIDE.
THEY GAVE US A NEW JOB.
YEAH, YEAH...
BUT THEY WENT BEHIND MY BACK TO MAKE A DEAL WITH ANOTHER FIRM.
SULK
Beep

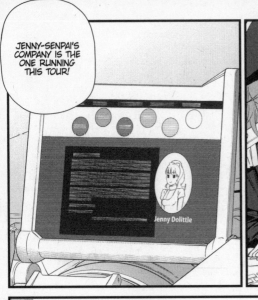

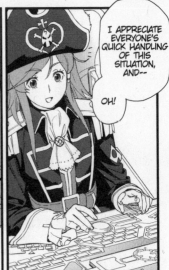

I APPRECIATE EVERYONE'S QUICK HANDLING OF THIS SITUATION, AND--
OH!
JENNY-SENPAI'S COMPANY IS THE ONE RUNNING THIS TOUR!
Jenny Dolittle
TRA
Boarding Passenger
D
Galaxy Pass Used
Kanat Mugen
PLIP
HUH?
Interstellar Travel Company Fairy Jane
Category: VIP
Name: Kanata Mugen
ID: 794E55788
Pass: Galaxy Pass
Destination: As far as possible
Address: Mugen Worksho

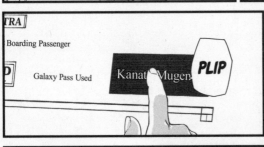

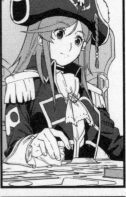

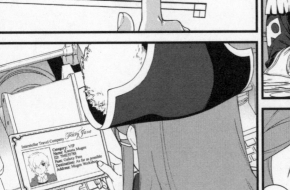

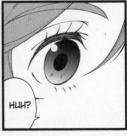

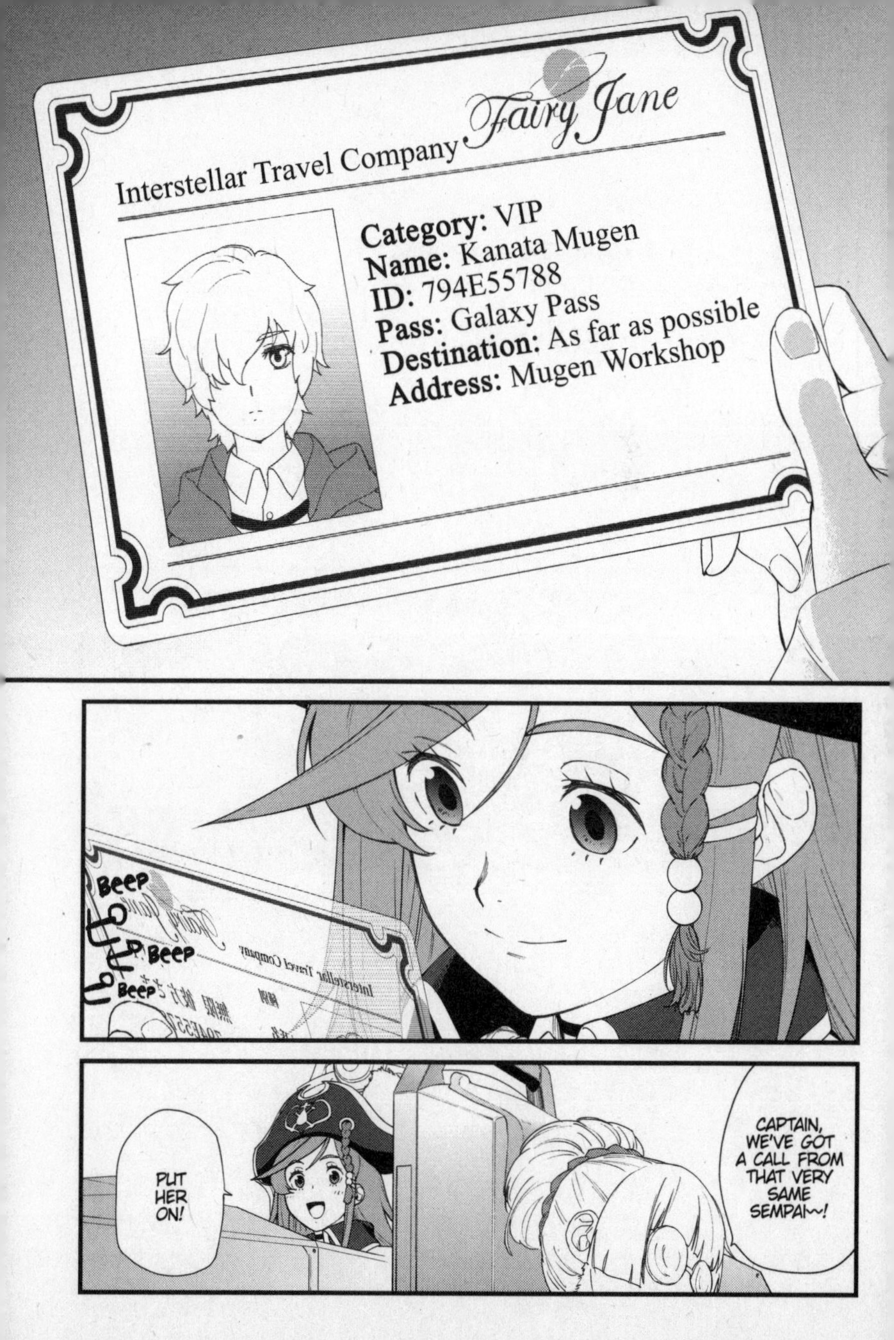

Interstellar Travel Company
Fairy Jane
Category: VIP
Name: Kanata Mugen
ID: 794E55788
Pass: Galaxy Pass
Destination: As far as possible
Address: Mugen Workshop
Beep
Beep
Beep
CAPTAIN, WE'VE GOT A CALL FROM THAT VERY SAME SEMPAI~!
PUT HER ON!

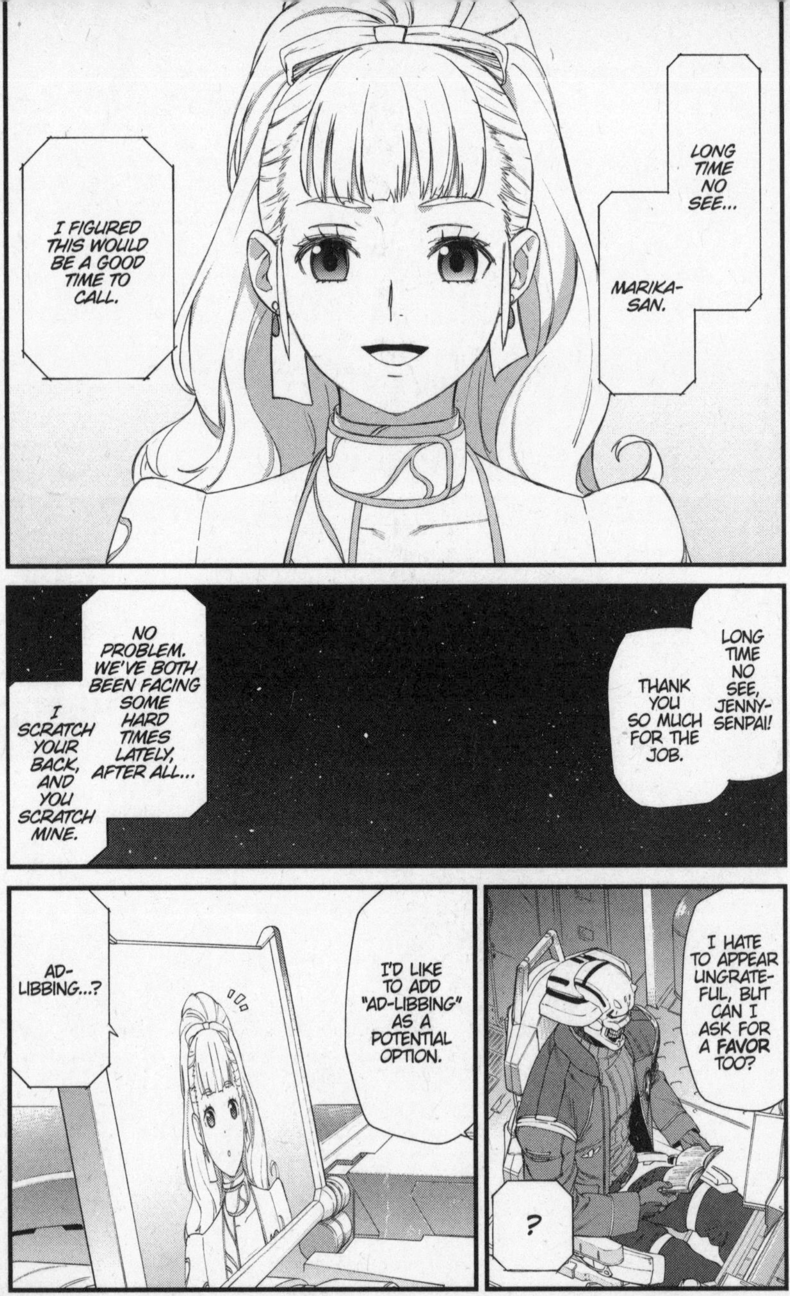
LONG TIME NO SEE... MARIKA-SAN.
I FIGURED THIS WOULD BE A GOOD TIME TO CALL.
LONG TIME NO SEE, JENNY-SENPAI!
THANK YOU SO MUCH FOR THE JOB.
NO PROBLEM. WE'VE BOTH BEEN FACING SOME HARD TIMES LATELY, AFTER ALL...
I SCRATCH YOUR BACK, AND YOU SCRATCH MINE.
I HATE TO APPEAR UNGRATEFUL, BUT CAN I ASK FOR A FAVOR TOO?
?
I'D LIKE TO ADD "AD-LIBBING" AS A POTENTIAL OPTION.
AD-LIBBING...?

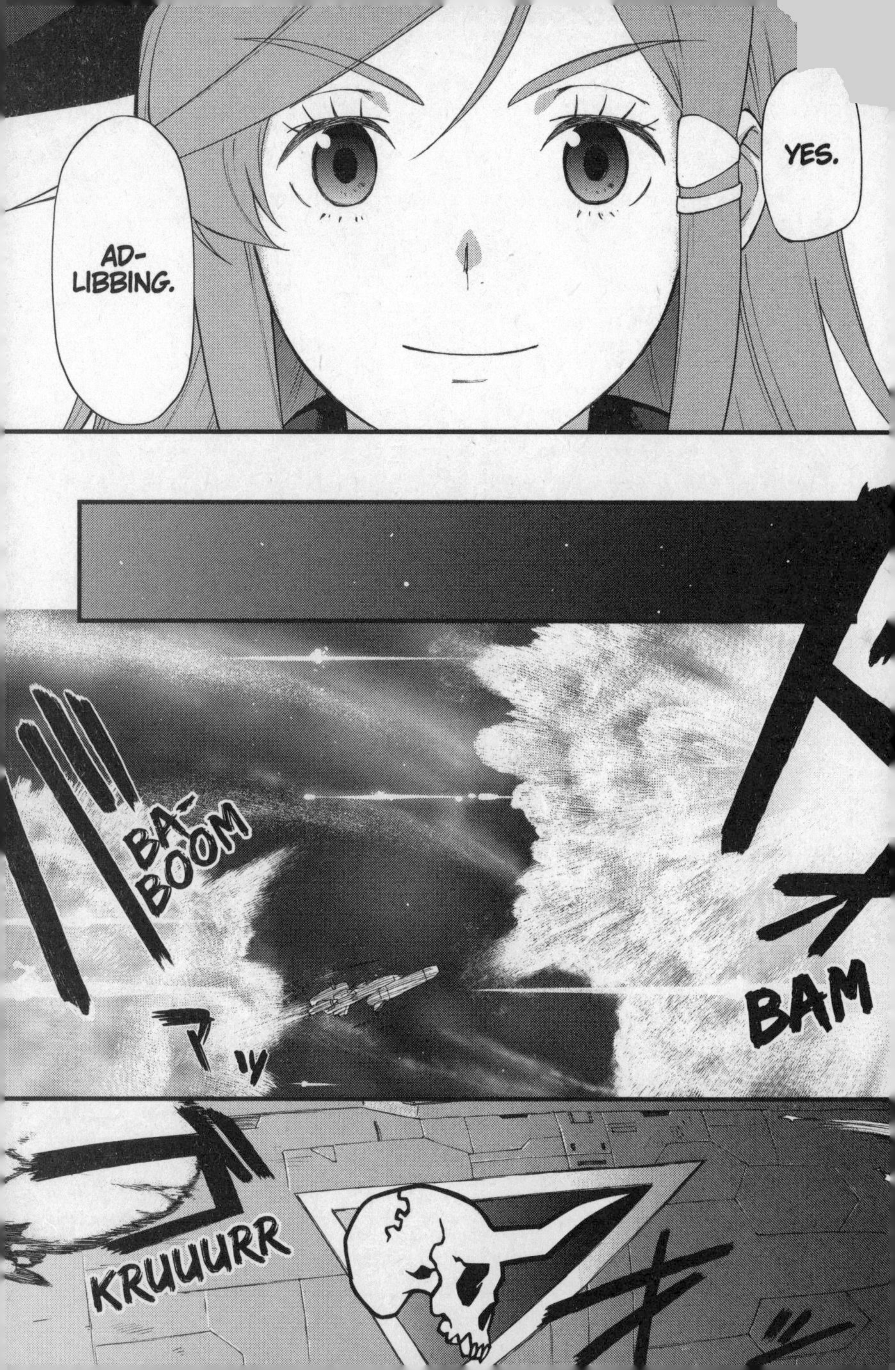
YES.
AD-LIBBING.
BAM
BA-BOOM
KRUUURR

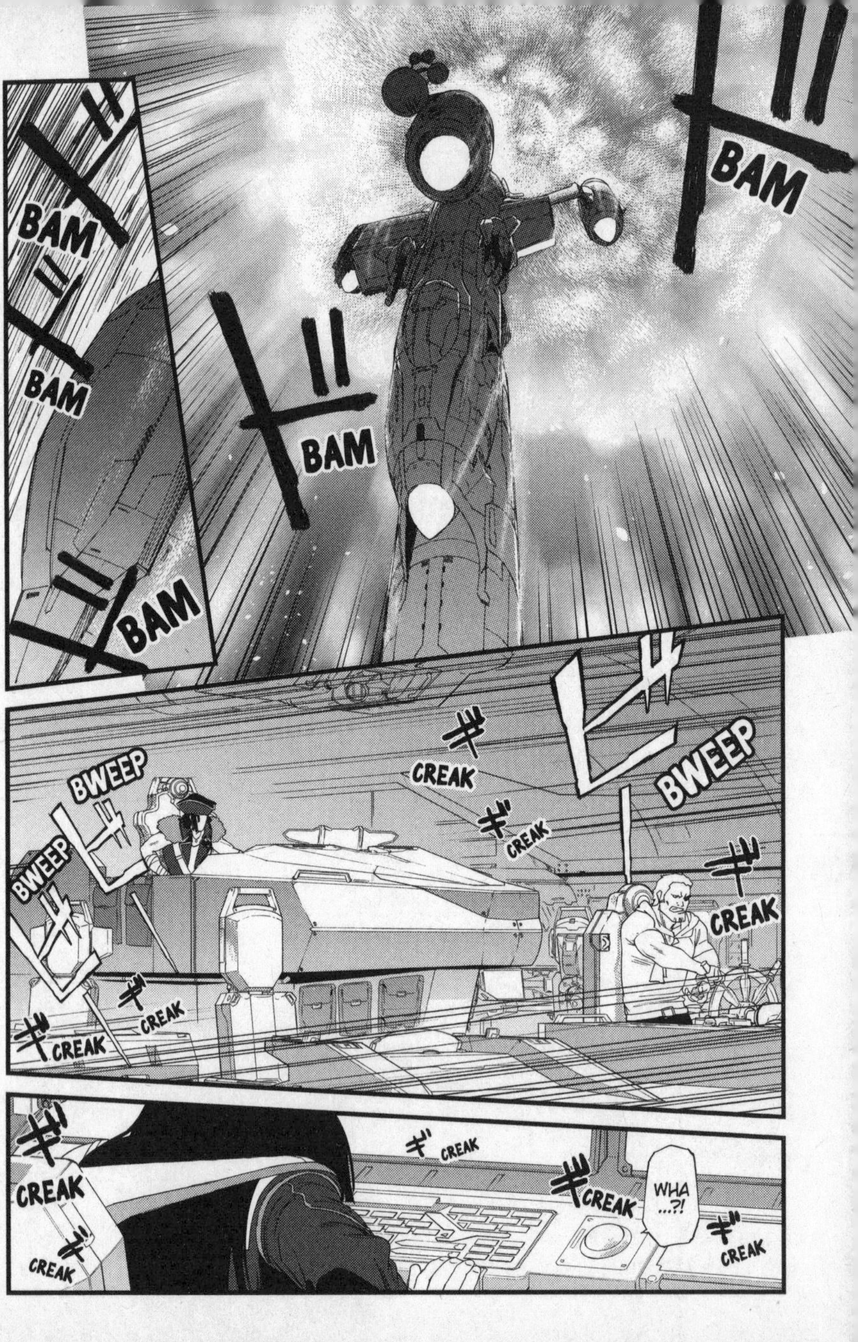
BAM
BAM
BAM
BAM
BAM
BWEEP
CREAK
CREAK
CREAK
BWEEP
BWEEP
CREAK
CREAK
CREAK
WHA ...?!
CREAK
CREAK
CREAK
CREAK

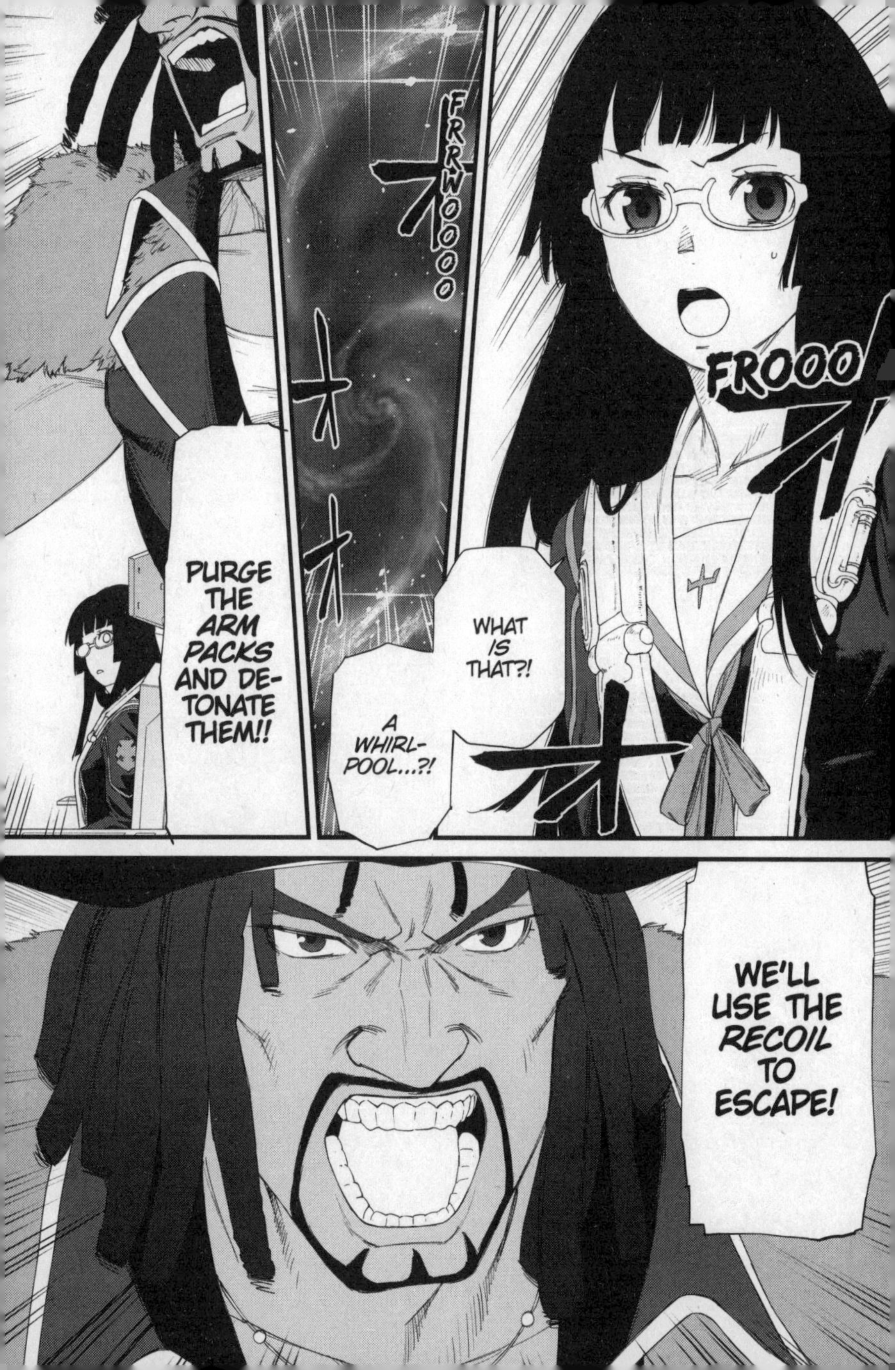
FROOO
WHAT IS THAT?!
A WHIRL-POOL...?!
FRRWOOOOO
PURGE THE ARM PACKS AND DE-TONATE THEM!!
WE'LL USE THE RECOIL TO ESCAPE!

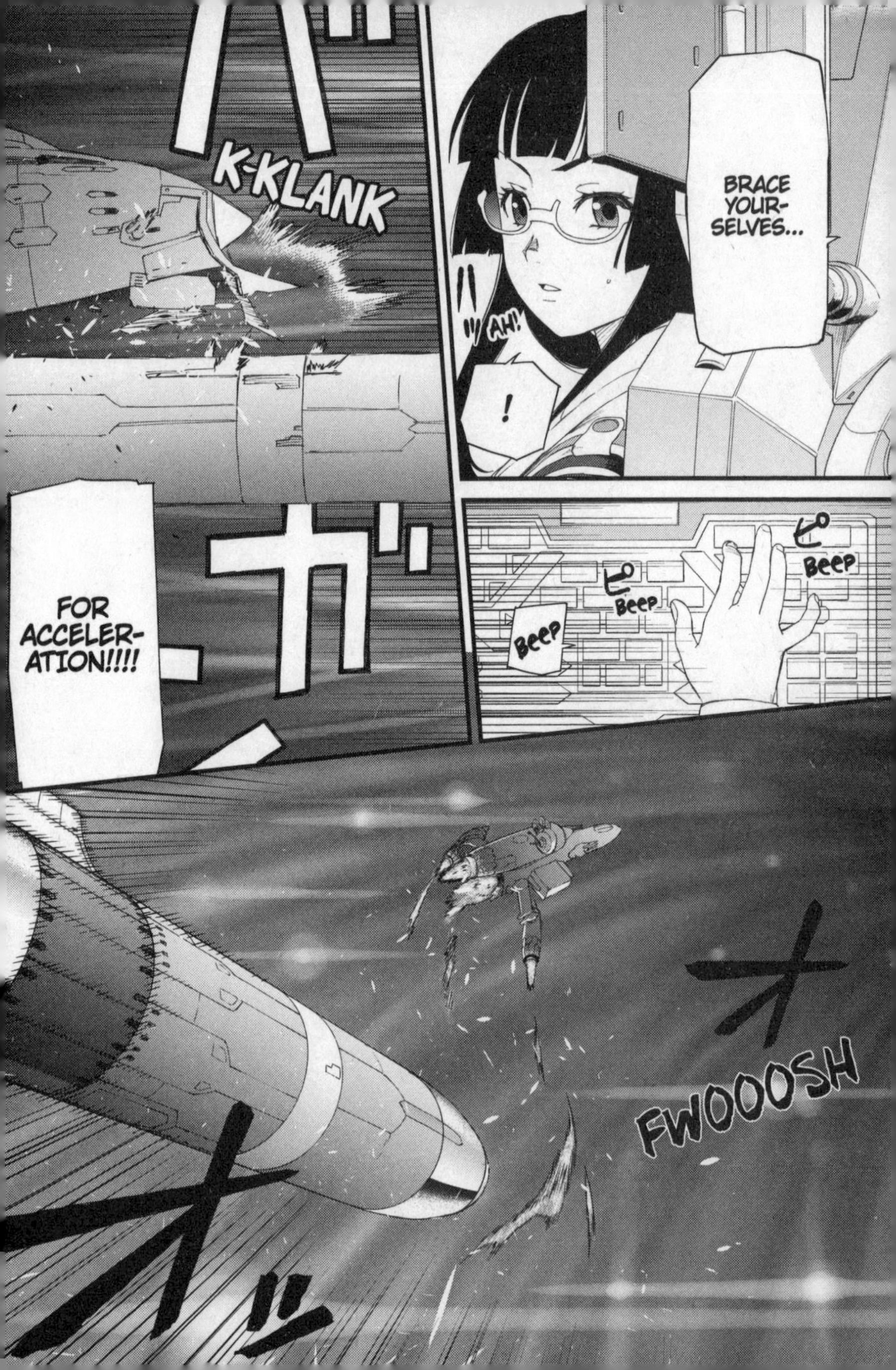

BRACE YOUR-SELVES...
AH!
!
バ
K-KLANK
ピ
Beep
ピ
Beep
Beep
FOR ACCELER-ATION!!!!
ガ
オ
FWOOOSH
オッ

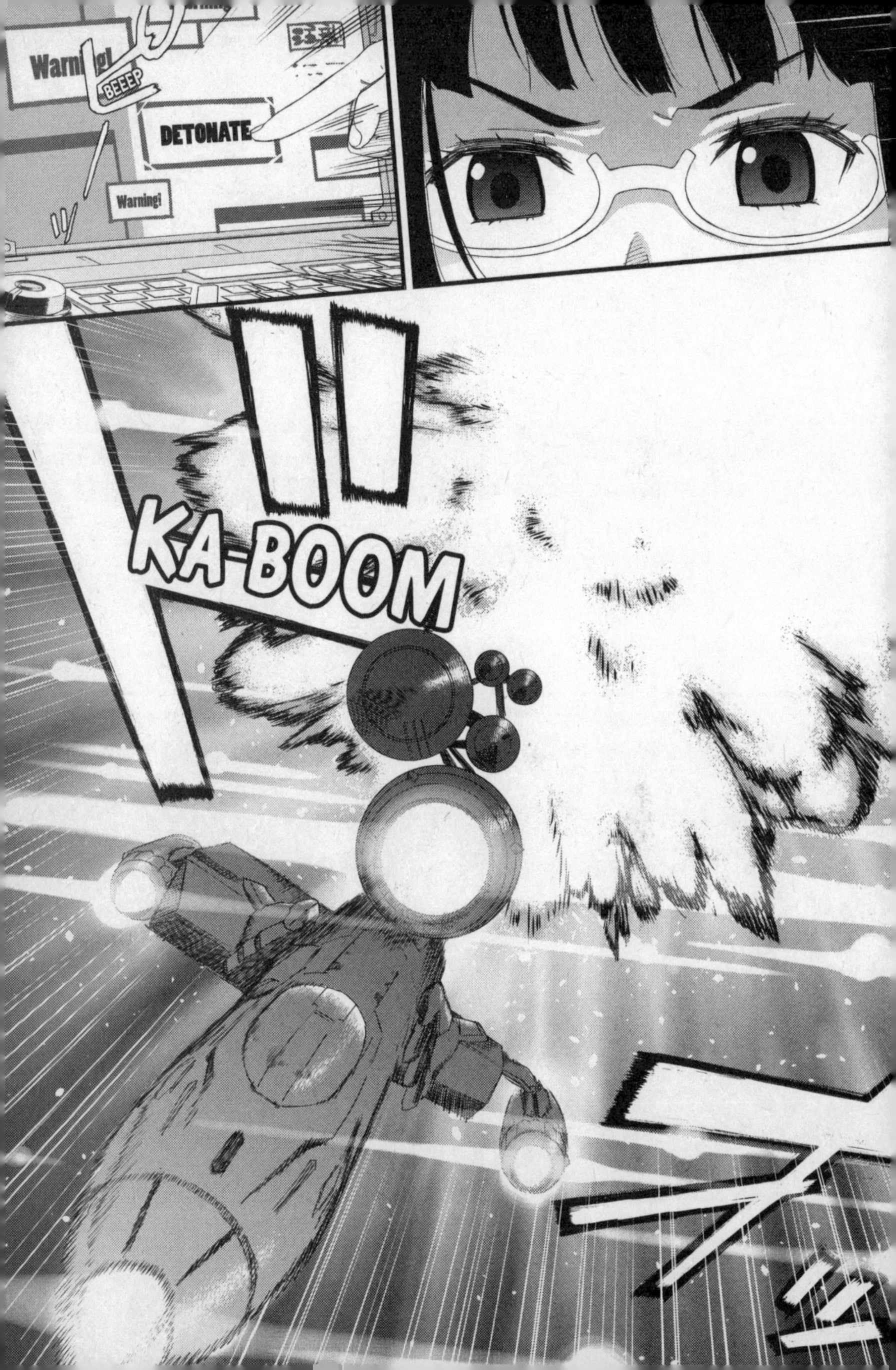
Warning!
BEEEP
DETONATE
Warning!
KA-BOOM

BRWOO

XOOOOSH

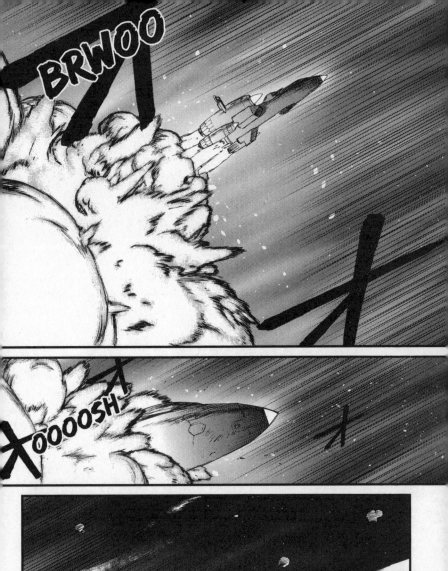

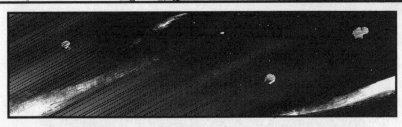

WE HAVE SUCCESSFULLY COMPLETED OUR FOURTH FTL JUMP.

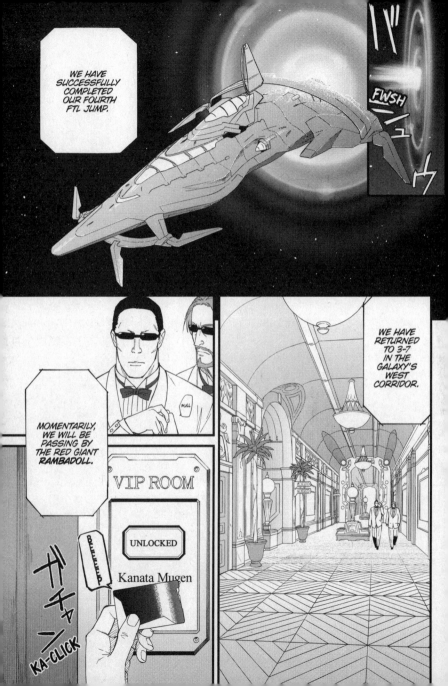

バ

FWSH

ニュ

ウ

WE HAVE RETURNED TO 3-7 IN THE GALAXY'S WEST CORRIDOR.

MOMENTARILY, WE WILL BE PASSING BY THE RED GIANT RAMBADOLL.

VIP ROOM

UNLOCKED

Kanata Mugen

PULL

ギ

ギ

ギ

KA-CLICK

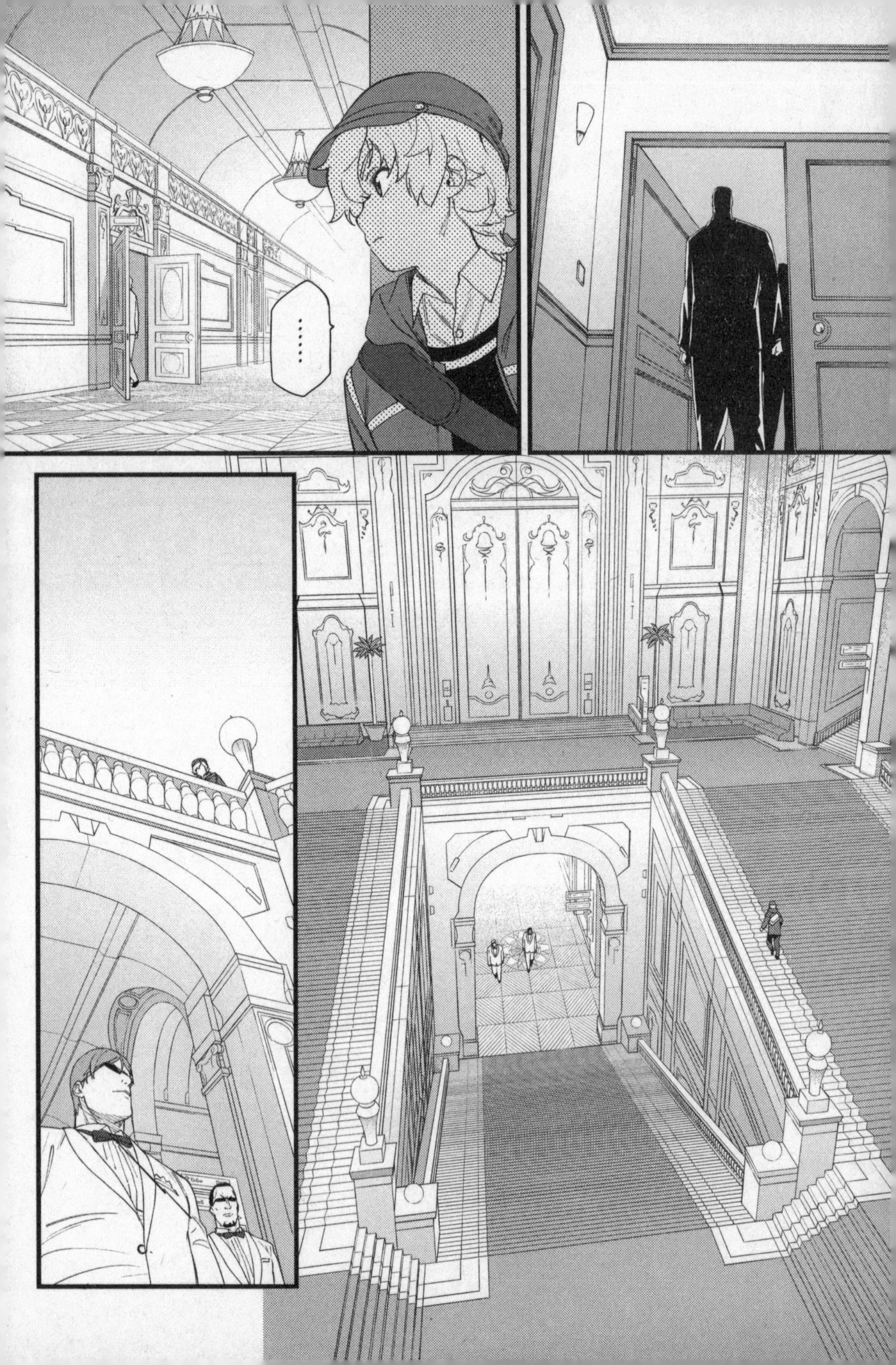
......

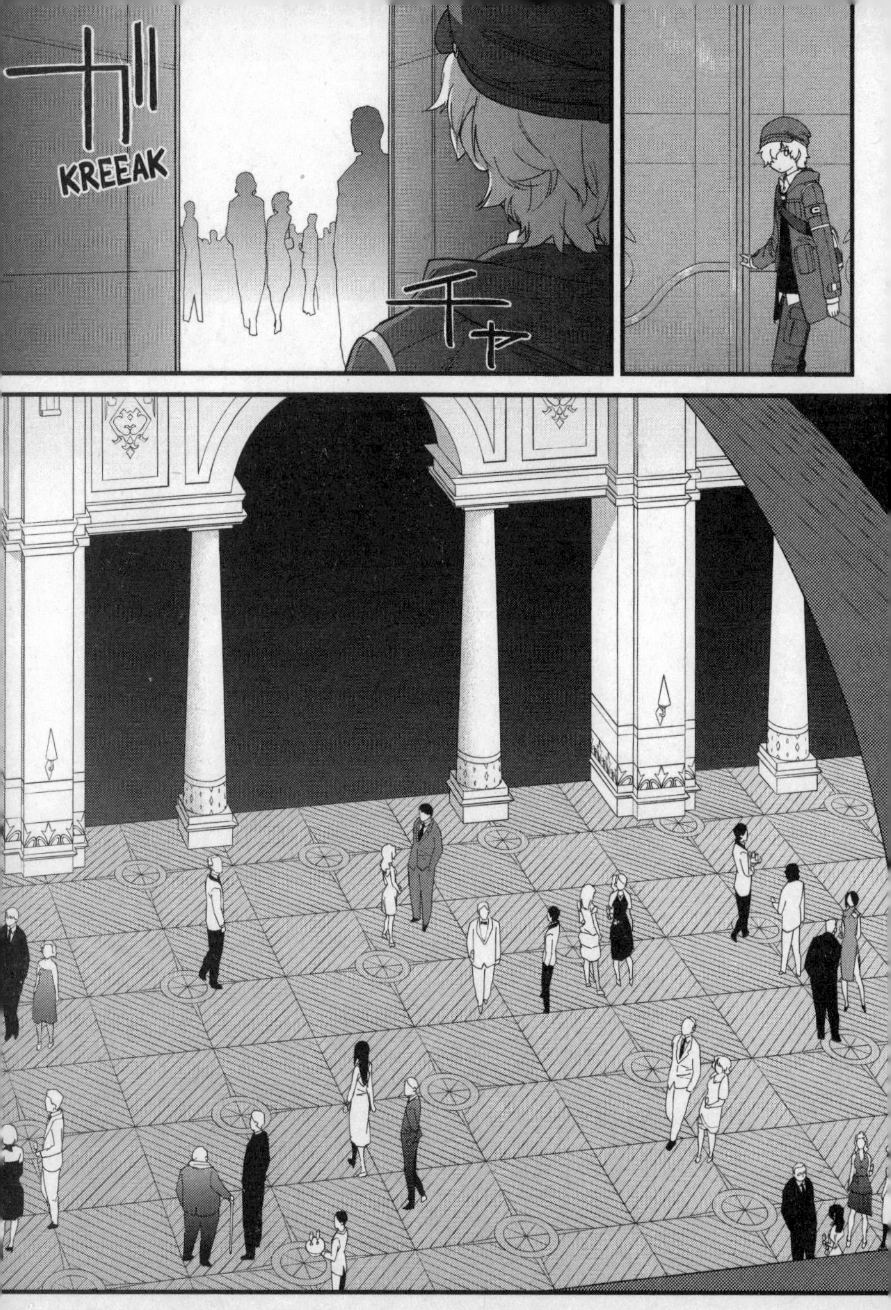
チャ
ガ
KREEAK

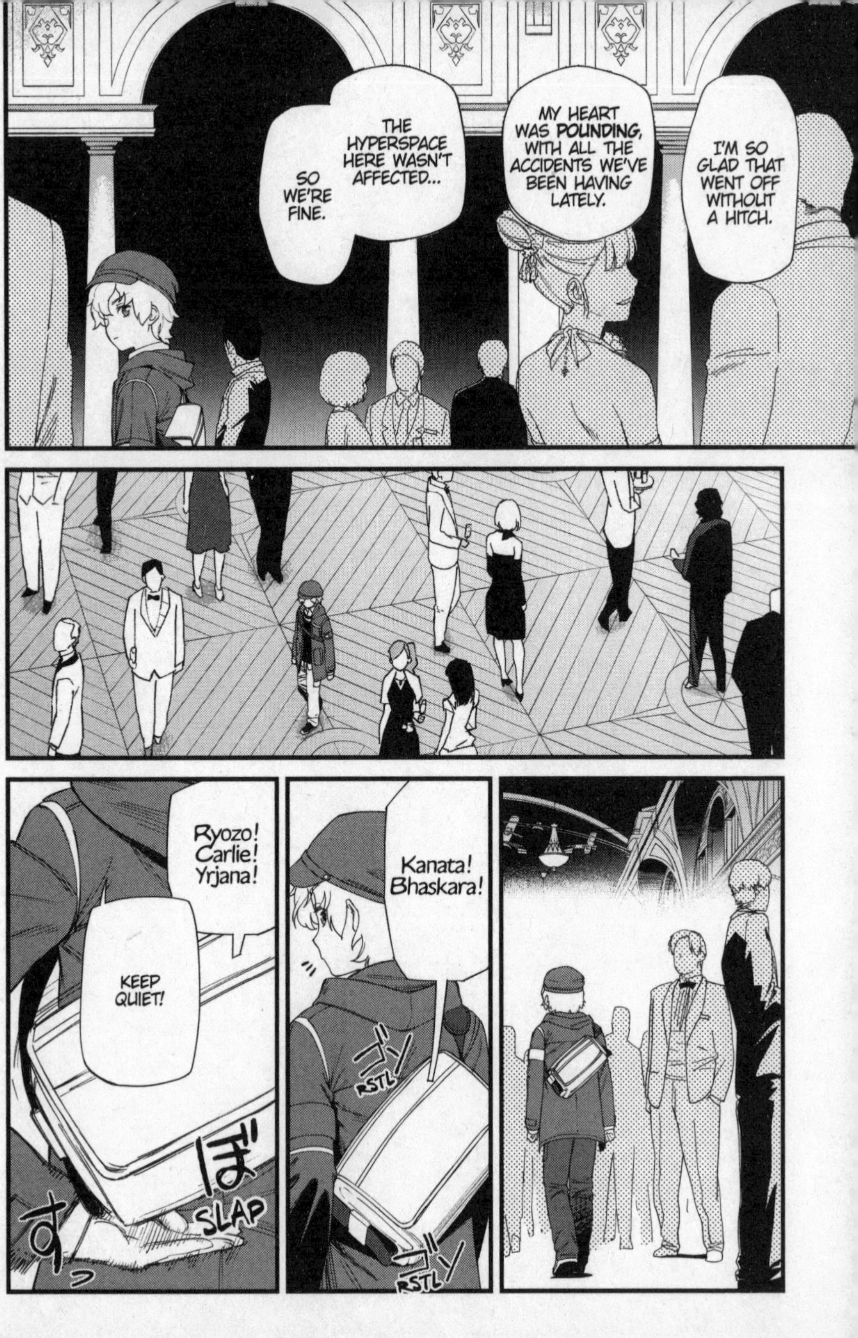
I'M SO GLAD THAT WENT OFF WITHOUT A HITCH.
MY HEART WAS **POUNDING**, WITH ALL THE ACCIDENTS WE'VE BEEN HAVING LATELY.
THE HYPERSPACE HERE WASN'T AFFECTED...
SO WE'RE FINE.
Kanata! Bhaskara!
RSTL
RSTL
Ryozo! Carlie! Yrjana!
KEEP QUIET!
SLAP

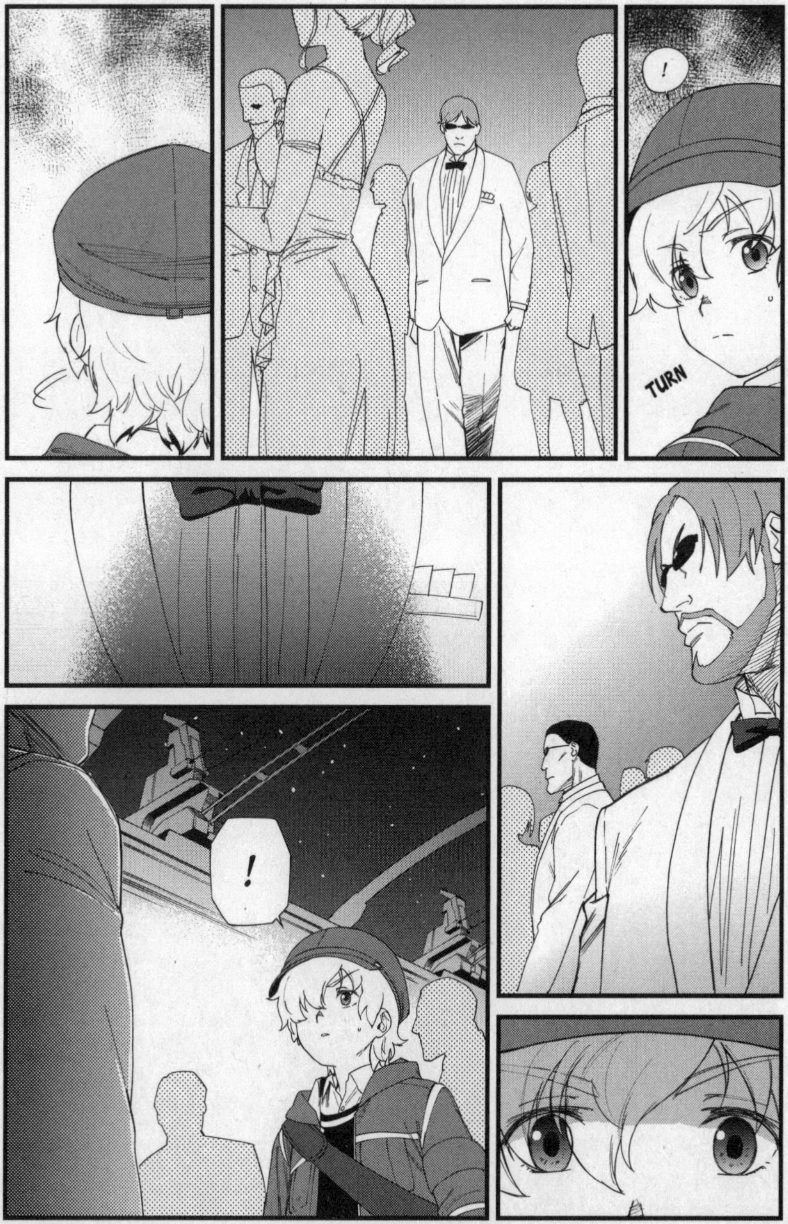
!
TURN
!

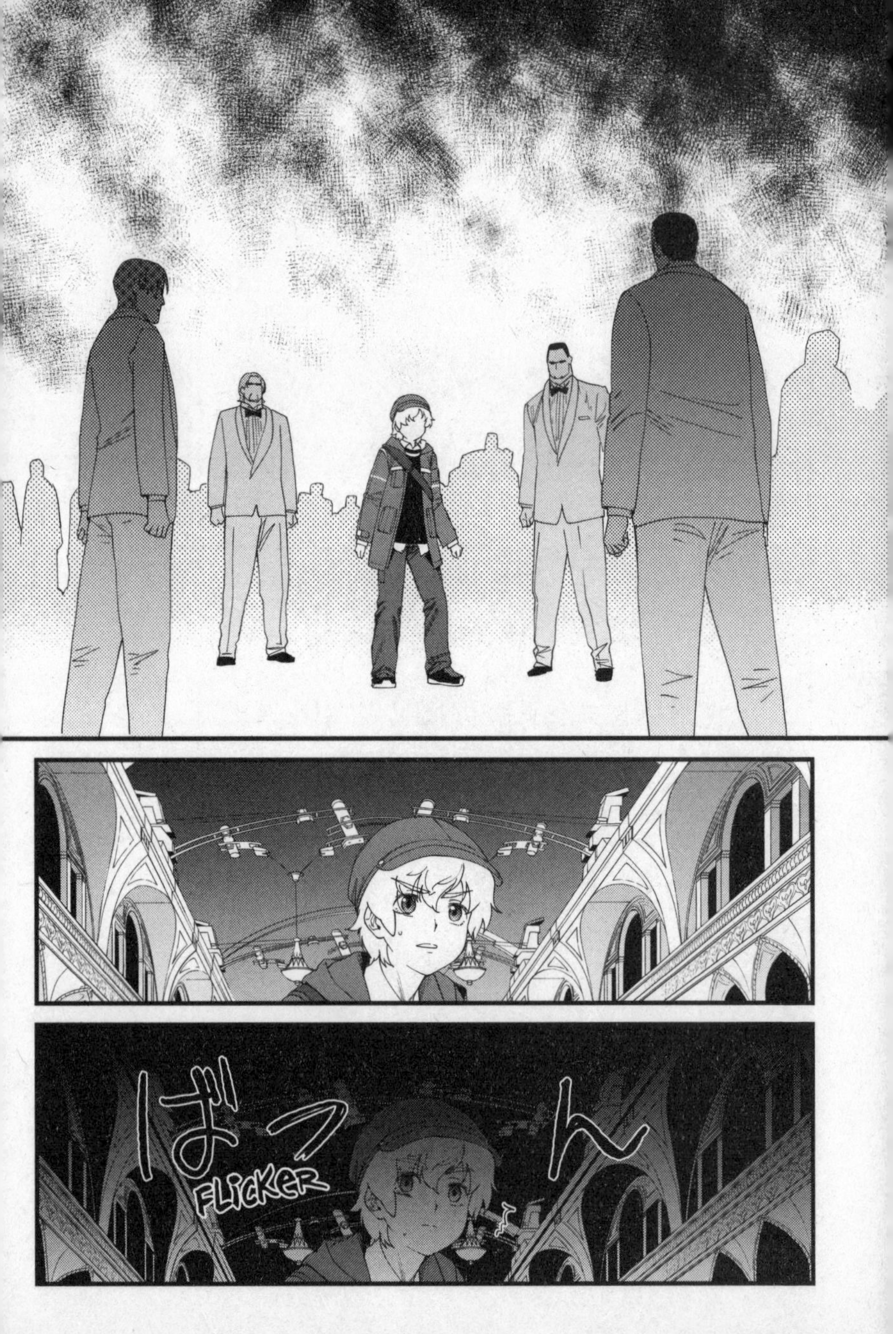
ぱっん
FLICKER

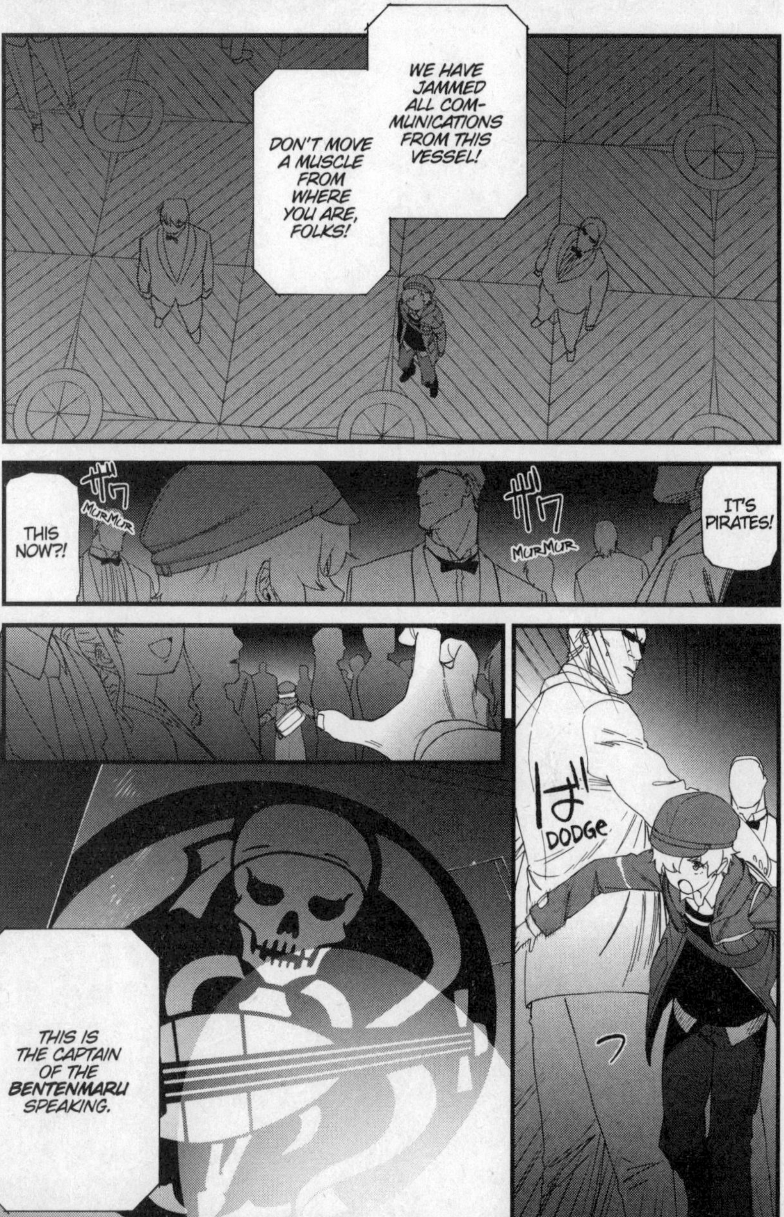
WE HAVE JAMMED ALL COM-MUNICATIONS FROM THIS VESSEL!
DON'T MOVE A MUSCLE FROM WHERE YOU ARE, FOLKS!
IT'S PIRATES!
ザワ
MURMUR
ザワ
MURMUR
THIS NOW?!
ぱ
DODGE
つ
THIS IS THE CAPTAIN OF THE BENTENMARU SPEAKING.

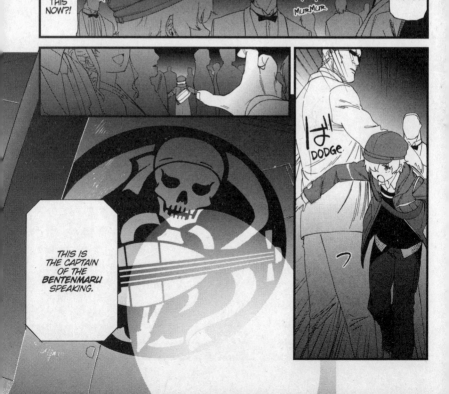

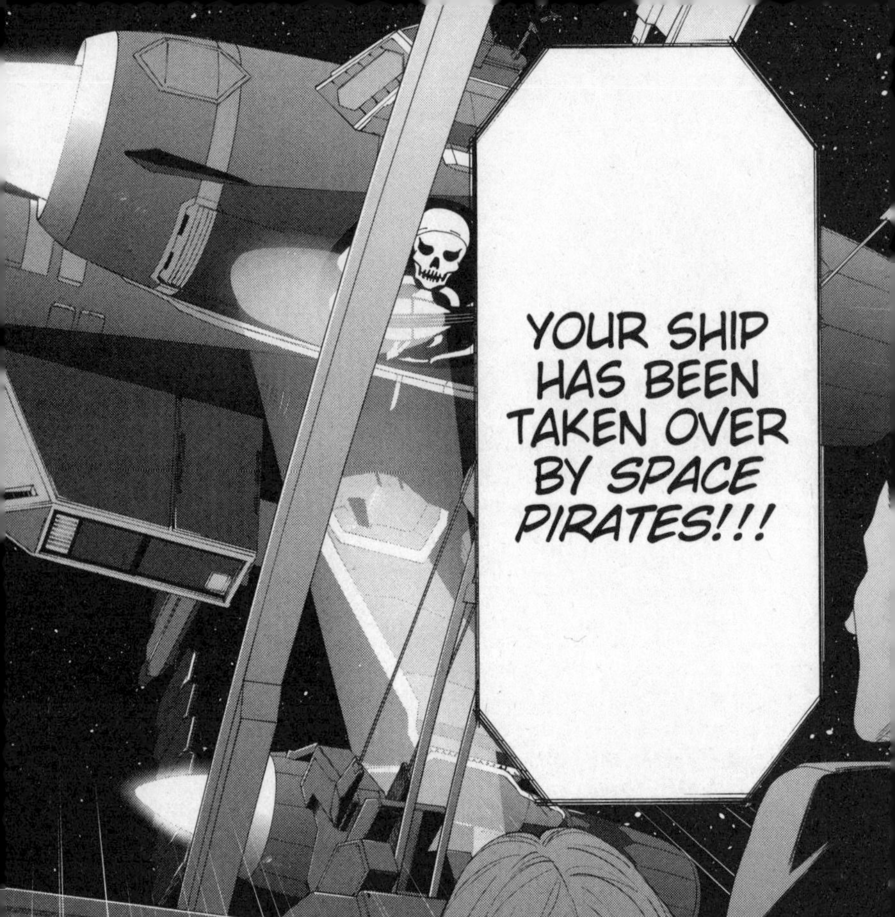
YOUR SHIP HAS BEEN TAKEN OVER BY *SPACE PIRATES*!!!
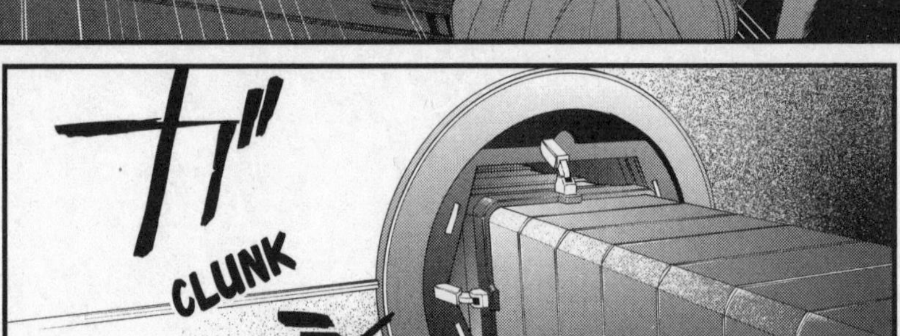
ガ
CLUNK
シュ

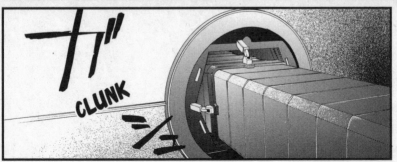

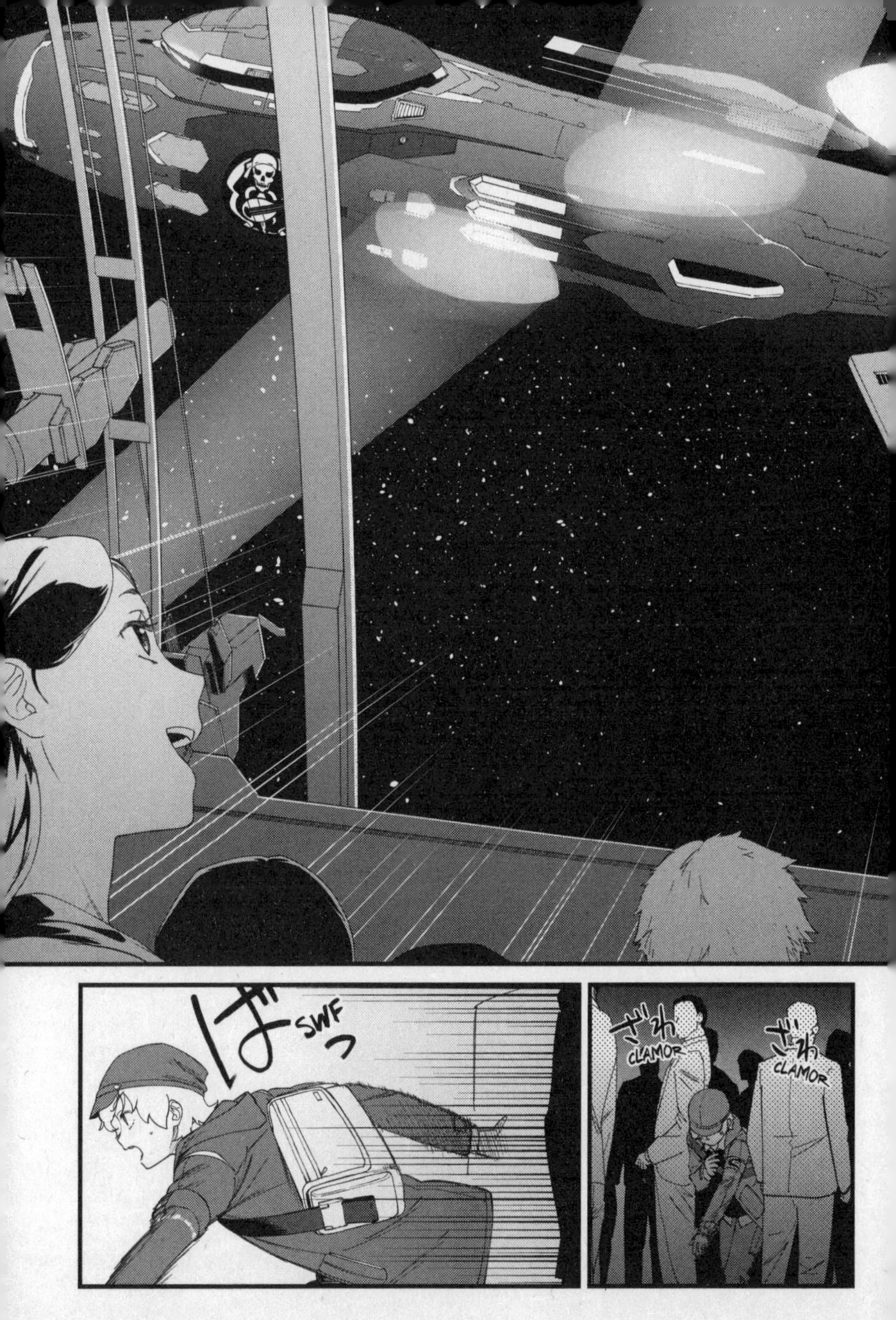
ざわ
CLAMOR
ざわ
CLAMOR
ぱっ
SWF

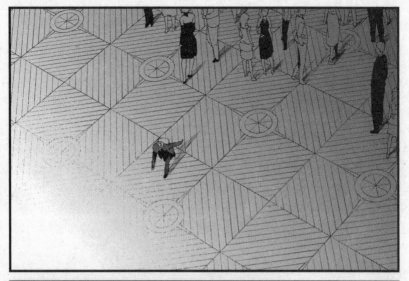

・・・・・・

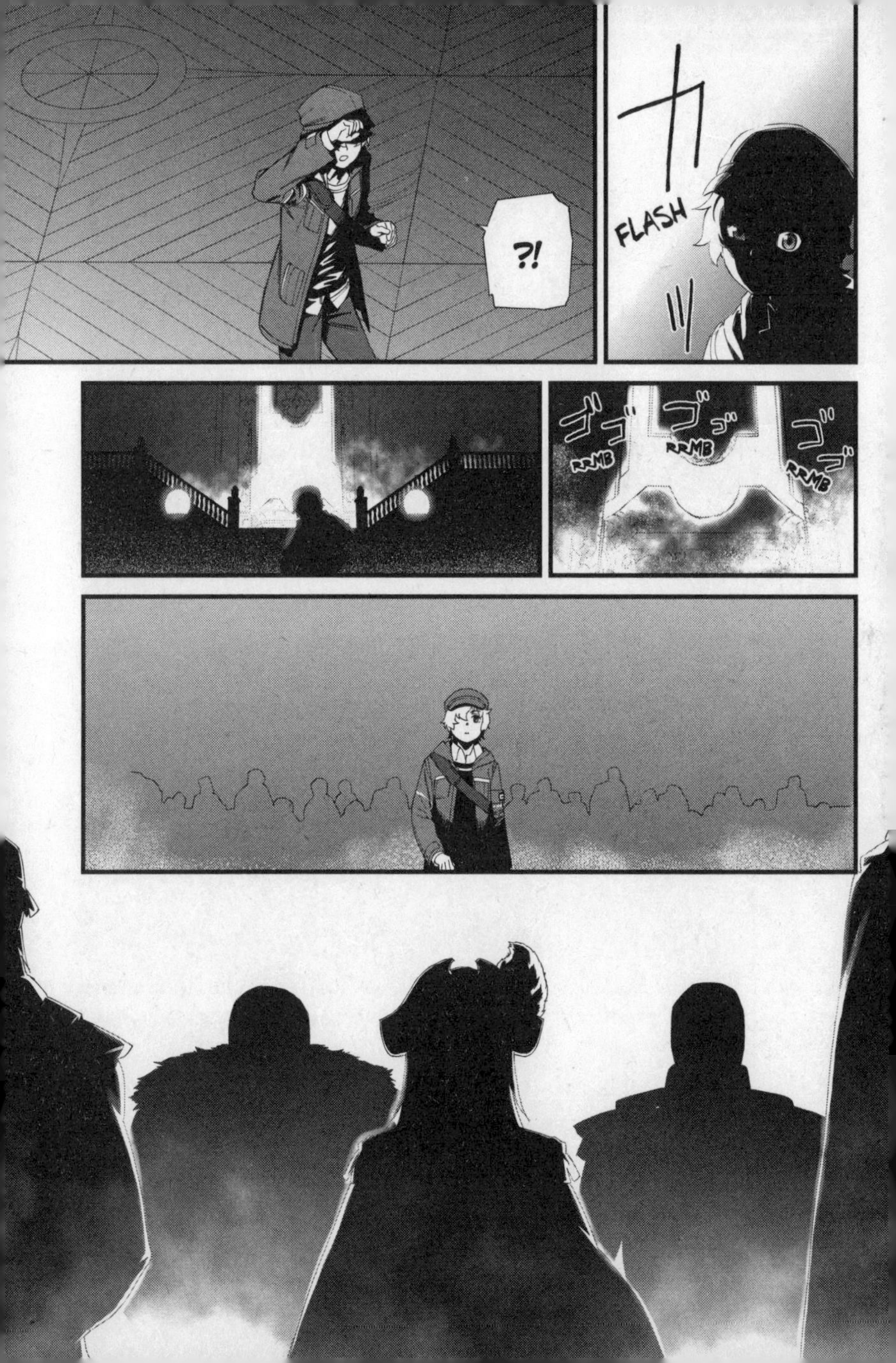
カ
FLASH
?!
ゴゴ
RRMB
ゴゴ
RRMB
ゴゴ
RRMB

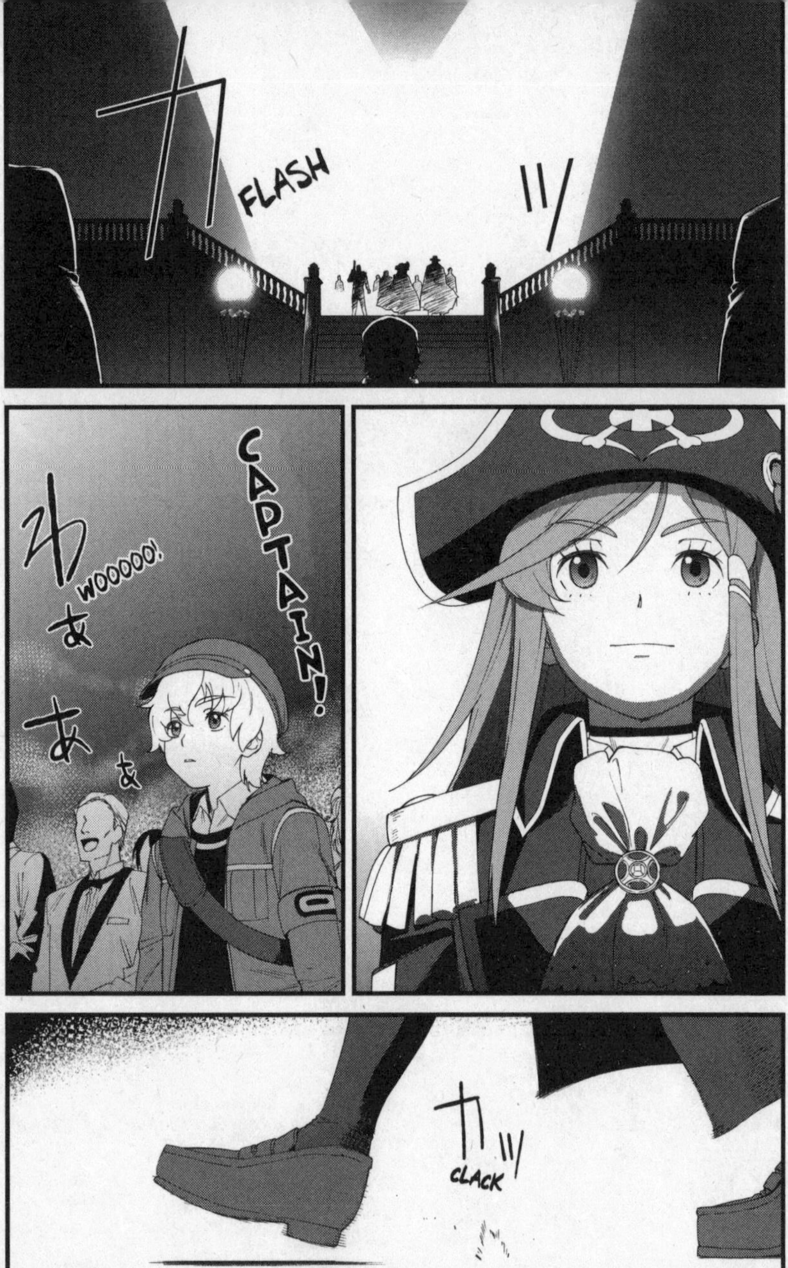
カッ
FLASH
CAPTAIN!
わぁぁぁ
WOOOOO!
カッ
CLACK

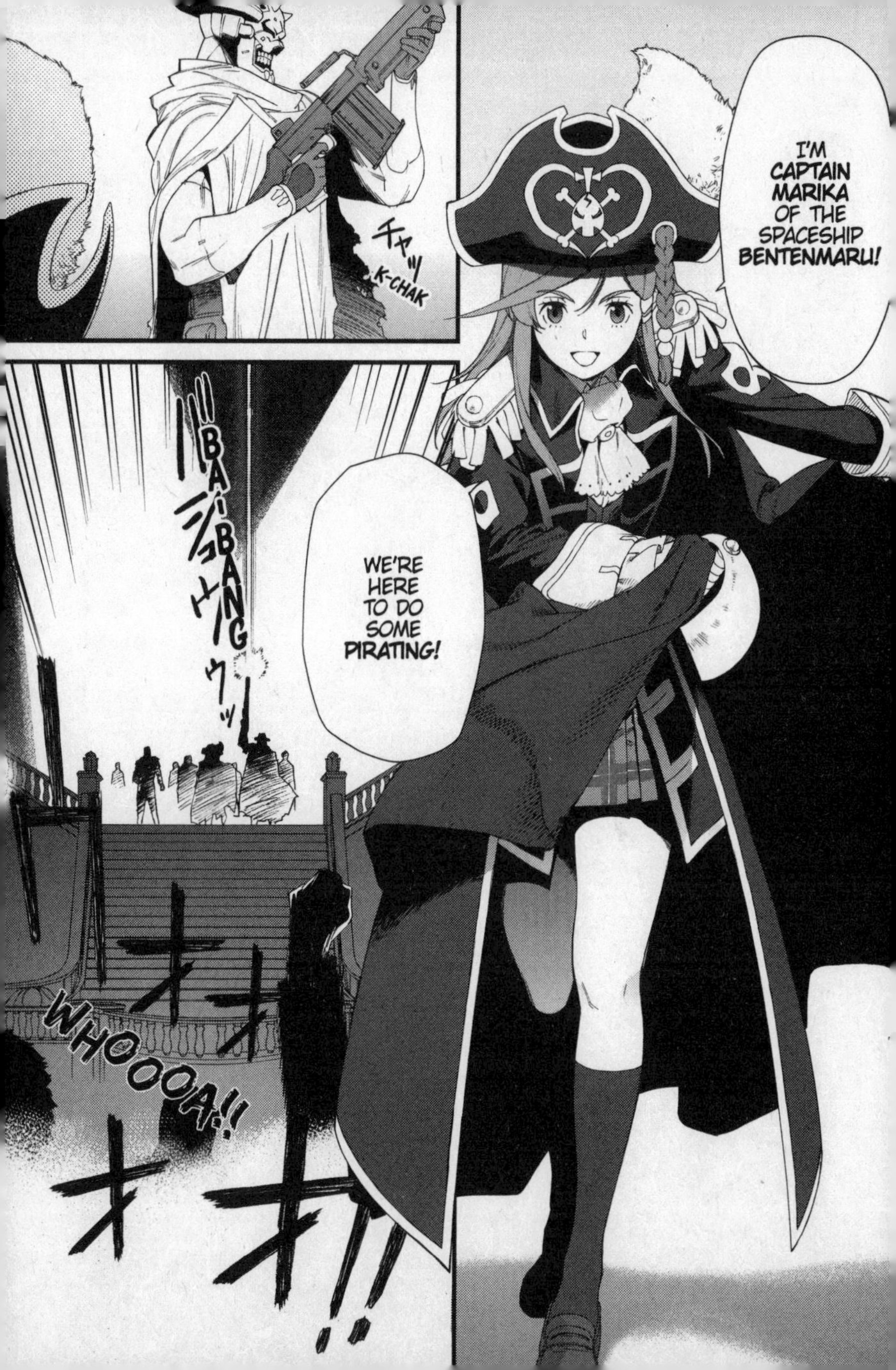
I'M CAPTAIN MARIKA OF THE SPACESHIP BENTENMARU!
WE'RE HERE TO DO SOME PIRATING!
チャッ
K-CHAK
BA-BANG
WHOOOA!!

IF YOU LISTEN TO MY **DEMANDS** LIKE PROPER LADIES AND GENTLEMEN...

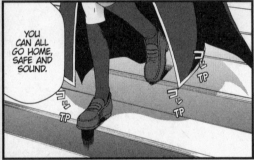

YOU CAN ALL GO HOME, SAFE AND SOUND.

YOU'LL EVEN BE ABLE TO **BRAG** TO ALL OF YOUR FRIENDS THAT YOU HAD A ONCE-IN-A-LIFETIME EXPERIENCE OF GETTING ATTACKED BY PIRATES.

I'D LIKE FOR EVERYONE TO CO-OPERATE...

GLANCE!

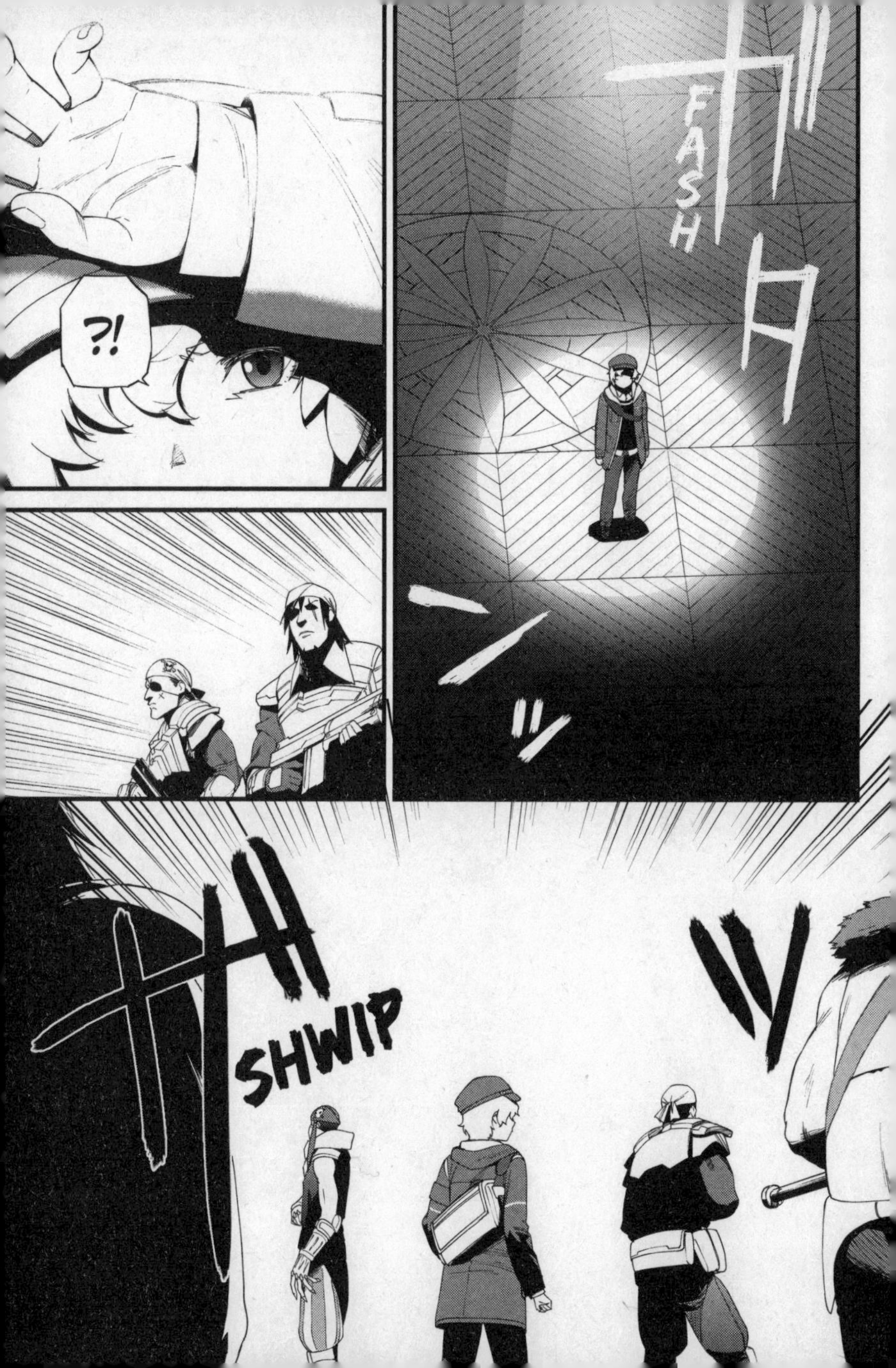
FASH
?!
SHWIP

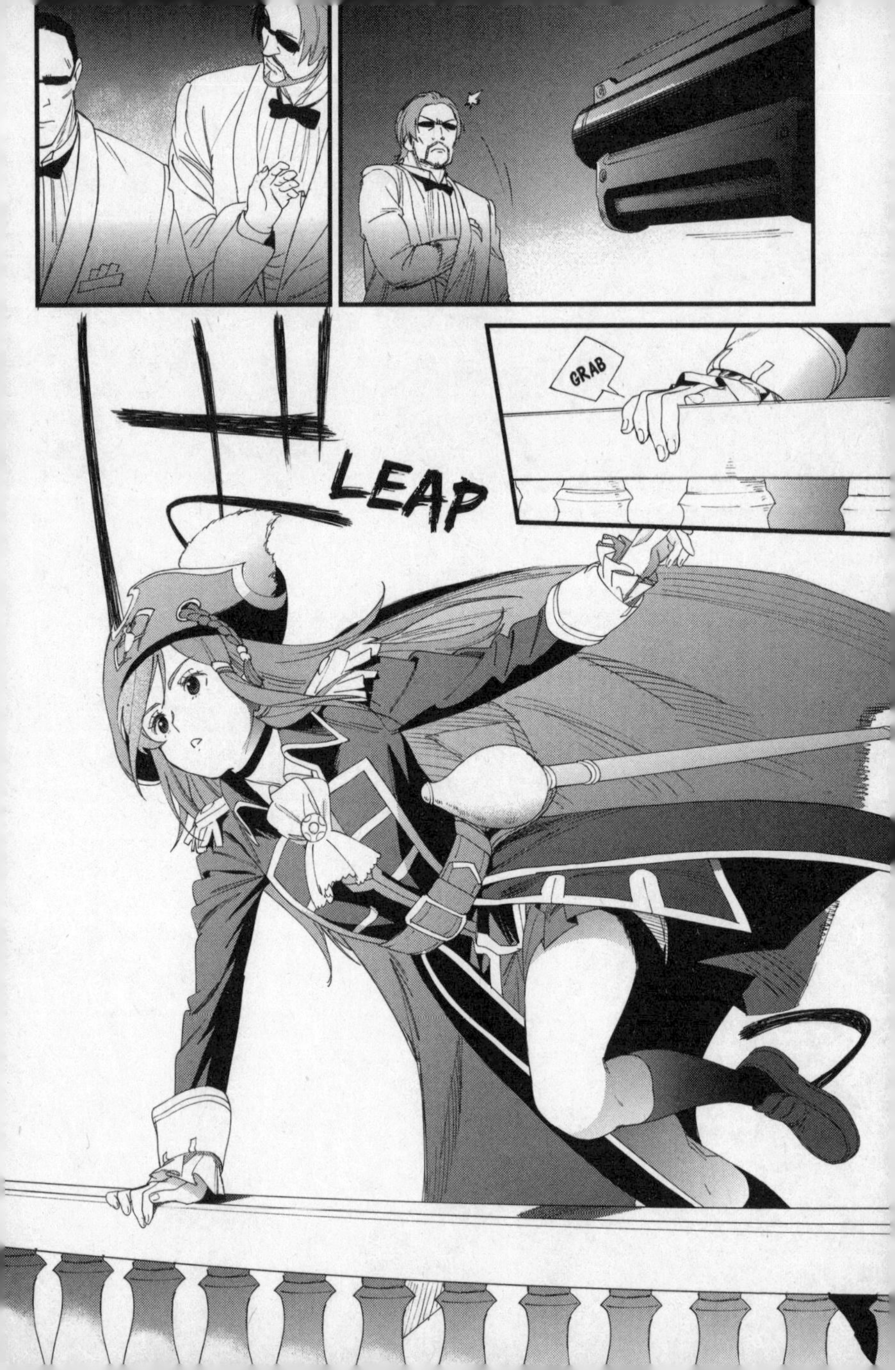
GRAB
LEAP

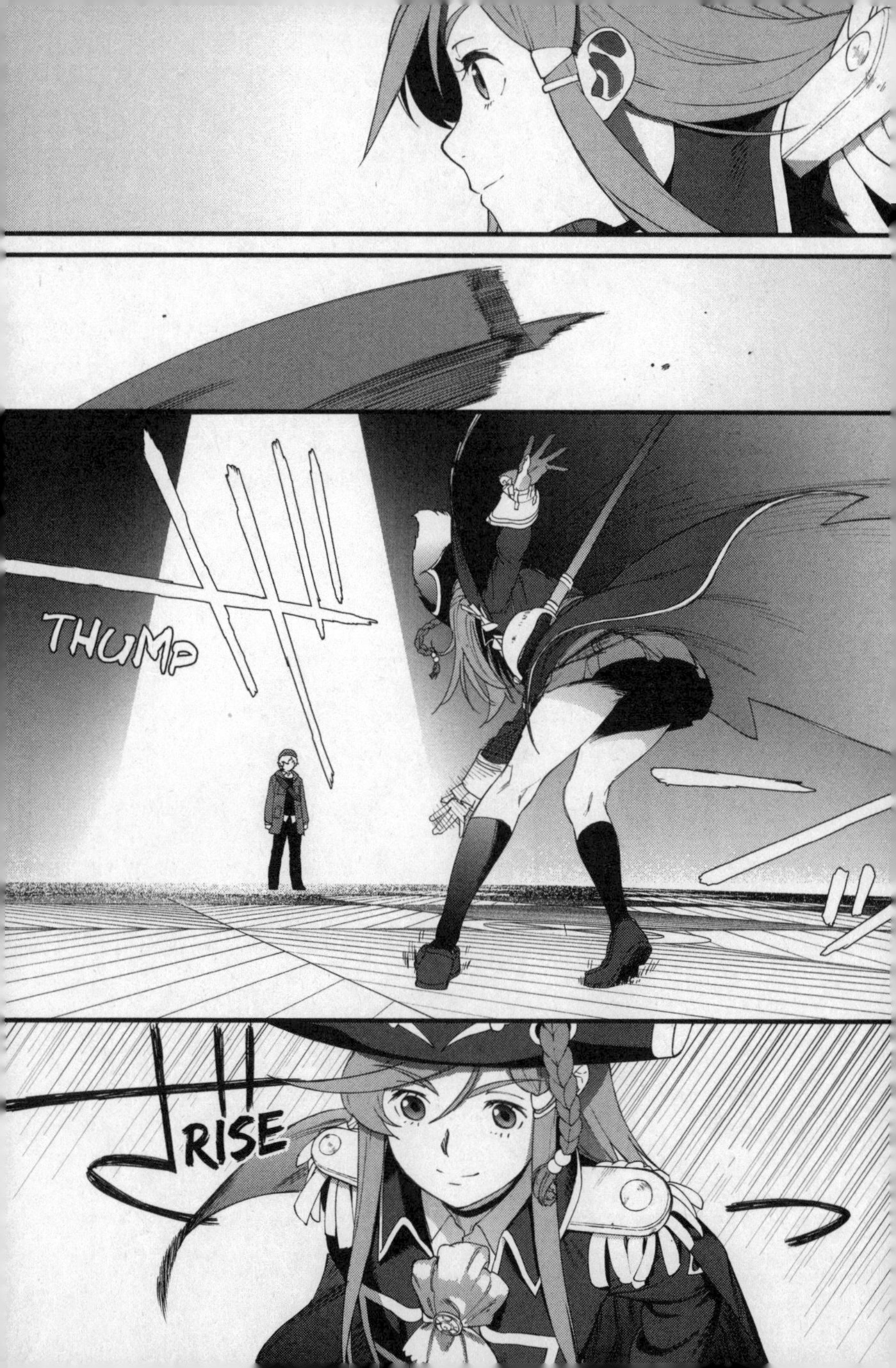
THUMP
RISE

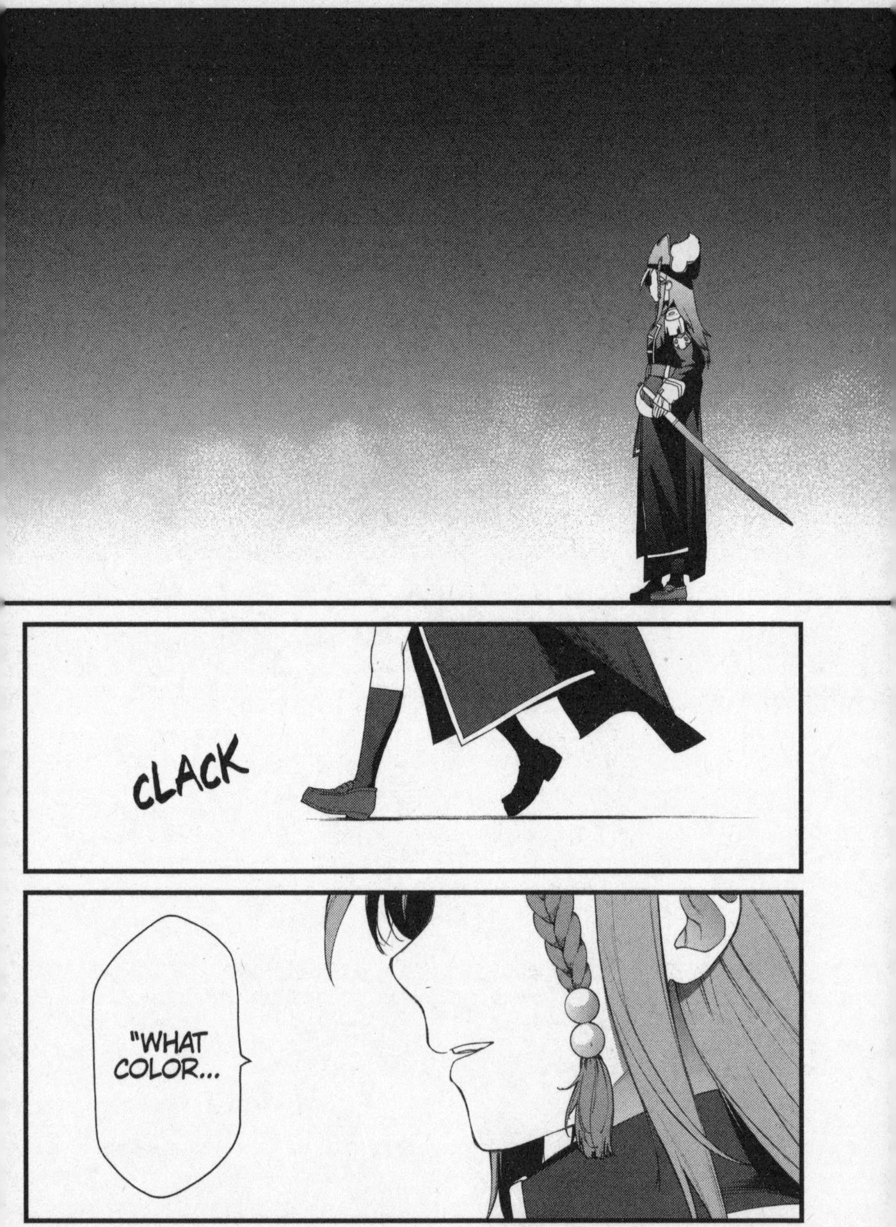
CLACK
"WHAT COLOR...

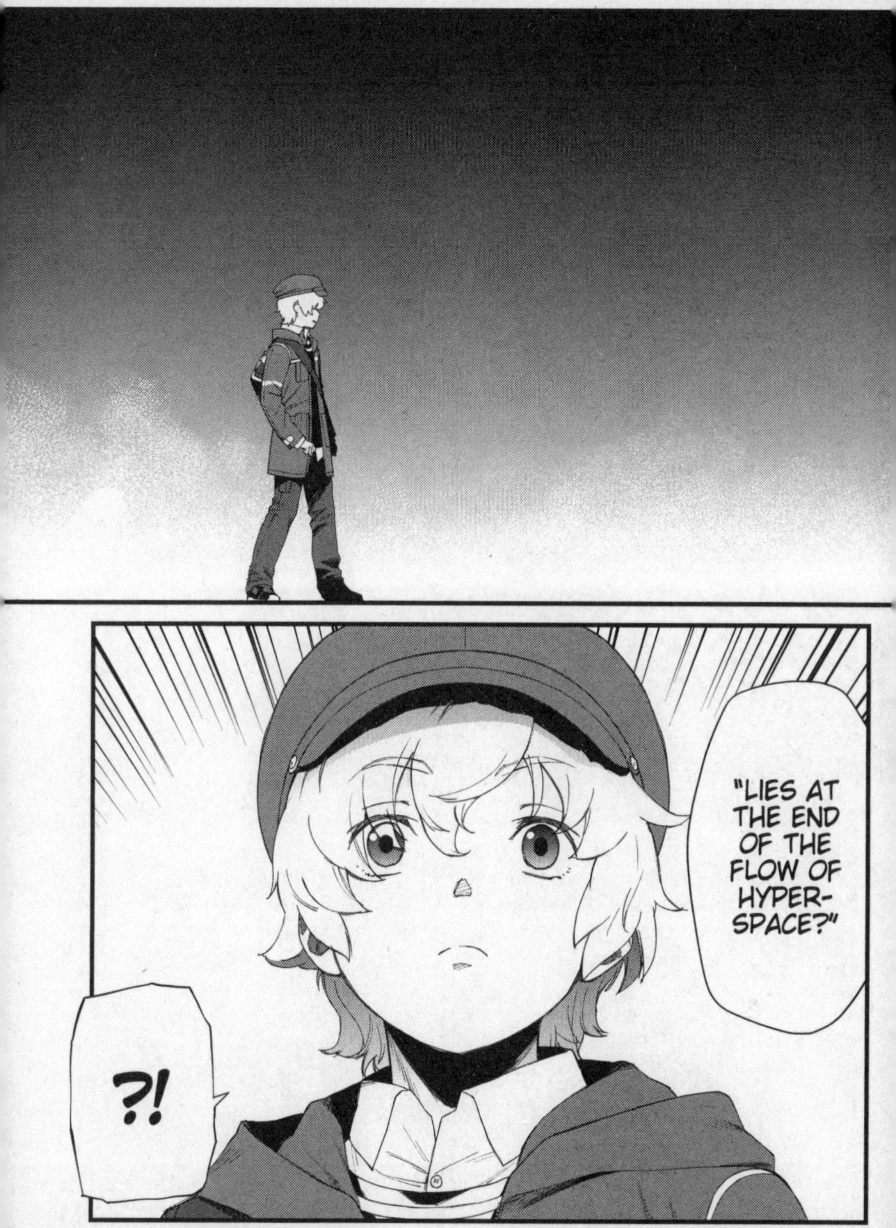
"LIES AT THE END OF THE FLOW OF HYPER-SPACE?"
?!

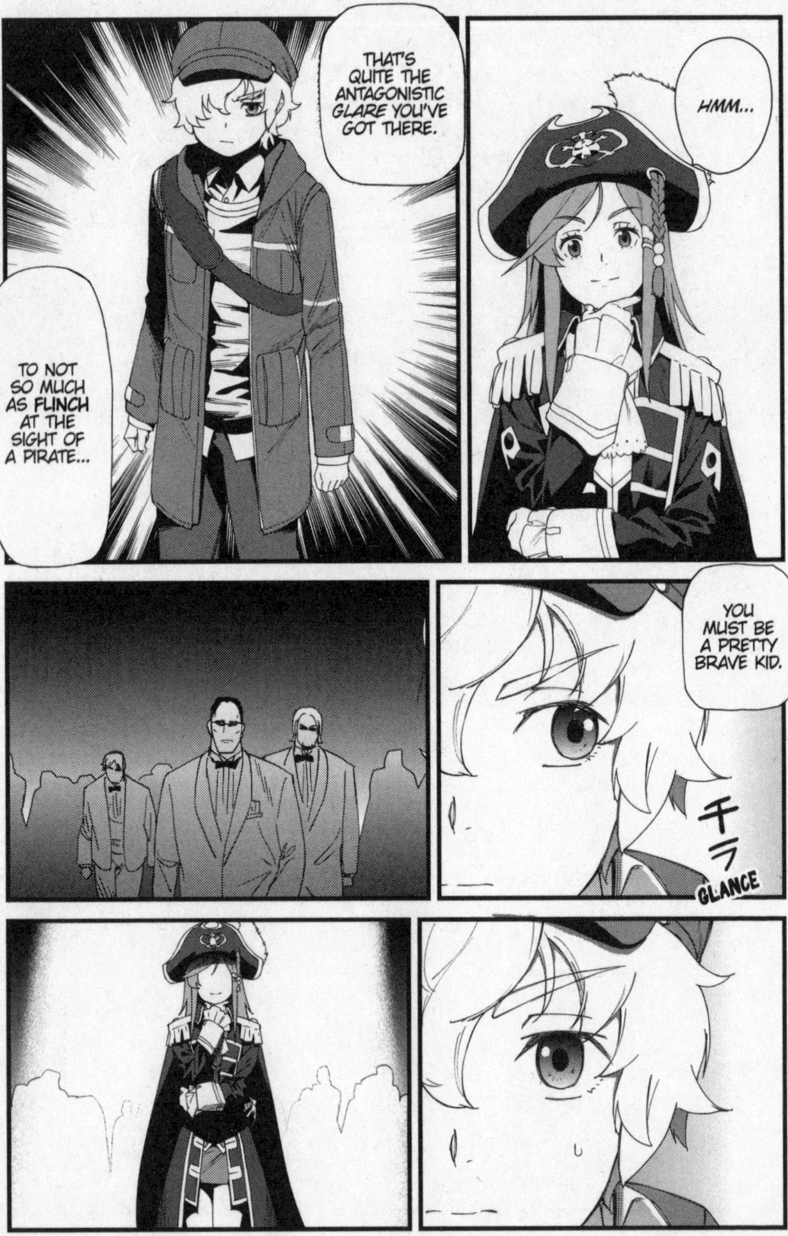
HMM...
THAT'S QUITE THE ANTAGONISTIC GLARE YOU'VE GOT THERE.
TO NOT SO MUCH AS FLINCH AT THE SIGHT OF A PIRATE...
YOU MUST BE A PRETTY BRAVE KID.
チラ
GLANCE

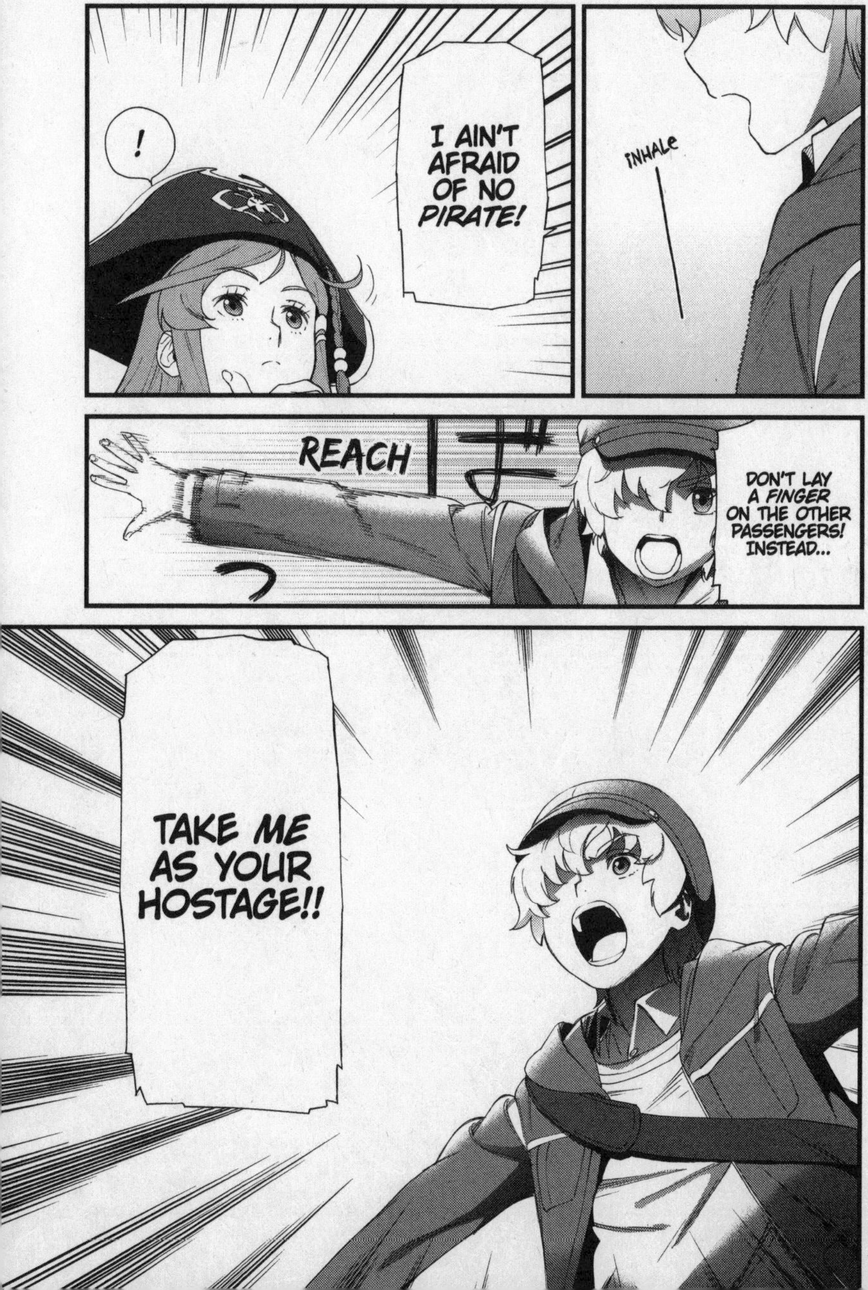

INHALE
I AIN'T AFRAID OF NO PIRATE!
!
DON'T LAY A FINGER ON THE OTHER PASSENGERS! INSTEAD...
REACH
TAKE ME AS YOUR HOSTAGE!!

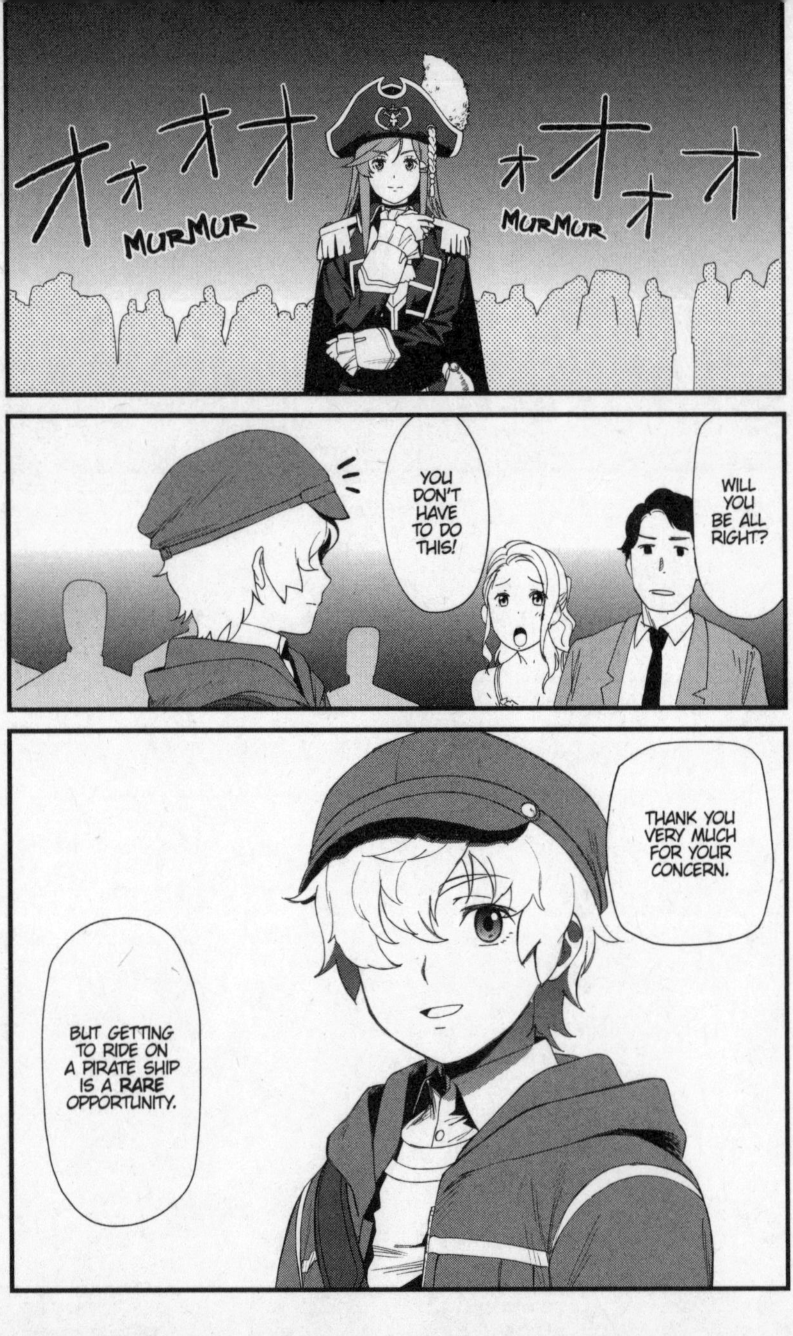
ォオォオ
MURMUR
オォオオ
MURMUR
WILL YOU BE ALL RIGHT?
YOU DON'T HAVE TO DO THIS!
THANK YOU VERY MUCH FOR YOUR CONCERN.
BUT GETTING TO RIDE ON A PIRATE SHIP IS A RARE OPPORTUNITY.

MY, MY.

I LIKE YOU, KID.

WHAT'S YOUR NAME, BOY?

KANATA...

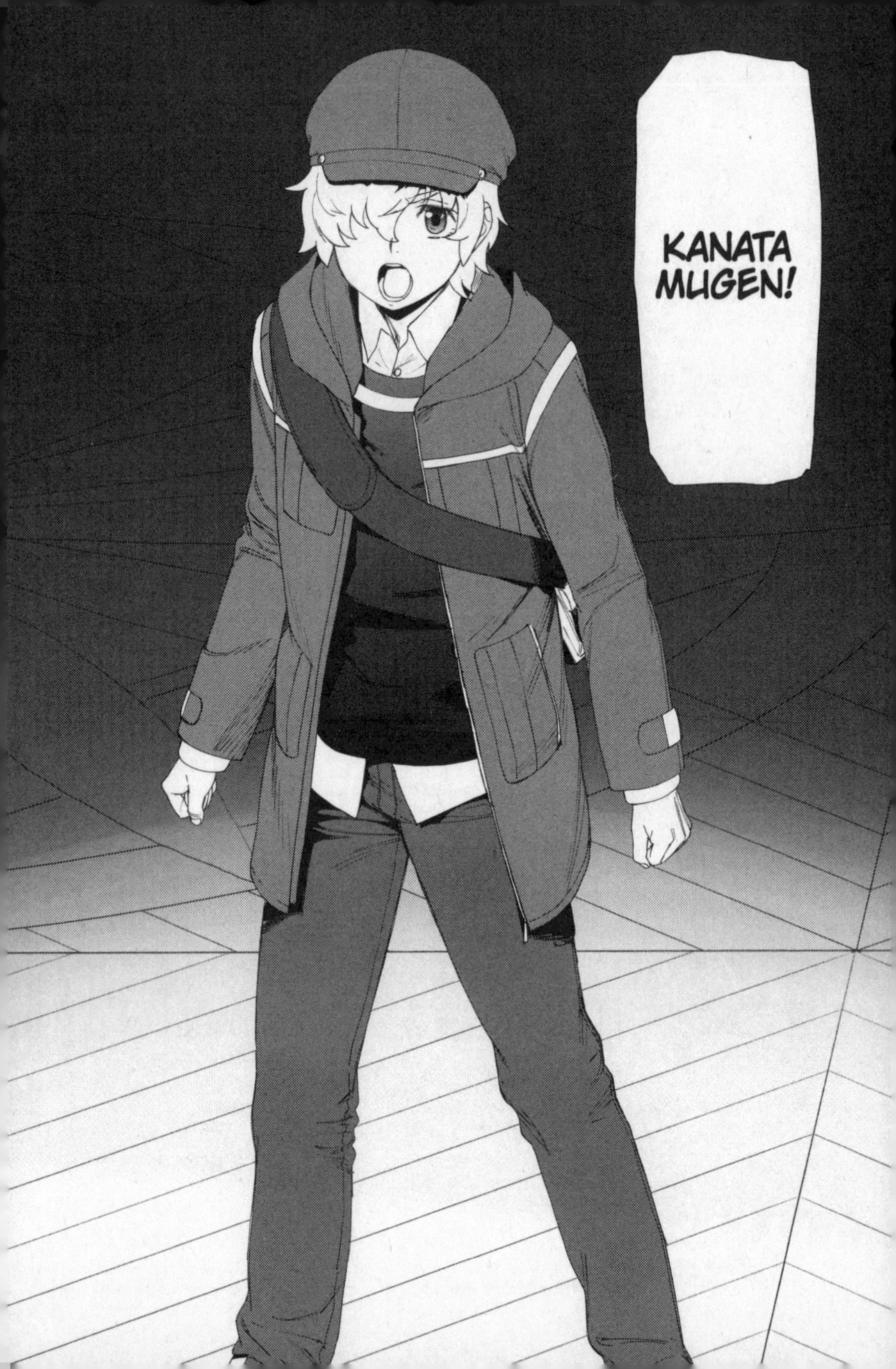
KANATA MUGEN!

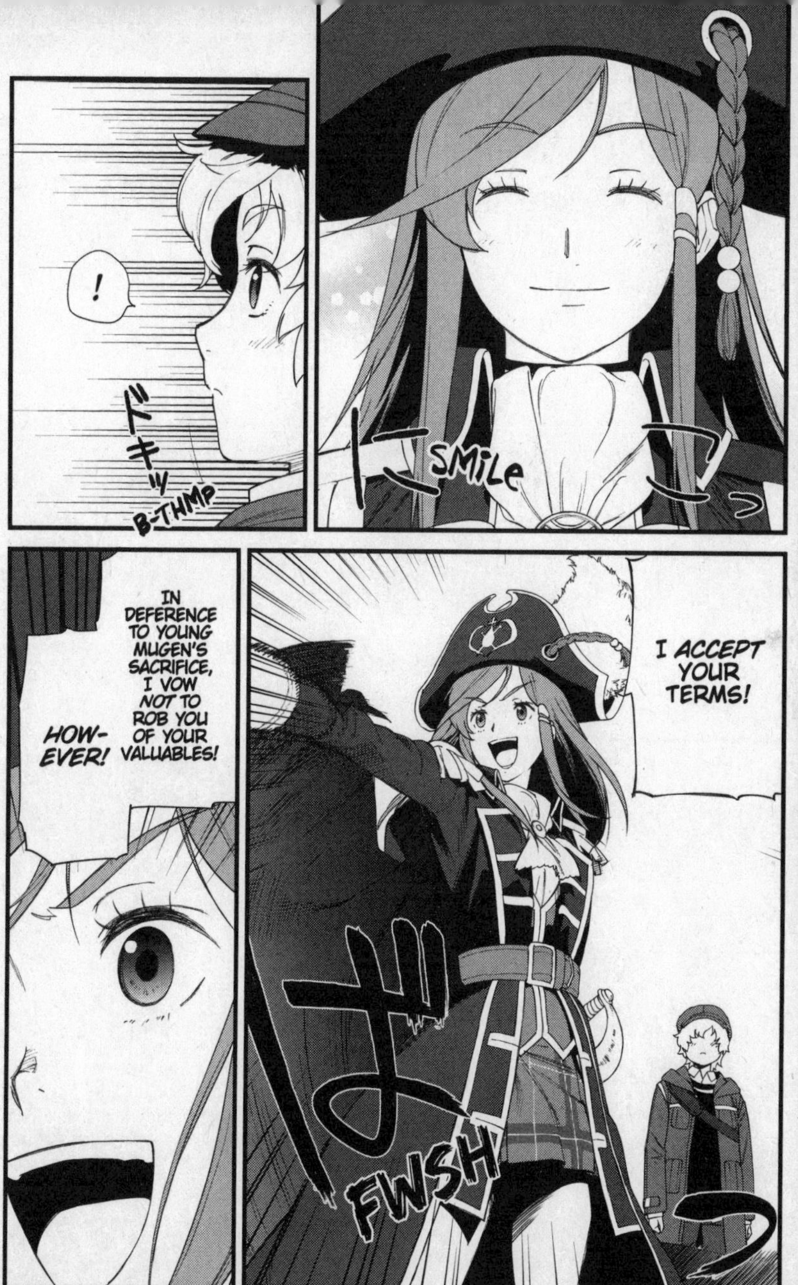
SMILE
!
ドキッ
B-THMP
I ACCEPT YOUR TERMS!
FWSH
IN DEFERENCE TO YOUNG MUGEN'S SACRIFICE, I VOW NOT TO ROB YOU OF YOUR VALUABLES!
HOW-EVER!

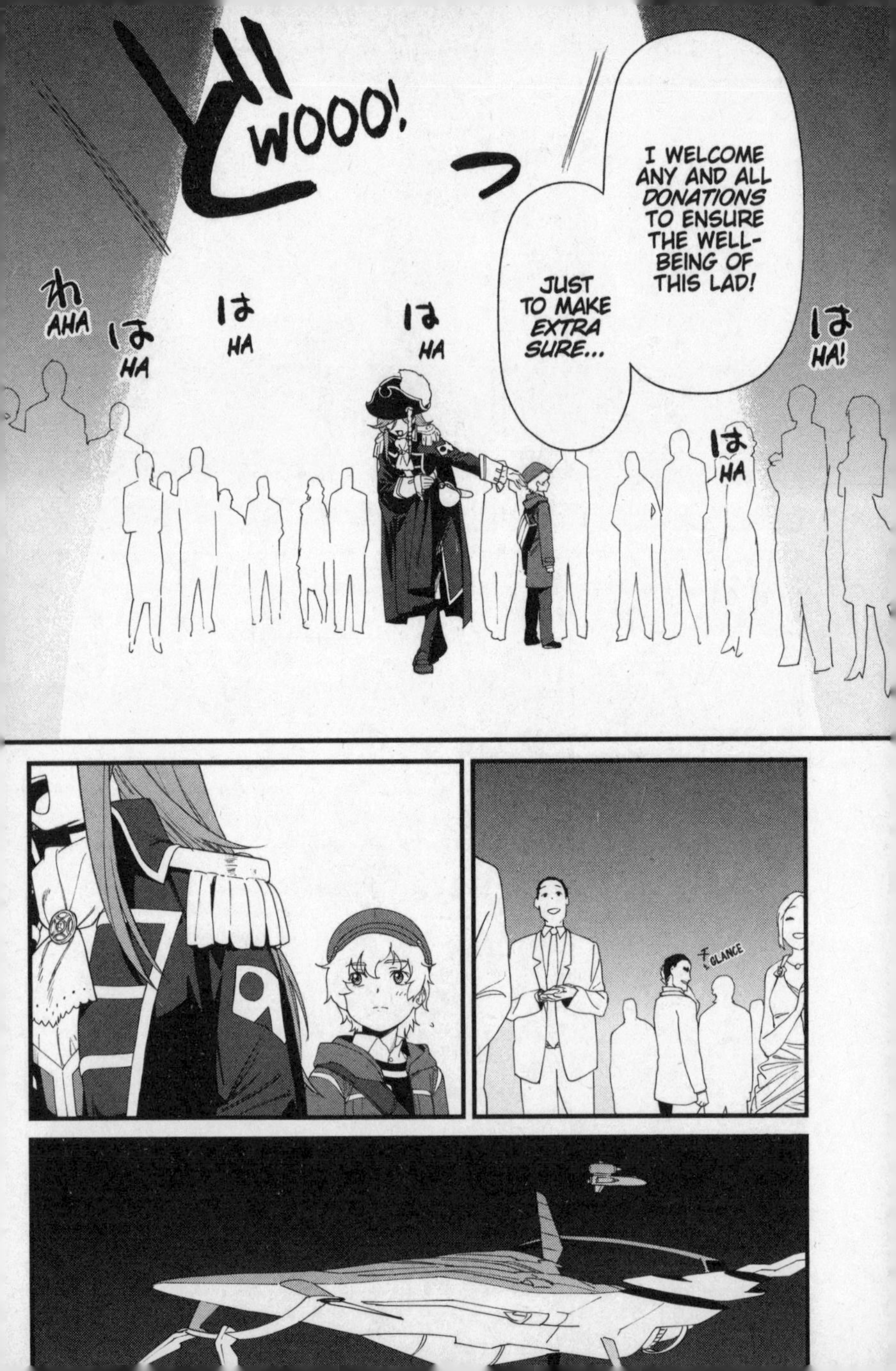

JUST TO MAKE EXTRA SURE...
I WELCOME ANY AND ALL DONATIONS TO ENSURE THE WELL-BEING OF THIS LAD!
は HA!
は HA
は HA
は HA
は HA
わ AHA
WOOO!
GLANCE

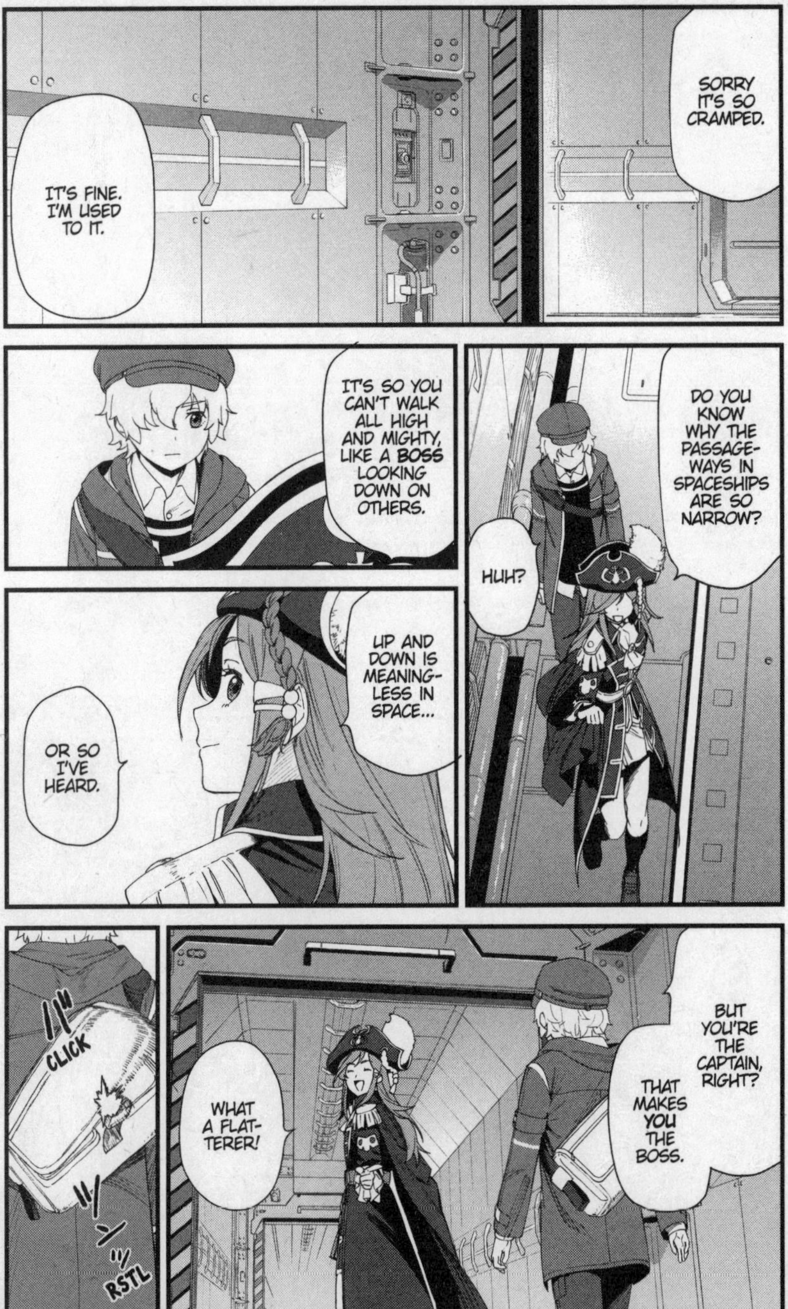
SORRY IT'S SO CRAMPED.
IT'S FINE. I'M USED TO IT.
DO YOU KNOW WHY THE PASSAGE-WAYS IN SPACESHIPS ARE SO NARROW?
HUH?
IT'S SO YOU CAN'T WALK ALL HIGH AND MIGHTY, LIKE A **BOSS** LOOKING DOWN ON OTHERS.
UP AND DOWN IS MEANING-LESS IN SPACE...
OR SO I'VE HEARD.
BUT YOU'RE THE CAPTAIN, RIGHT?
THAT MAKES **YOU** THE BOSS.
WHAT A FLAT-TERER!
CLICK
RSTL

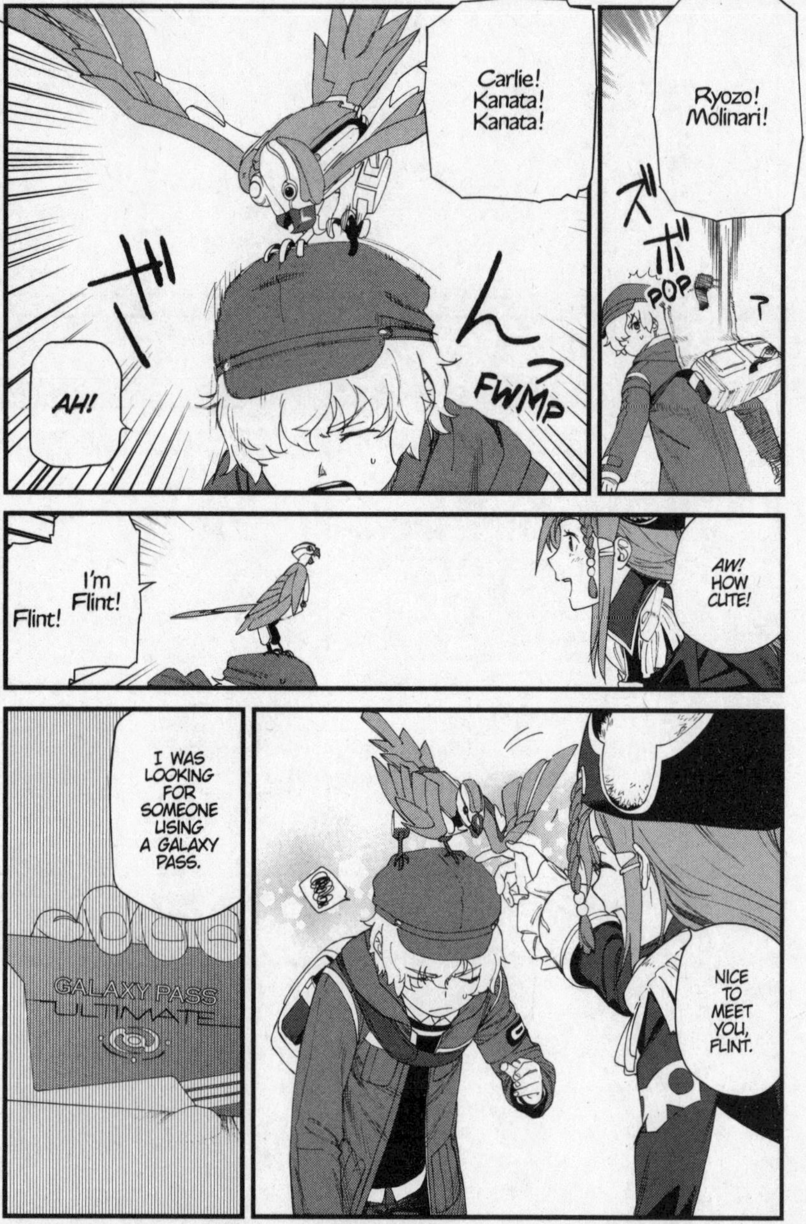
Ryozo! Molinari!
ズボ
POP
?
Carlie! Kanata! Kanata!
ギー
んっ
FWMP
AH!
AW! HOW CUTE!
I'm Flint!
Flint!
NICE TO MEET YOU, FLINT.
I WAS LOOKING FOR SOMEONE USING A GALAXY PASS.
GALAXY PASS ULTIMATE

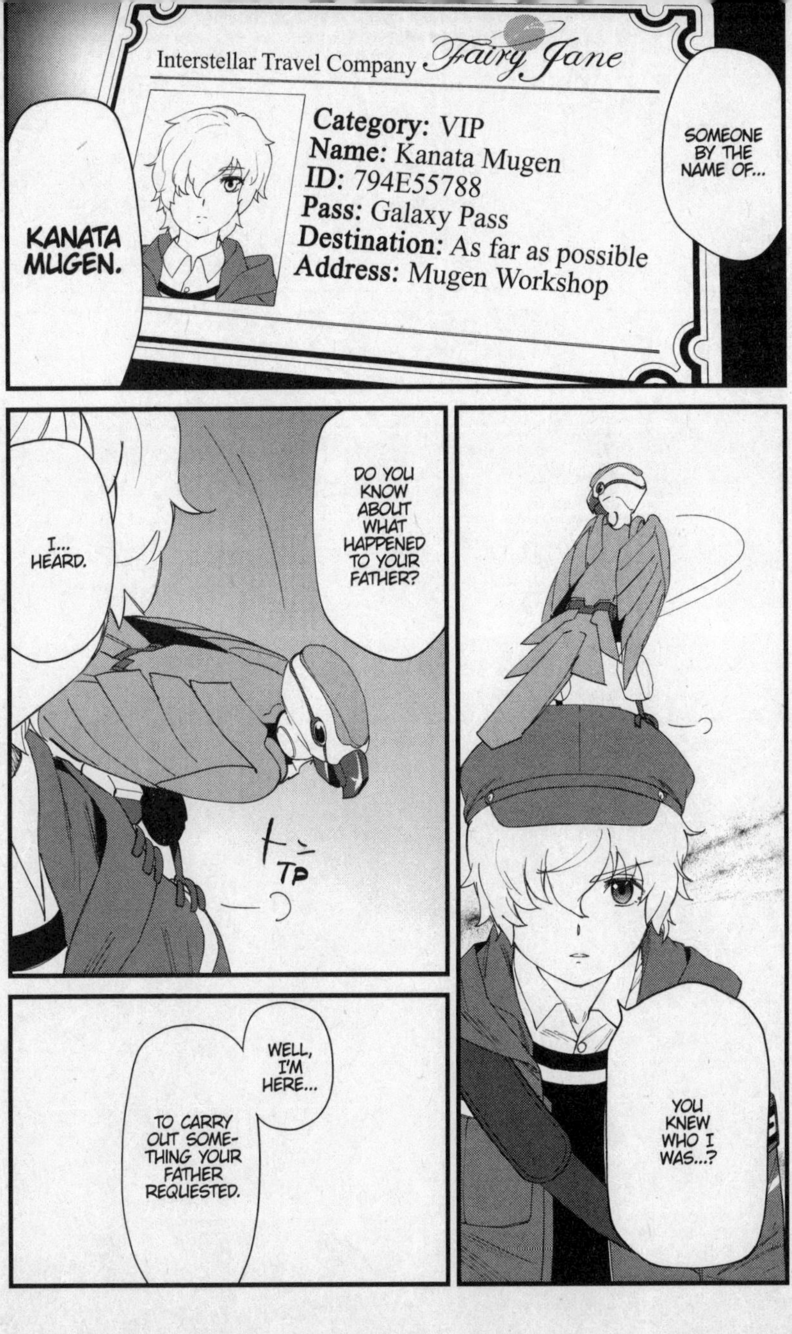
SOMEONE BY THE NAME OF...
Interstellar Travel Company Fairy Jane
Category: VIP
Name: Kanata Mugen
ID: 794E55788
Pass: Galaxy Pass
Destination: As far as possible
Address: Mugen Workshop
KANATA MUGEN.
YOU KNEW WHO I WAS...?
DO YOU KNOW ABOUT WHAT HAPPENED TO YOUR FATHER?
I... HEARD.
TP
WELL, I'M HERE...
TO CARRY OUT SOME-THING YOUR FATHER REQUESTED.

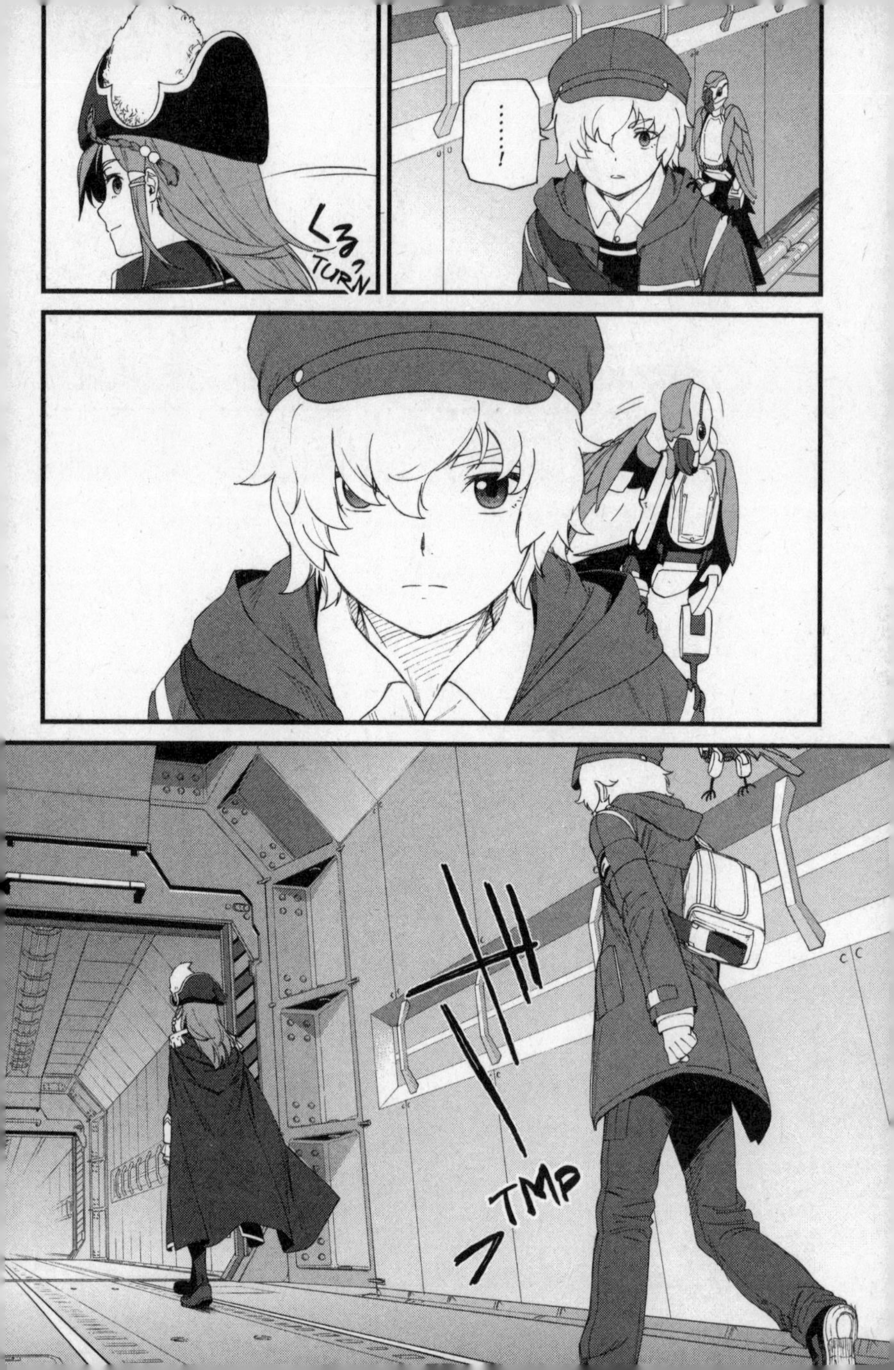
......!
くるっ
TURN
TMP

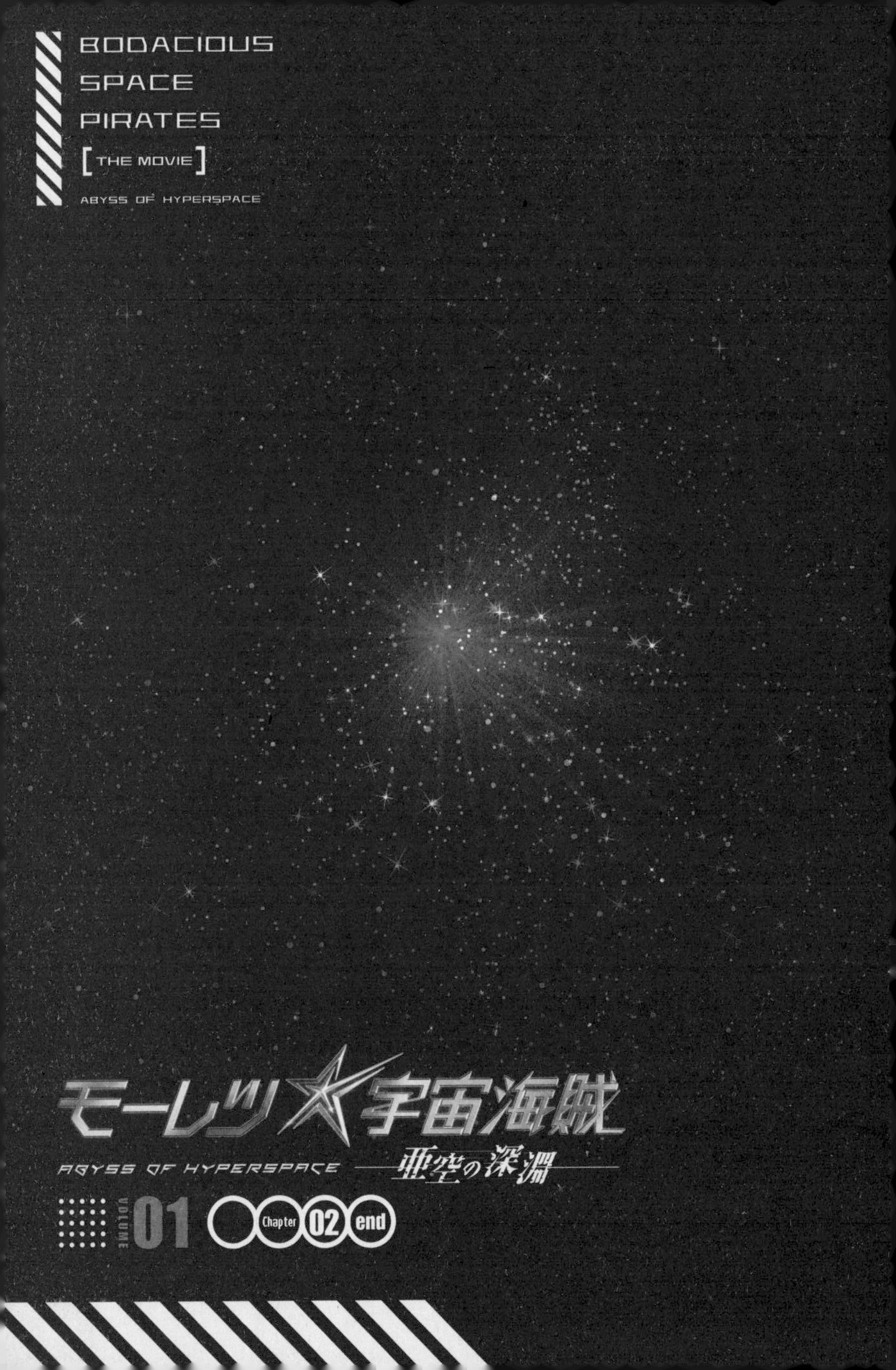
BODACIOUS
SPACE
PIRATES
[THE MOVIE]
ABYSS OF HYPERSPACE
モーレツ★宇宙海賊
ABYSS OF HYPERSPACE
亜空の深淵
VOLUME 01
Chapter 02 end

BODACIOUS
SPACE
PIRATES
[THE MOVIE]
ABYSS OF HYPERSPACE

VOLUME 01

Chapter 03

[START]

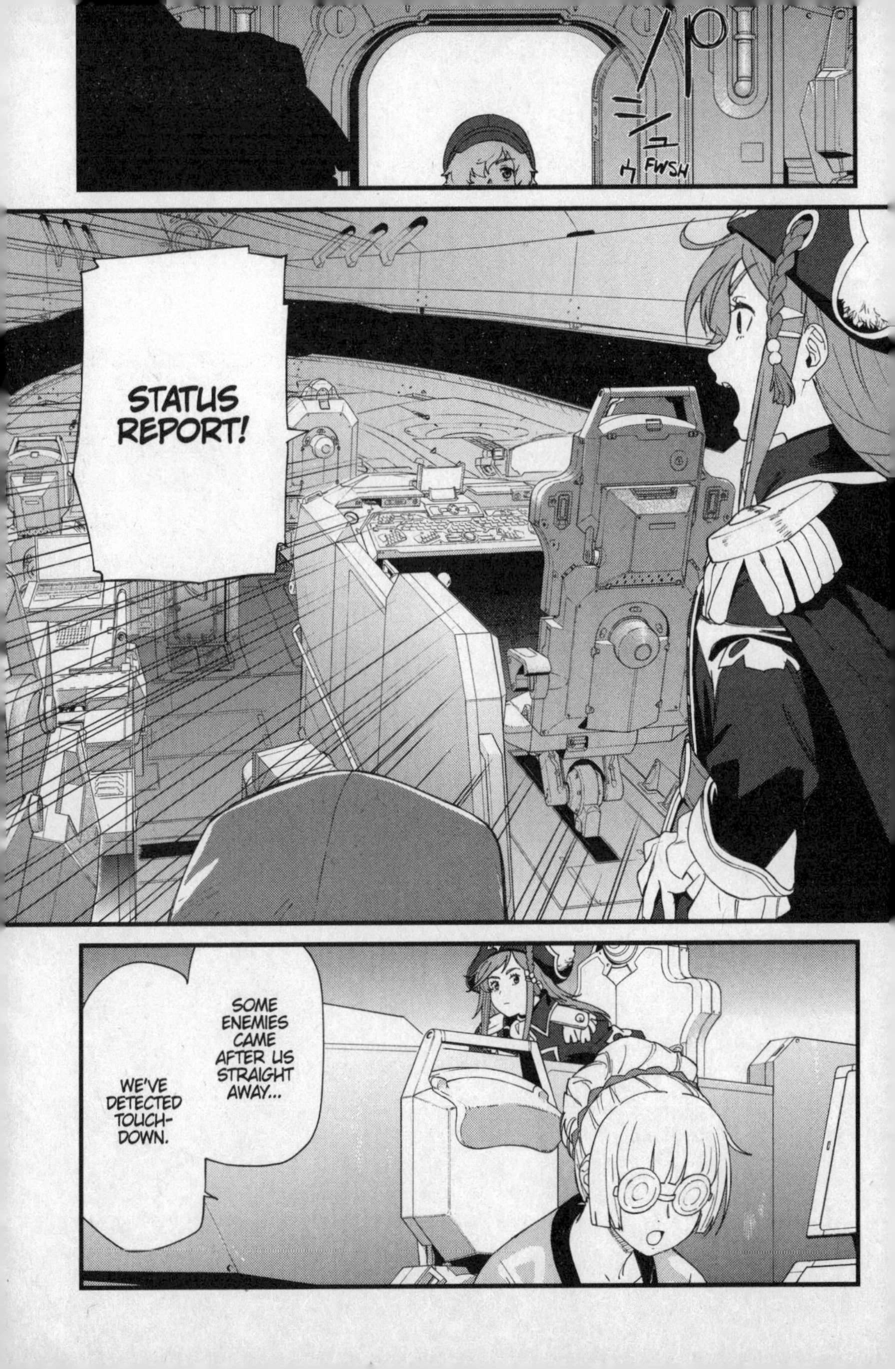
FWSH
STATUS REPORT!
SOME ENEMIES CAME AFTER US STRAIGHT AWAY...
WE'VE DETECTED TOUCH-DOWN.

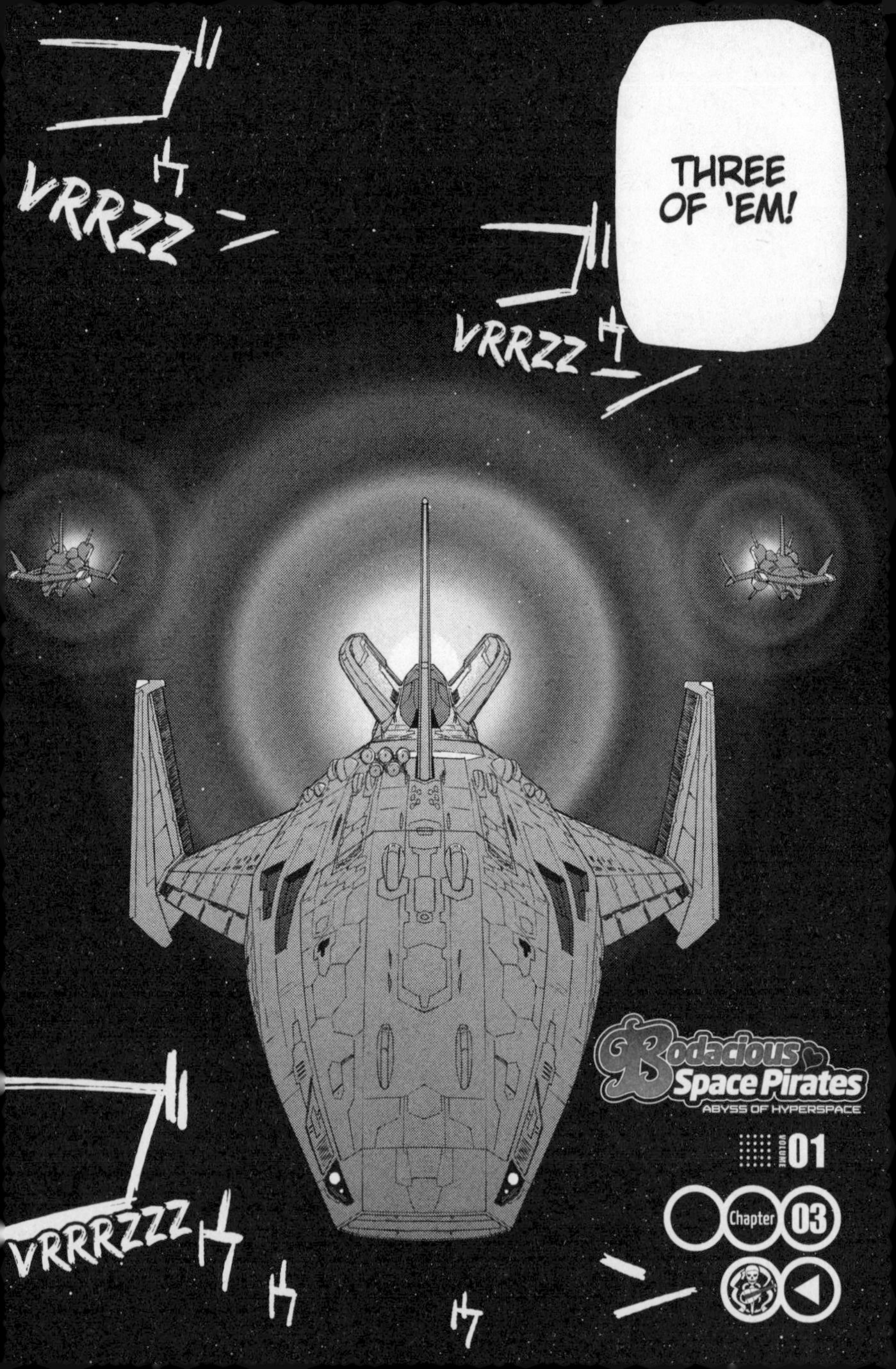
THREE OF 'EM!
VRRZZ
VRRZZ
Bodacious Space Pirates
ABYSS OF HYPERSPACE
VOLUME 01
Chapter 03
VRRRZZZ

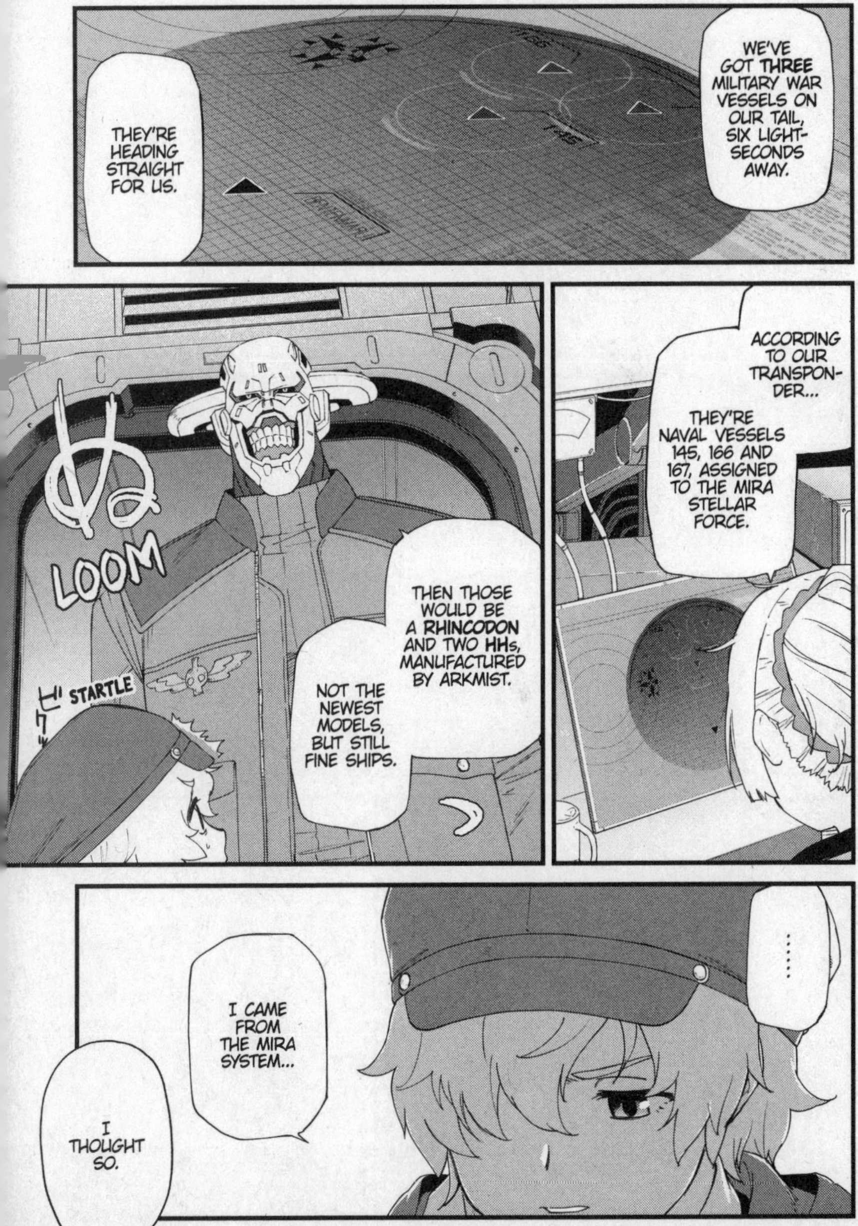
WE'VE GOT THREE MILITARY WAR VESSELS ON OUR TAIL, SIX LIGHT-SECONDS AWAY.
THEY'RE HEADING STRAIGHT FOR US.
ACCORDING TO OUR TRANSPONDER...
THEY'RE NAVAL VESSELS 145, 166 AND 167, ASSIGNED TO THE MIRA STELLAR FORCE.
LOOM
THEN THOSE WOULD BE A RHINCODON AND TWO HHs, MANUFACTURED BY ARKMIST.
NOT THE NEWEST MODELS, BUT STILL FINE SHIPS.
STARTLE
......
I CAME FROM THE MIRA SYSTEM...
I THOUGHT SO.

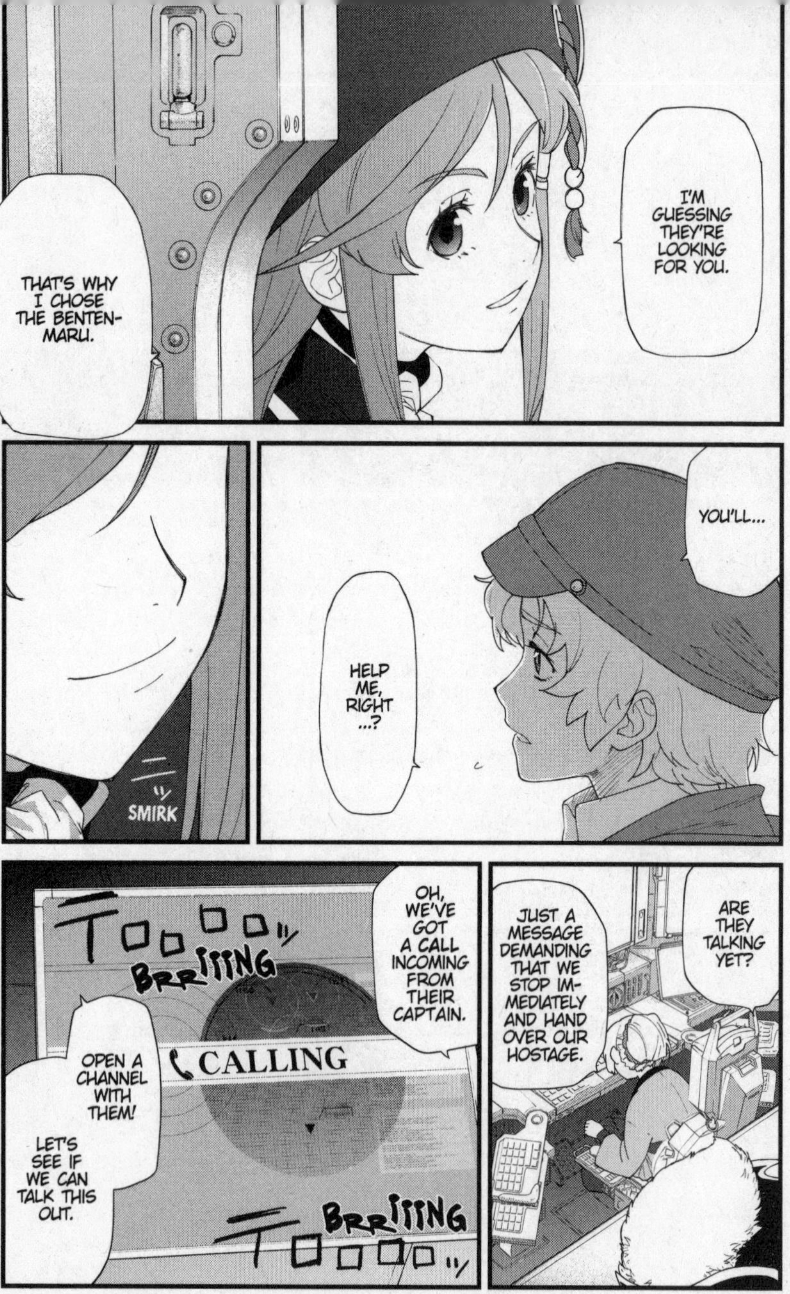
I'M GUESSING THEY'RE LOOKING FOR YOU.
THAT'S WHY I CHOSE THE BENTEN-MARU.
YOU'LL...
HELP ME, RIGHT ...?
SMIRK
ARE THEY TALKING YET?
JUST A MESSAGE DEMANDING THAT WE STOP IM-MEDIATELY AND HAND OVER OUR HOSTAGE.
OH, WE'VE GOT A CALL INCOMING FROM THEIR CAPTAIN.
BRRIIING
CALLING
OPEN A CHANNEL WITH THEM!
LET'S SEE IF WE CAN TALK THIS OUT.
BRRIIING

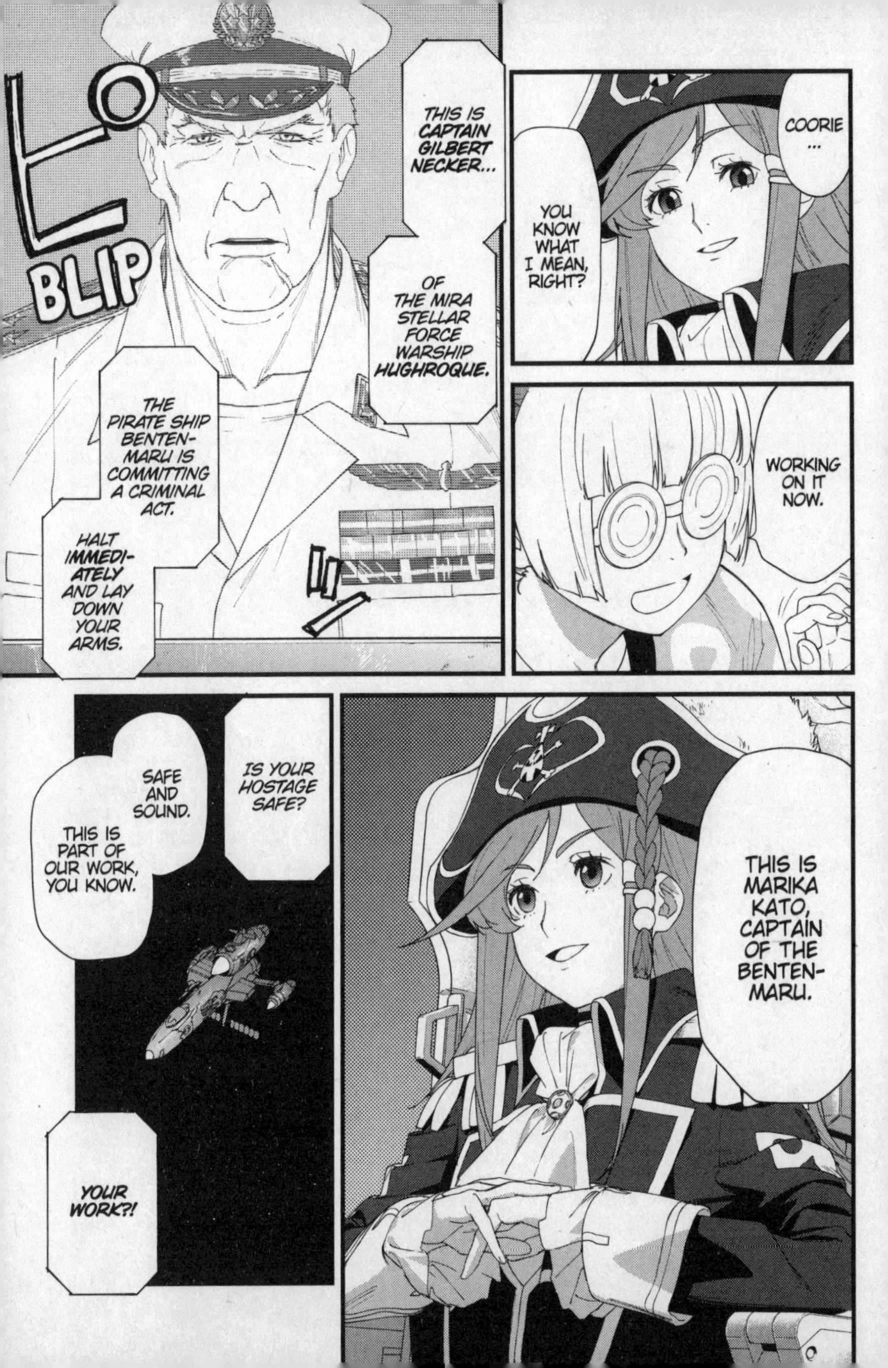
COORIE ...
YOU KNOW WHAT I MEAN, RIGHT?
WORKING ON IT NOW.
BLIP
THIS IS CAPTAIN GILBERT NECKER...
OF THE MIRA STELLAR FORCE WARSHIP HUGHROQUE.
THE PIRATE SHIP BENTEN-MARU IS COMMITTING A CRIMINAL ACT.
HALT IMMEDIATELY AND LAY DOWN YOUR ARMS.
THIS IS MARIKA KATO, CAPTAIN OF THE BENTEN-MARU.
IS YOUR HOSTAGE SAFE?
SAFE AND SOUND.
THIS IS PART OF OUR WORK, YOU KNOW.
YOUR WORK?!

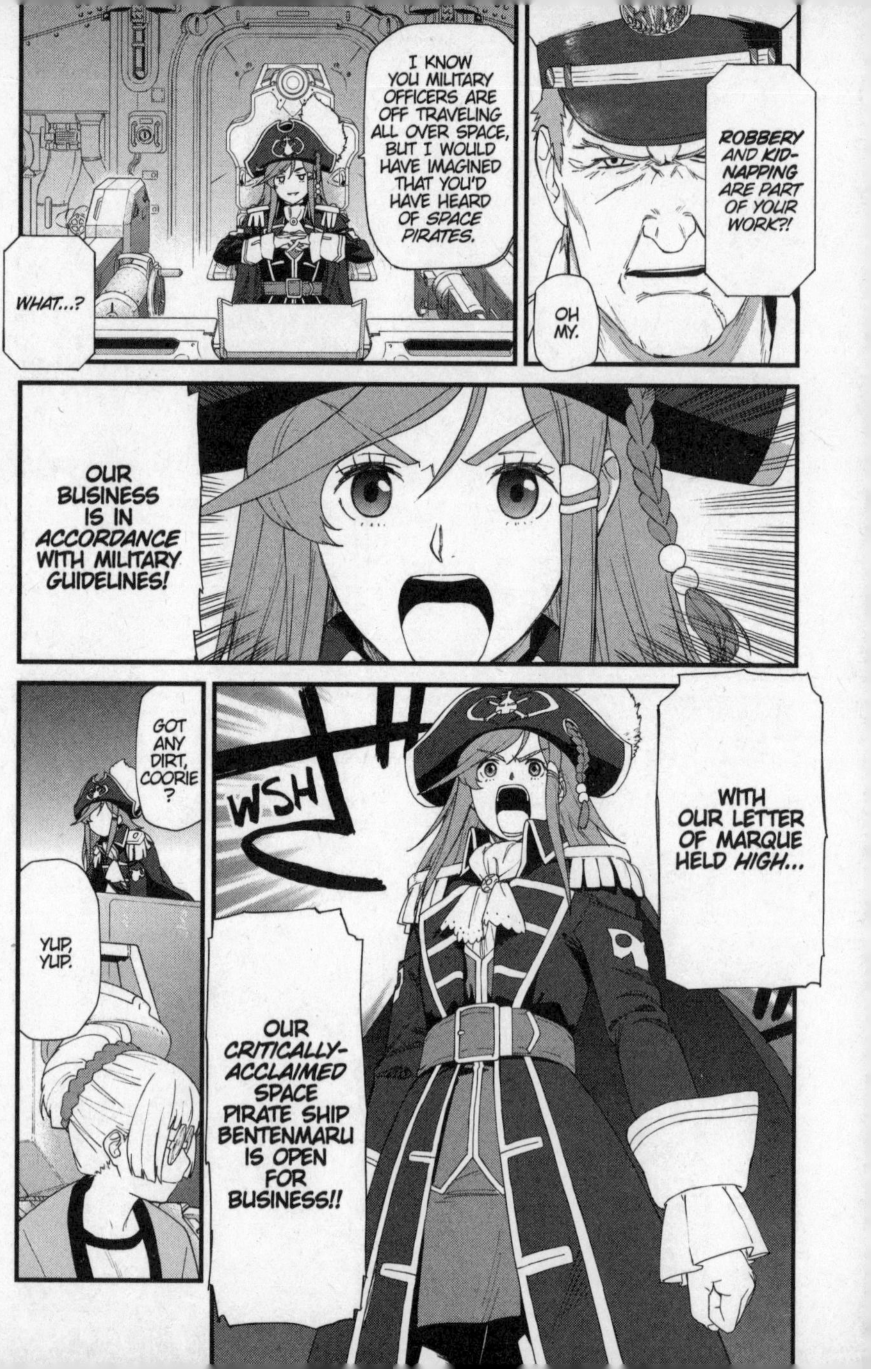
ROBBERY AND KID-NAPPING ARE PART OF YOUR WORK?!
OH MY.
I KNOW YOU MILITARY OFFICERS ARE OFF TRAVELING ALL OVER SPACE, BUT I WOULD HAVE IMAGINED THAT YOU'D HAVE HEARD OF SPACE PIRATES.
WHAT...?
OUR BUSINESS IS IN ACCORDANCE WITH MILITARY GUIDELINES!
WITH OUR LETTER OF MARQUE HELD HIGH...
WSH
OUR CRITICALLY-ACCLAIMED SPACE PIRATE SHIP BENTENMARU IS OPEN FOR BUSINESS!!
GOT ANY DIRT, COORIE?
YUP, YUP.

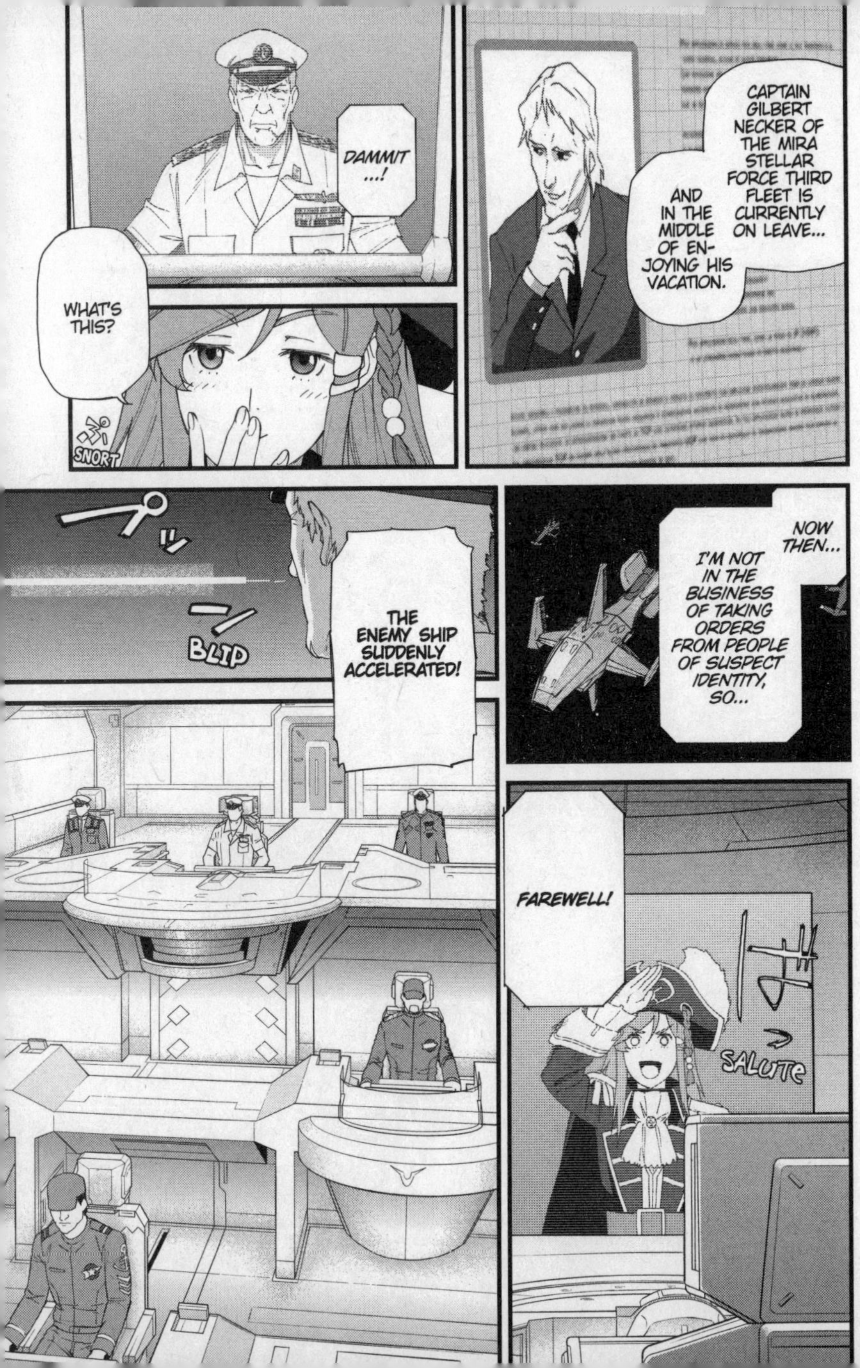
CAPTAIN GILBERT NECKER OF THE MIRA STELLAR FORCE THIRD FLEET IS CURRENTLY ON LEAVE...
AND IN THE MIDDLE OF EN-JOYING HIS VACATION.
DAMMIT ...!
WHAT'S THIS?
SNORT
NOW THEN...
I'M NOT IN THE BUSINESS OF TAKING ORDERS FROM PEOPLE OF SUSPECT IDENTITY, SO...
FAREWELL!
SALUTE
BLIP
THE ENEMY SHIP SUDDENLY ACCELERATED!

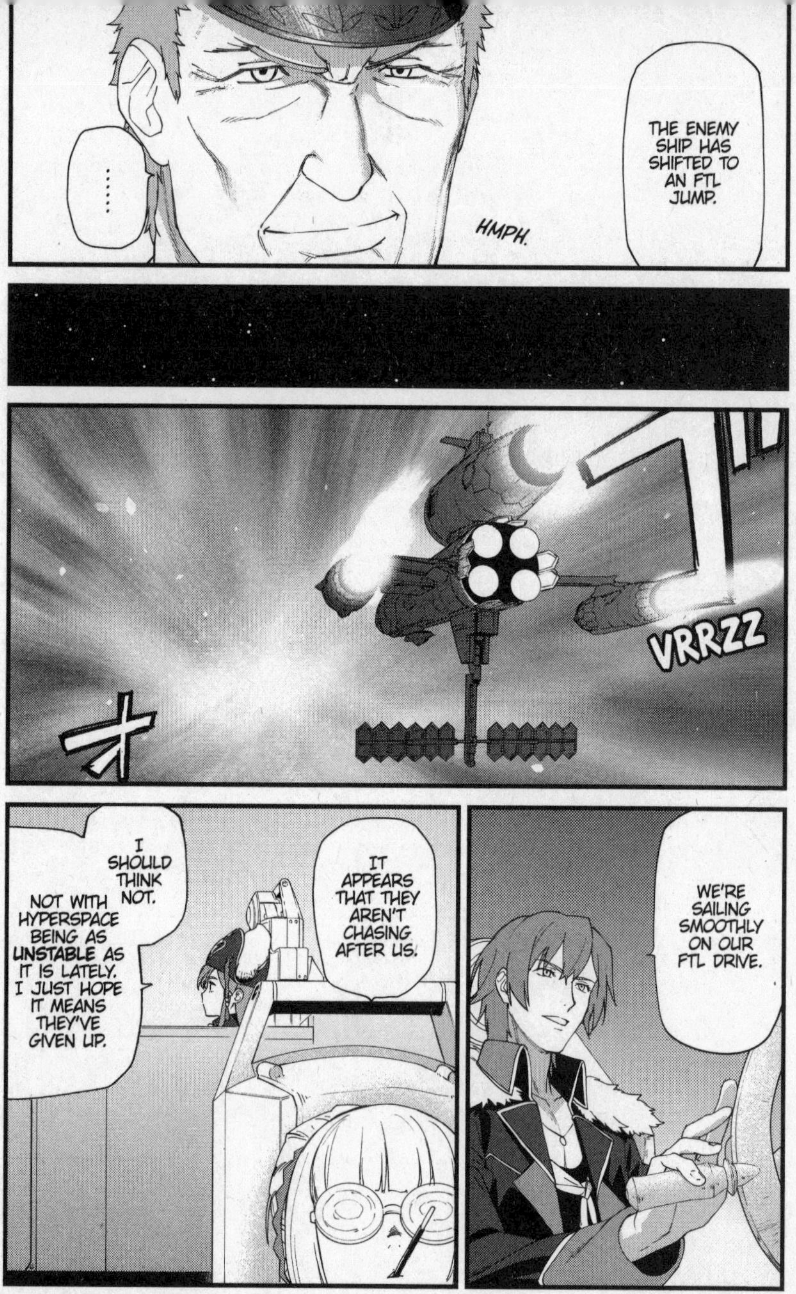
THE ENEMY SHIP HAS SHIFTED TO AN FTL JUMP.
HMPH.
......
VRRZZ
WE'RE SAILING SMOOTHLY ON OUR FTL DRIVE.
IT APPEARS THAT THEY AREN'T CHASING AFTER US.
I SHOULD THINK NOT.
NOT WITH HYPERSPACE BEING AS UNSTABLE AS IT IS LATELY. I JUST HOPE IT MEANS THEY'VE GIVEN UP.

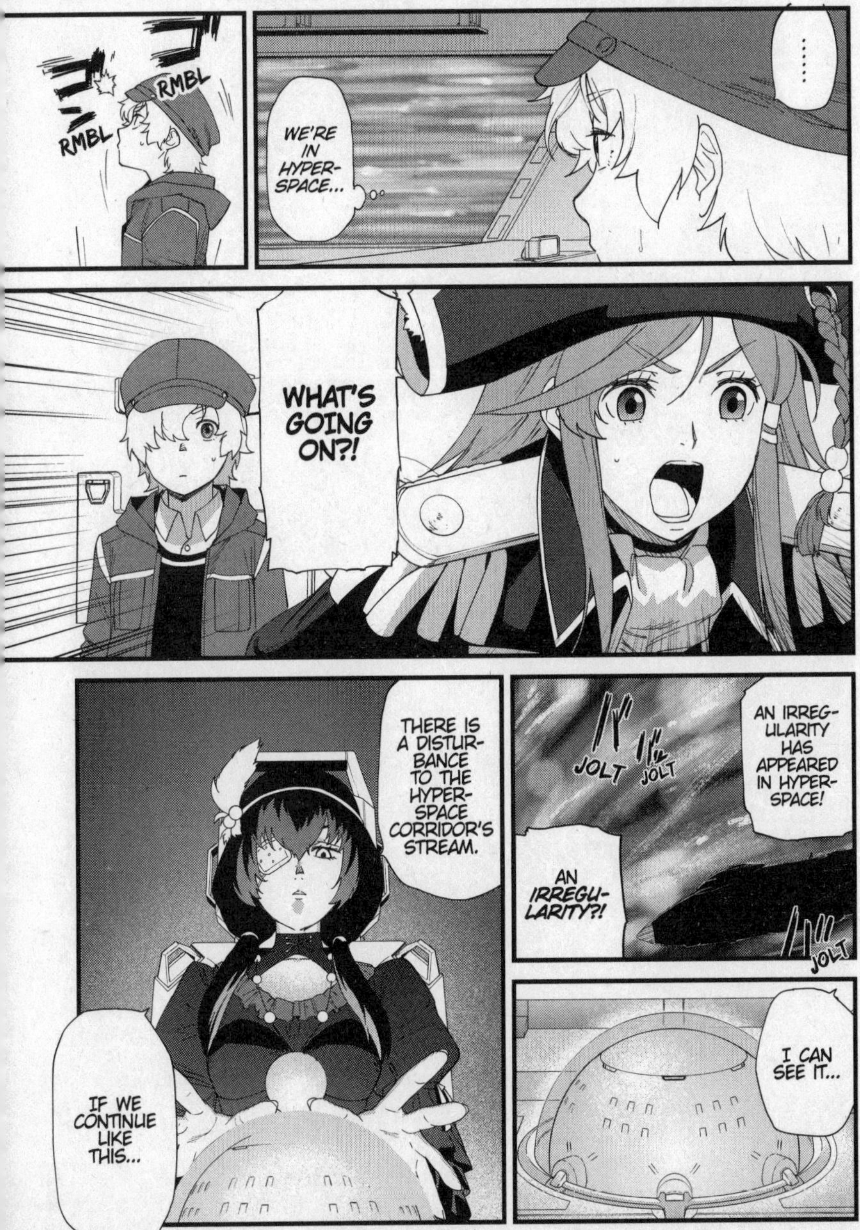
......
WE'RE IN HYPER-SPACE...
RMBL
RMBL
WHAT'S GOING ON?!
AN IRREG-ULARITY HAS APPEARED IN HYPER-SPACE!
JOLT
JOLT
AN IRREGU-LARITY?!
JOLT
I CAN SEE IT...
THERE IS A DISTUR-BANCE TO THE HYPER-SPACE CORRIDOR'S STREAM.
IF WE CONTINUE LIKE THIS...

WELL...

WHAT ABOUT ALTERNATIVE ROUTES?!

HEAVEN WILL--

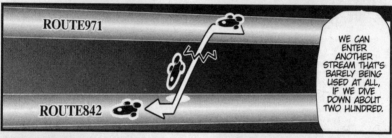

ROUTE971

ROUTE842

WE CAN ENTER ANOTHER STREAM THAT'S BARELY BEING USED AT ALL, IF WE DIVE DOWN ABOUT TWO HUNDRED.

......

LET'S GO...

BENTEN-MARU!

AYE-AYE!

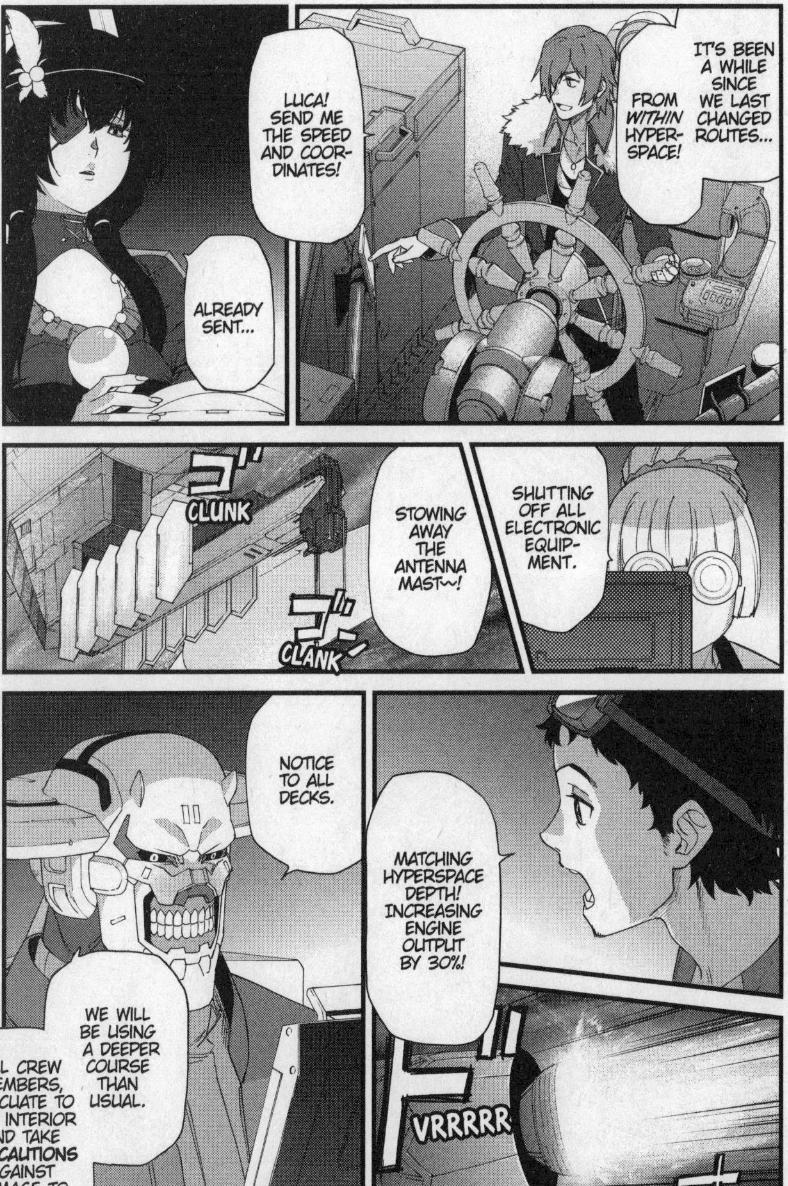
IT'S BEEN A WHILE SINCE WE LAST CHANGED ROUTES...
FROM WITHIN HYPER-SPACE!
LUCA! SEND ME THE SPEED AND COOR-DINATES!
ALREADY SENT...
SHUTTING OFF ALL ELECTRONIC EQUIP-MENT.
STOWING AWAY THE ANTENNA MAST~!
CLUNK
CLANK
MATCHING HYPERSPACE DEPTH! INCREASING ENGINE OUTPUT BY 30%!
VRRRRR
NOTICE TO ALL DECKS.
WE WILL BE USING A DEEPER COURSE THAN USUAL.
ALL CREW MEMBERS, EVACUATE TO THE INTERIOR AND TAKE PRECAUTIONS AGAINST DAMAGE TO THE OUTER WALL.

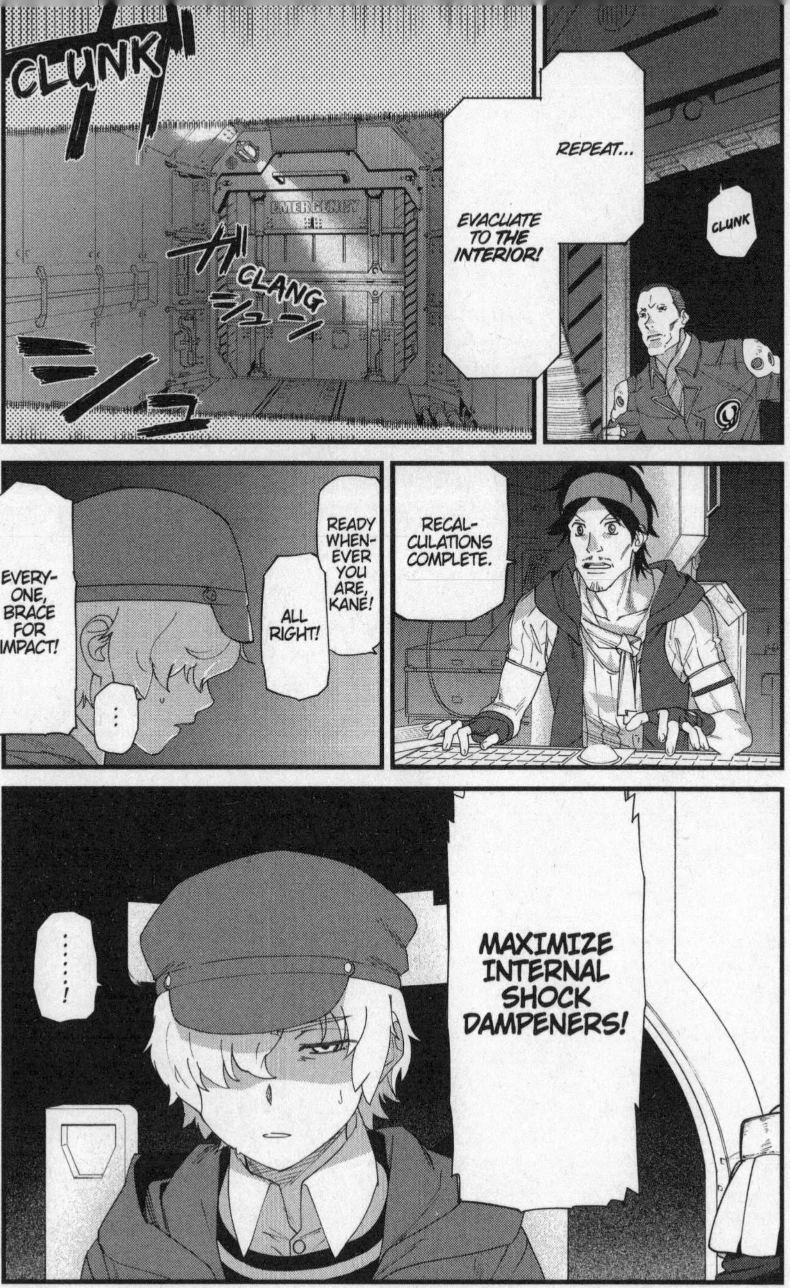
REPEAT...
EVACUATE TO THE INTERIOR!
CLUNK
CLUNK
EMERGENCY
CLANG
RECAL-CULATIONS COMPLETE.
READY WHEN-EVER YOU ARE, KANE!
ALL RIGHT!
EVERY-ONE, BRACE FOR IMPACT!
...
MAXIMIZE INTERNAL SHOCK DAMPENERS!
......!

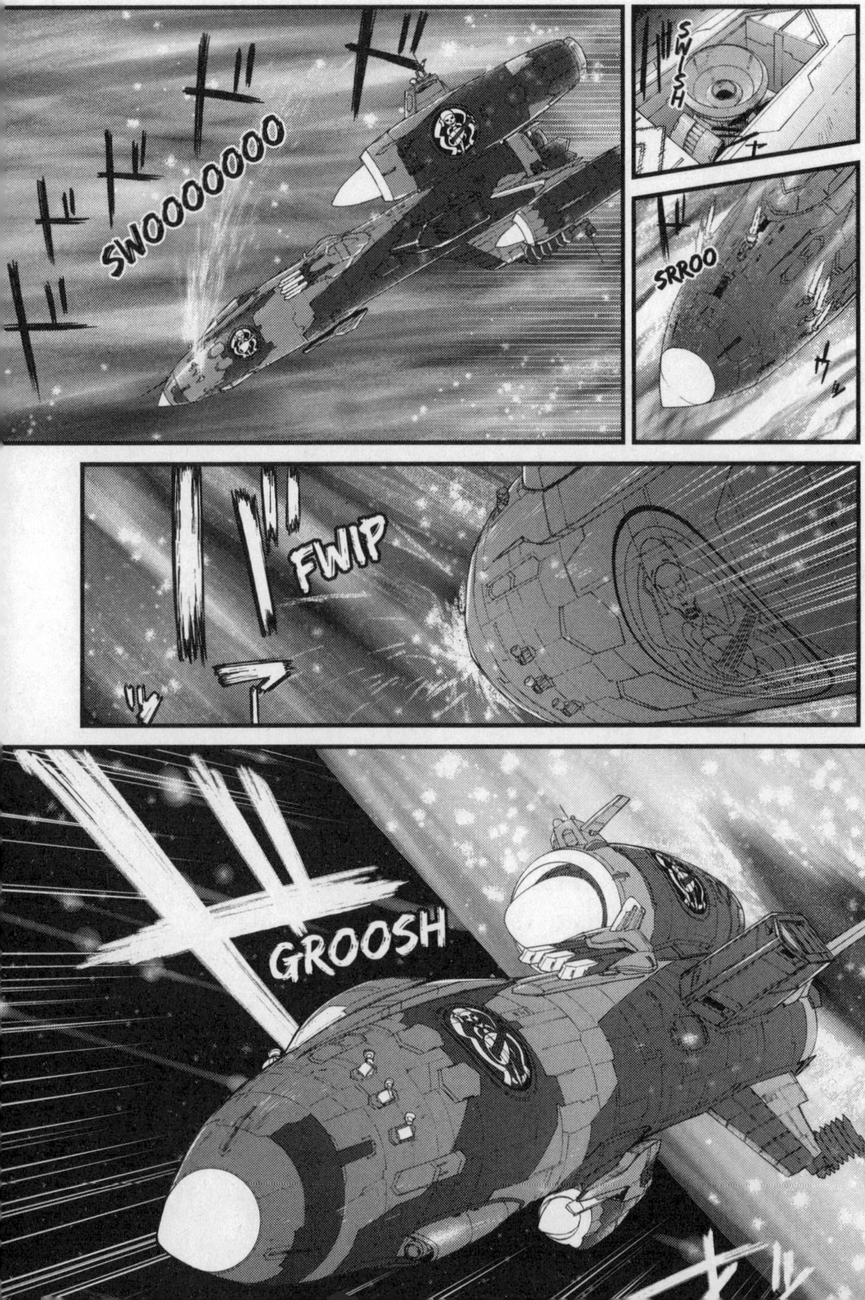
SWISH
SRROO
SWOOOOOOO
FWIP
GROOSH

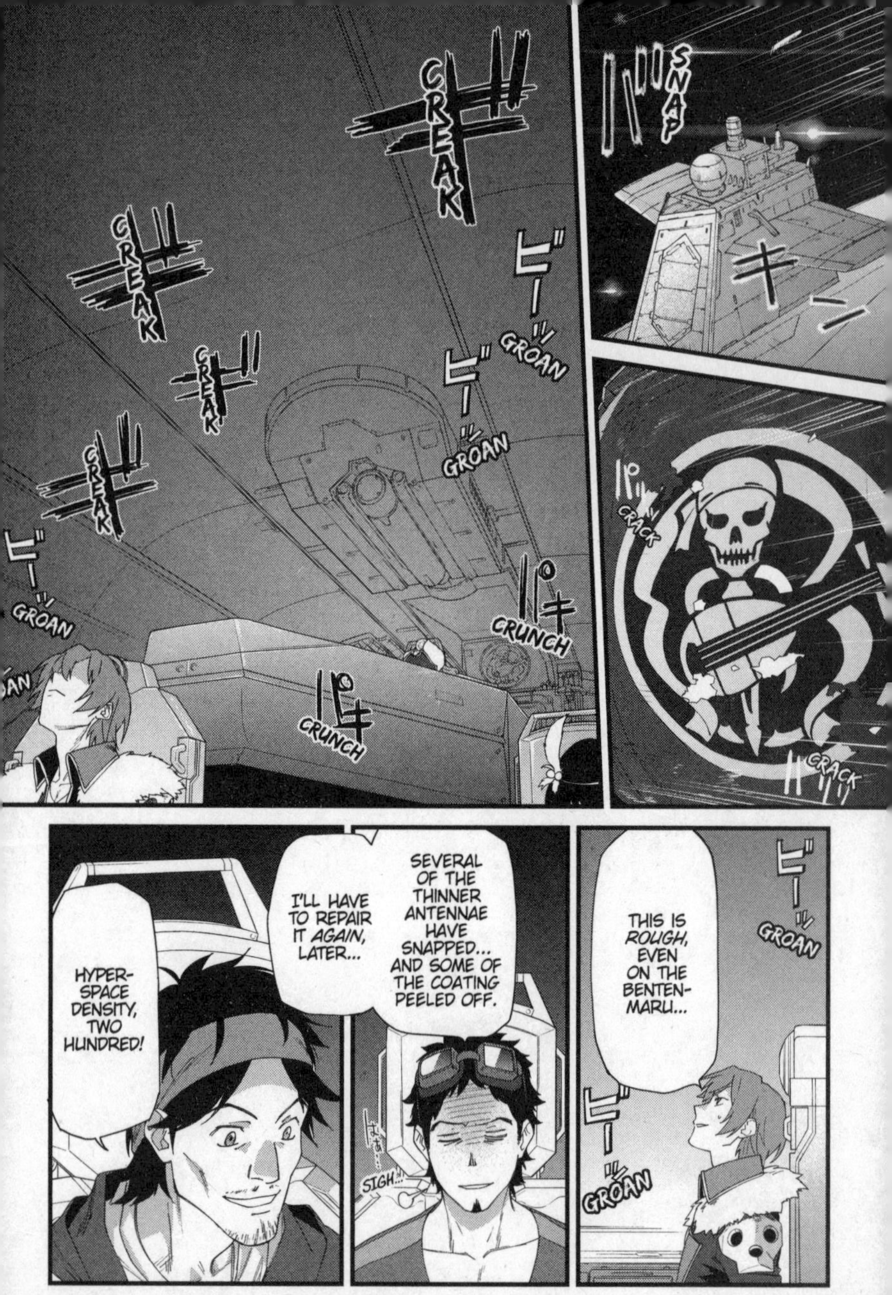
SNAP
CRACK
CRACK
CREAK
CREAK
CREAK
CREAK
GROAN
GROAN
GROAN
CRUNCH
CRUNCH
GROAN
THIS IS *ROUGH,* EVEN ON THE BENTEN-MARU...
GROAN
SEVERAL OF THE THINNER ANTENNAE HAVE SNAPPED... AND SOME OF THE COATING PEELED OFF.
I'LL HAVE TO REPAIR IT *AGAIN,* LATER...
SIGH...
HYPER-SPACE DENSITY, TWO HUNDRED!

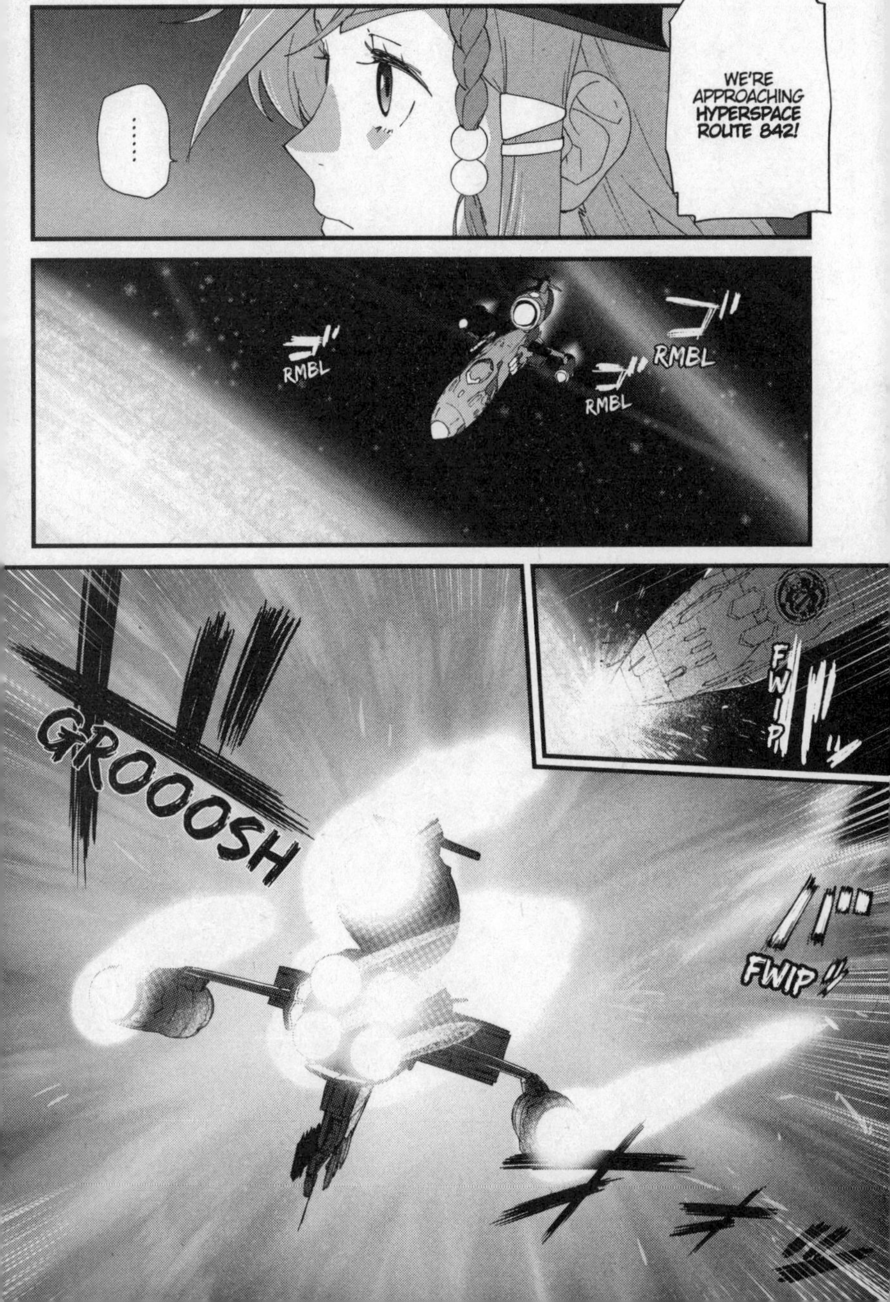
WE'RE APPROACHING HYPERSPACE ROUTE 842!
......
RMBL
RMBL
RMBL
FWIP
GROOOSH
FWIP!!

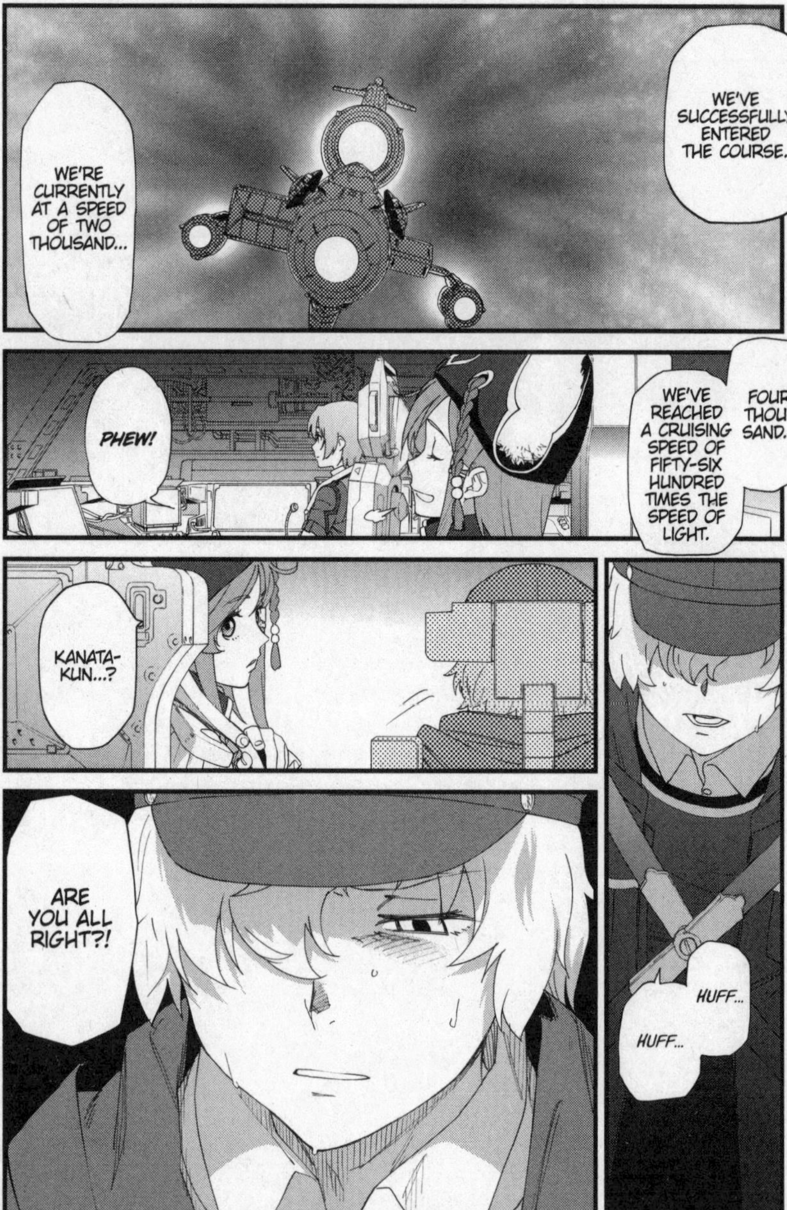
WE'VE SUCCESSFULLY ENTERED THE COURSE.
WE'RE CURRENTLY AT A SPEED OF TWO THOUSAND...
FOUR THOUSAND...
WE'VE REACHED A CRUISING SPEED OF FIFTY-SIX HUNDRED TIMES THE SPEED OF LIGHT.
PHEW!
HUFF...
HUFF...
KANATA-KUN...?
ARE YOU ALL RIGHT?!

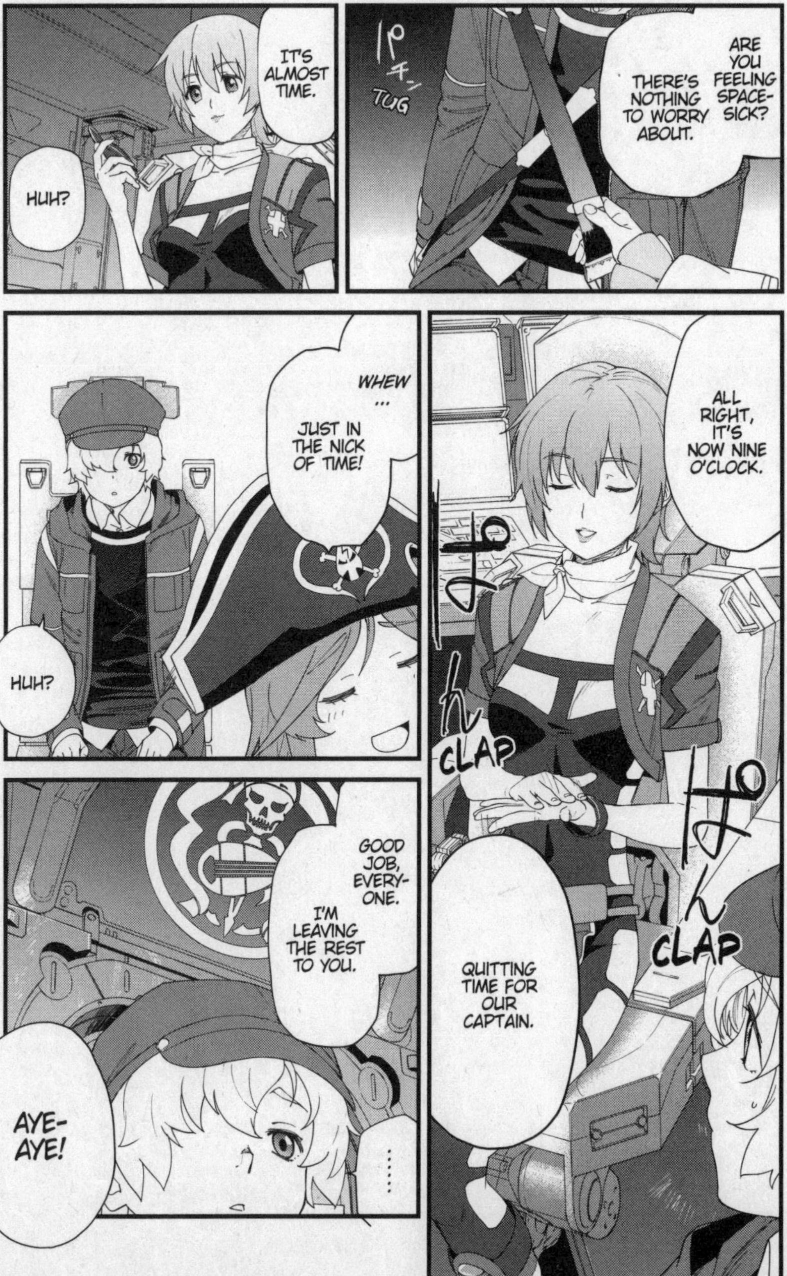

TUG
ARE YOU FEELING SPACE-SICK?
THERE'S NOTHING TO WORRY ABOUT.
IT'S ALMOST TIME.
HUH?
ALL RIGHT, IT'S NOW NINE O'CLOCK.
CLAP
CLAP
QUITTING TIME FOR OUR CAPTAIN.
WHEW ...
JUST IN THE NICK OF TIME!
HUH?
GOOD JOB, EVERY-ONE.
I'M LEAVING THE REST TO YOU.
AYE-AYE!
......

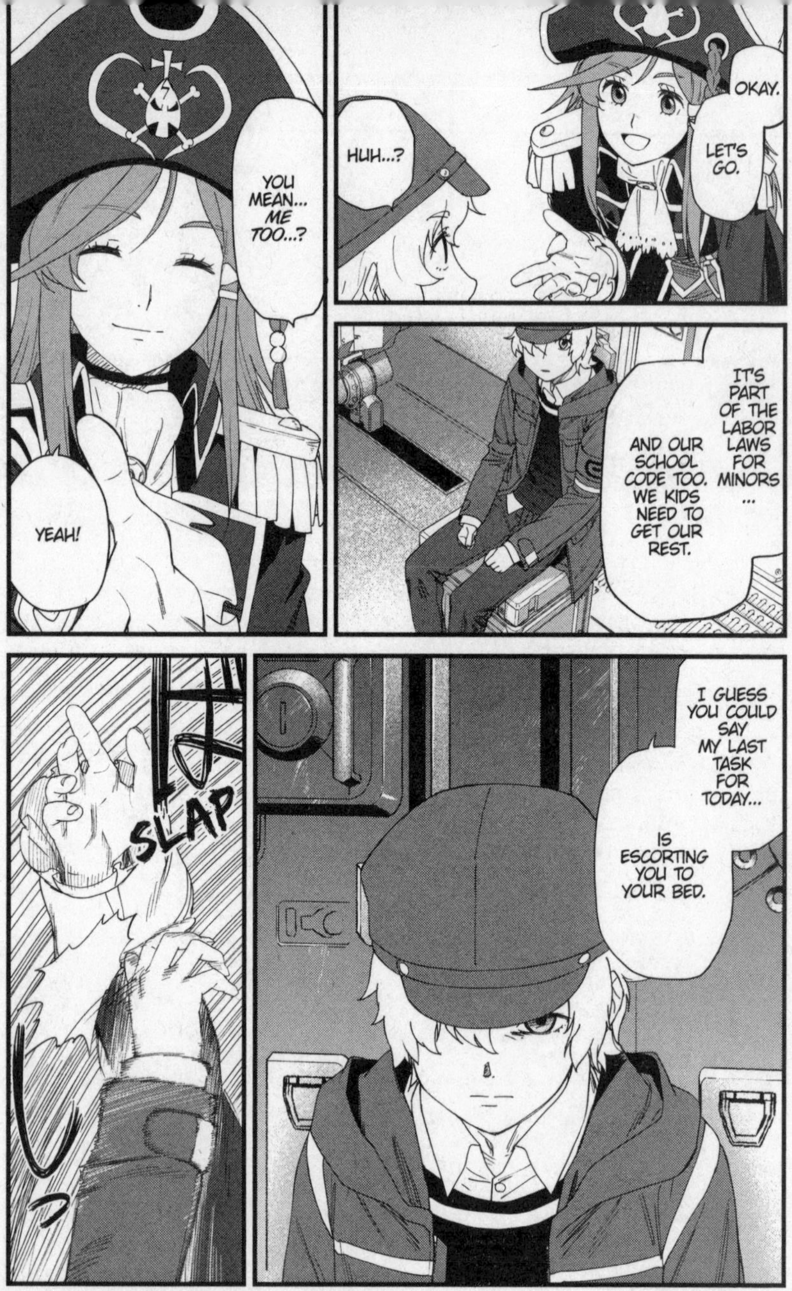
OKAY.
LET'S GO.
HUH...?
IT'S PART OF THE LABOR LAWS FOR MINORS...
AND OUR SCHOOL CODE TOO. WE KIDS NEED TO GET OUR REST.
YOU MEAN... ME TOO...?
YEAH!
I GUESS YOU COULD SAY MY LAST TASK FOR TODAY...
IS ESCORTING YOU TO YOUR BED.
SLAP

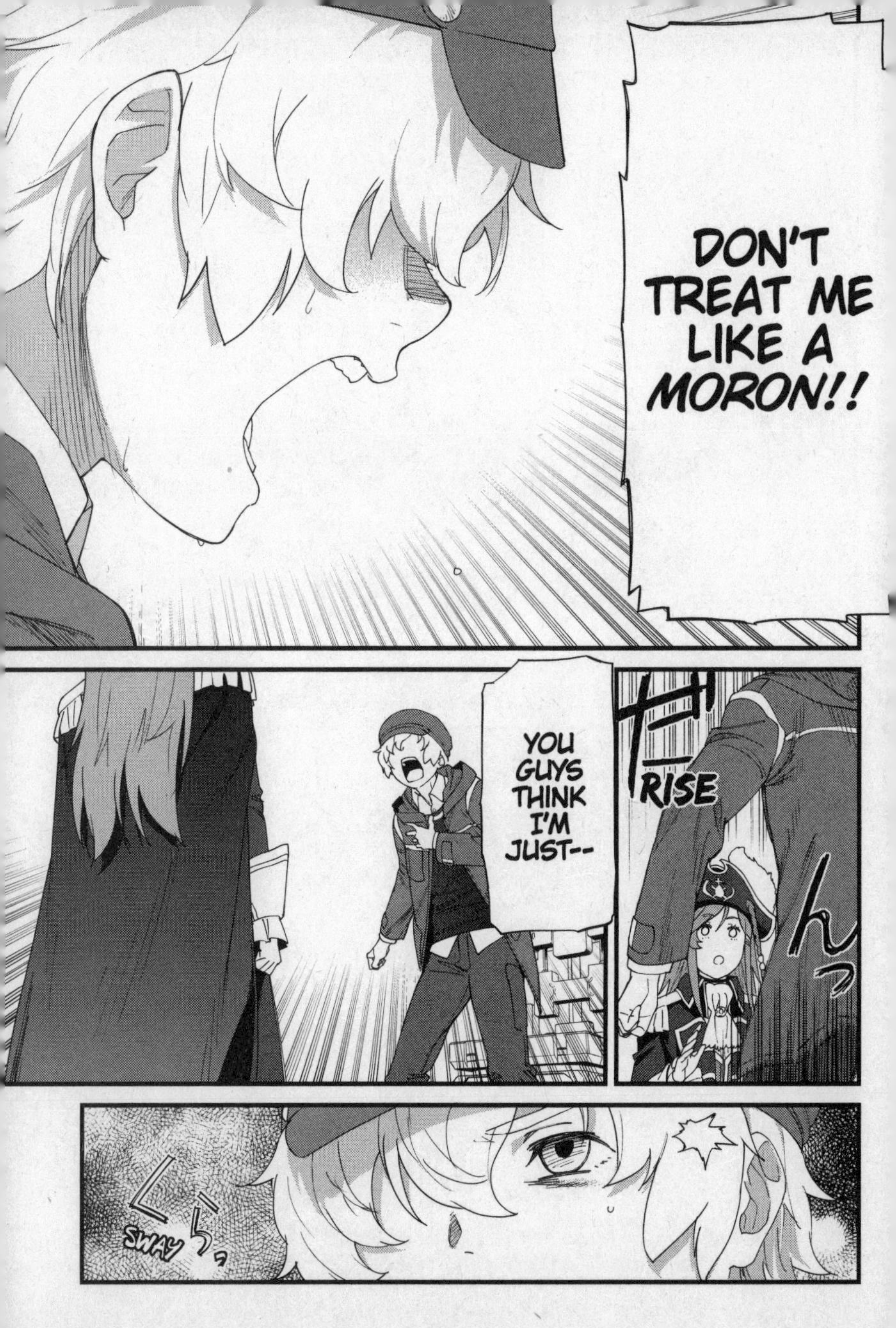
DON'T TREAT ME LIKE A MORON!!
RISE
YOU GUYS THINK I'M JUST--
SWAY

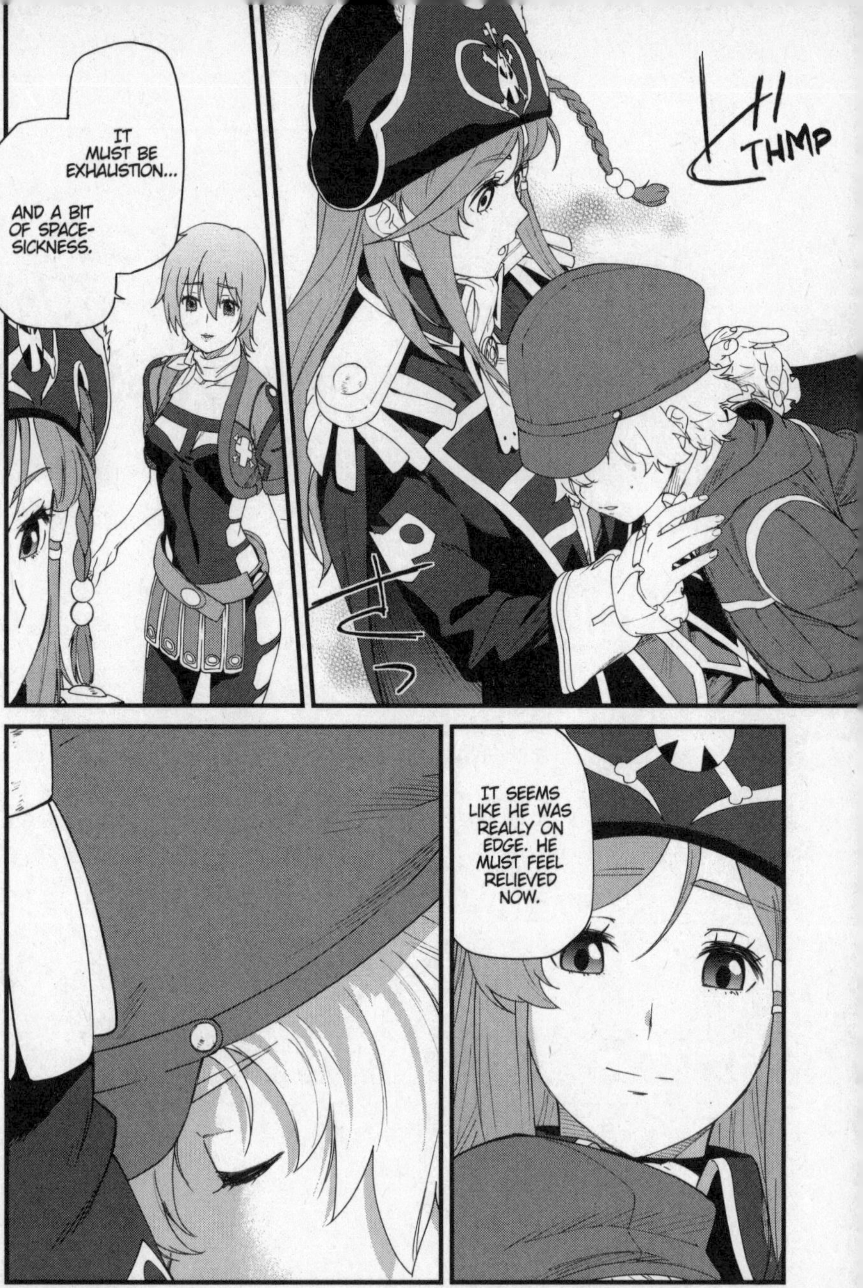
THMP
さっ
IT MUST BE EXHAUSTION...
AND A BIT OF SPACE-SICKNESS.
IT SEEMS LIKE HE WAS REALLY ON EDGE. HE MUST FEEL RELIEVED NOW.

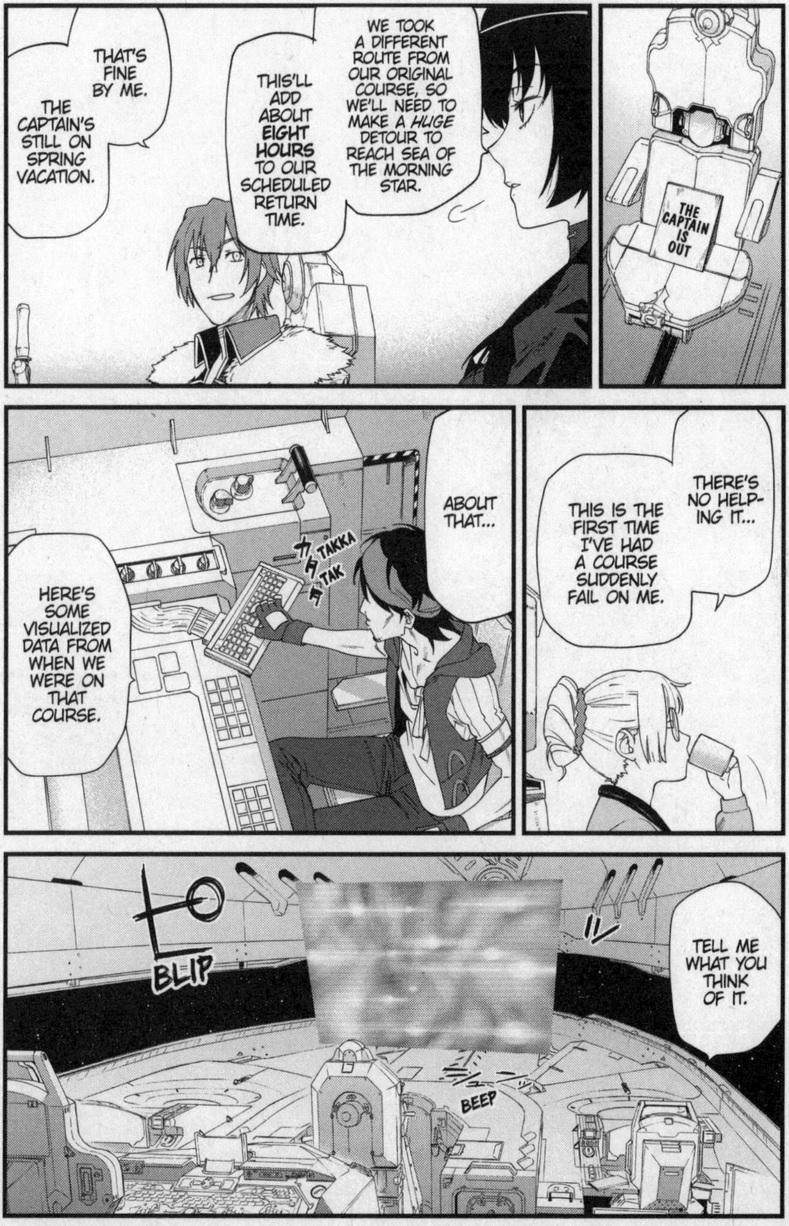
THE CAPTAIN IS OUT
WE TOOK A DIFFERENT ROUTE FROM OUR ORIGINAL COURSE, SO WE'LL NEED TO MAKE A *HUGE* DETOUR TO REACH SEA OF THE MORNING STAR.
THIS'LL ADD ABOUT **EIGHT HOURS** TO OUR SCHEDULED RETURN TIME.
THAT'S FINE BY ME.
THE CAPTAIN'S STILL ON SPRING VACATION.
THERE'S NO HELPING IT...
THIS IS THE FIRST TIME I'VE HAD A COURSE SUDDENLY FAIL ON ME.
ABOUT THAT...
TAKKA
TAK
HERE'S SOME VISUALIZED DATA FROM WHEN WE WERE ON THAT COURSE.
TELL ME WHAT YOU THINK OF IT.
BEEP
BLIP

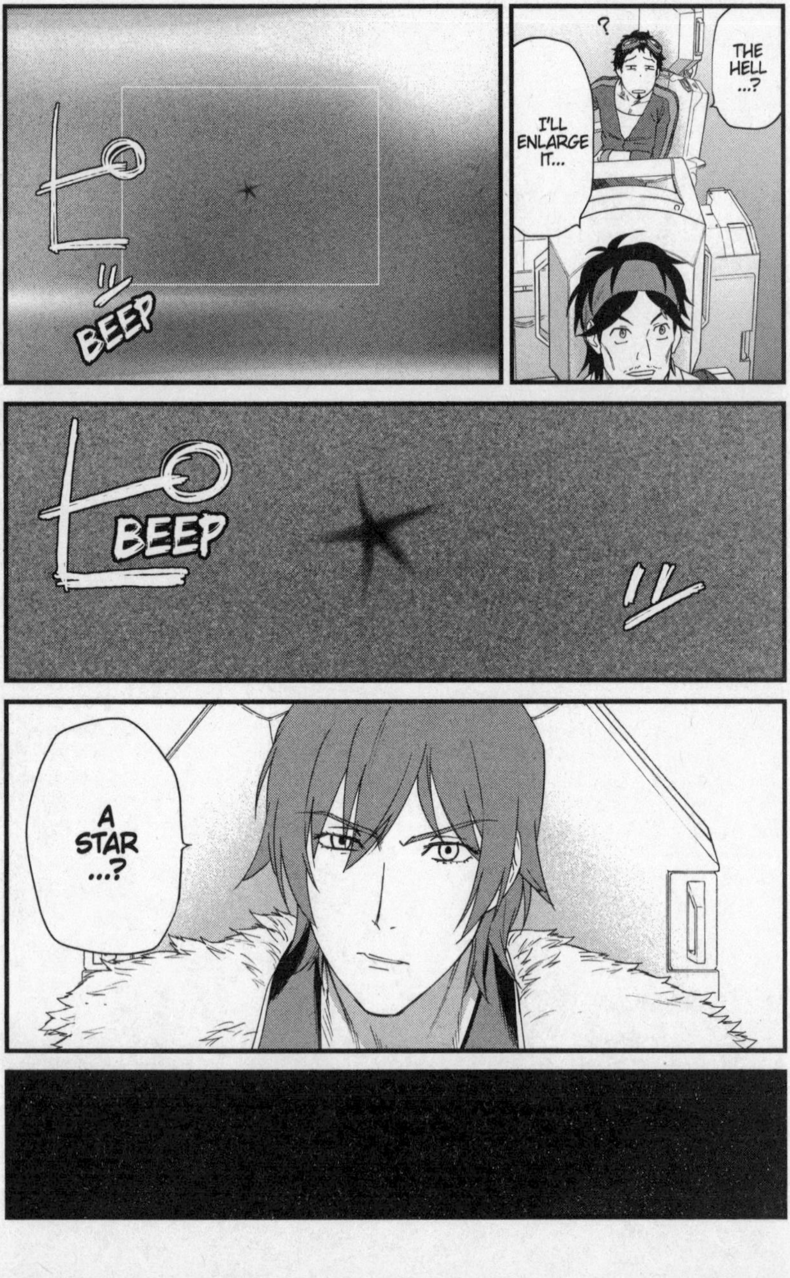
THE HELL ...?
?
I'LL ENLARGE IT...
ピッ
BEEP
ピッ
BEEP
A STAR ...?

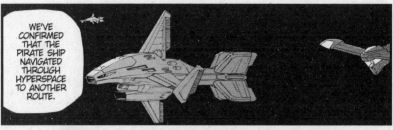

WE'VE CONFIRMED THAT THE PIRATE SHIP NAVIGATED THROUGH HYPERSPACE TO ANOTHER ROUTE.
WE'RE CALCULATING THEIR DESTINATION.
THEY SUDDENLY ENTERED ANOTHER COURSE? UNBELIEVABLE...
HURRY UP AND RECOVER THE FLAWEN!
TOK
ROGER!
HMPH...

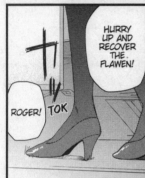

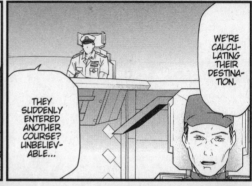

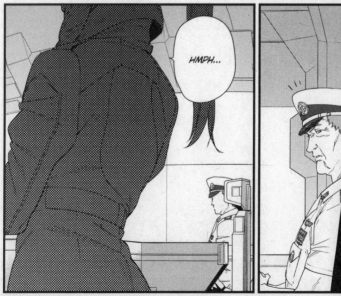

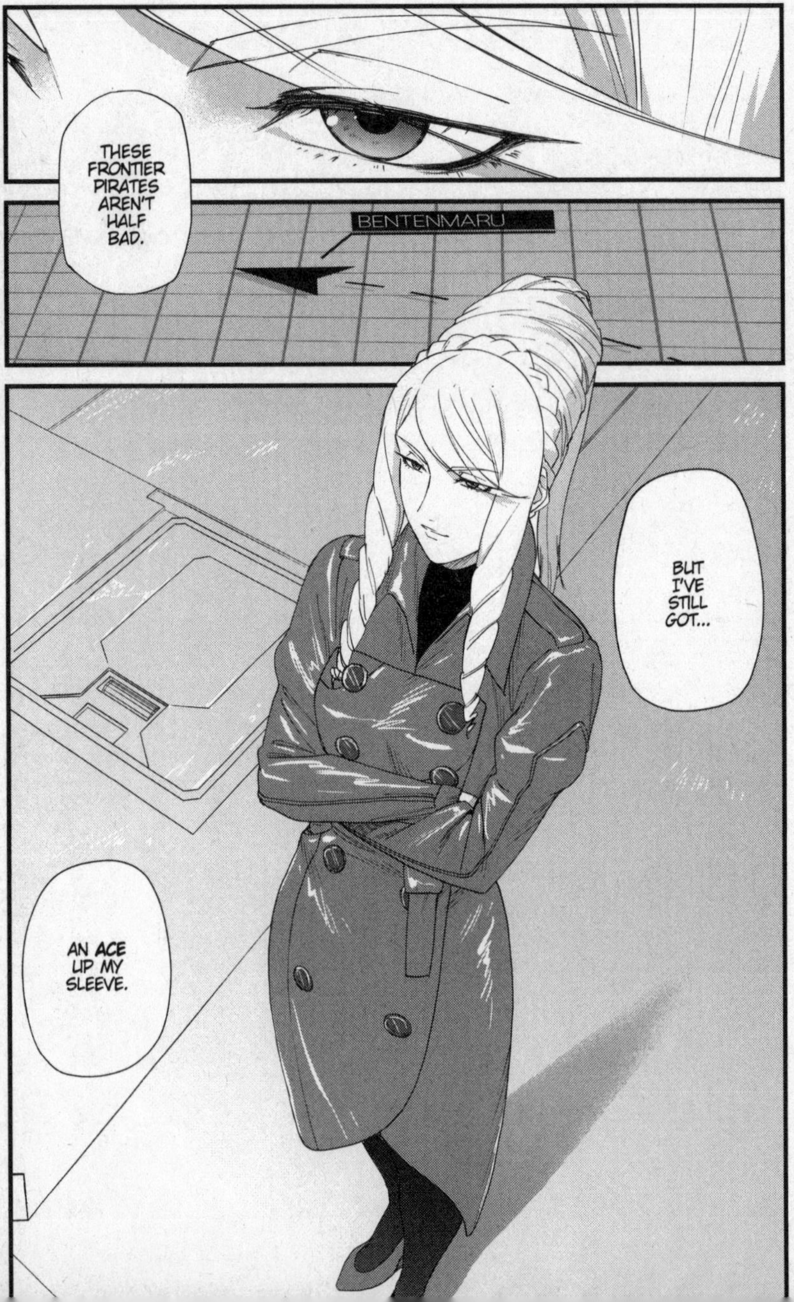
THESE FRONTIER PIRATES AREN'T HALF BAD.
BENTENMARU
BUT I'VE STILL GOT...
AN ACE UP MY SLEEVE.

BODACIOUS
SPACE
PIRATES
[THE MOVIE]
ABYSS OF HYPERSPACE

モーレツ★宇宙海賊
ABYSS OF HYPERSPACE
亜空の深淵

VOLUME 01 Chapter 03 end

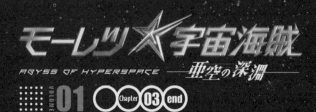

BODACIOUS
SPACE
PIRATES
[THE MOVIE]

ABYSS OF HYPERSPACE

VOLUME 01

Chapter 04

[START]

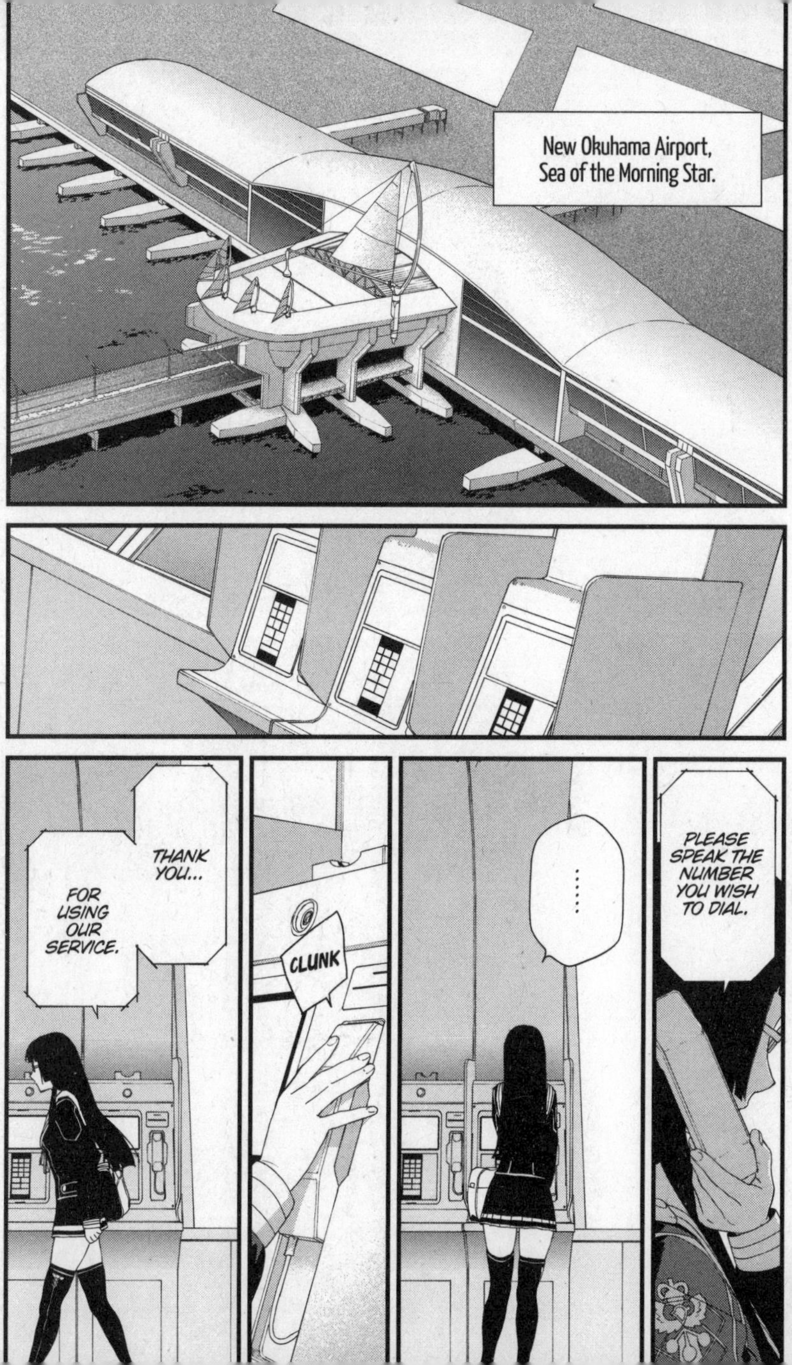
New Okuhama Airport, Sea of the Morning Star.
PLEASE SPEAK THE NUMBER YOU WISH TO DIAL.
......
CLUNK
THANK YOU...
FOR USING OUR SERVICE.

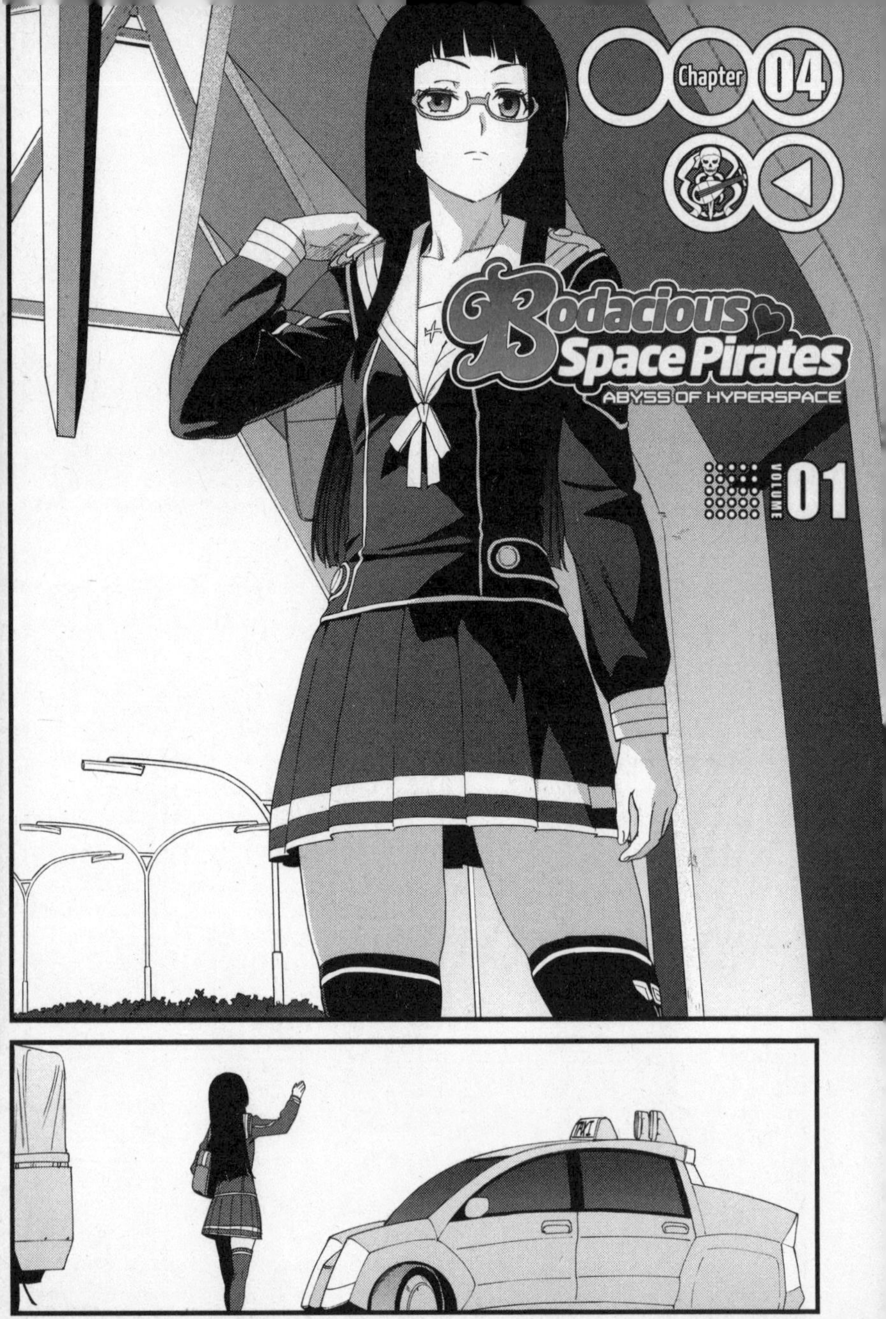
Chapter 04
Bodacious Space Pirates
ABYSS OF HYPERSPACE
VOLUME 01

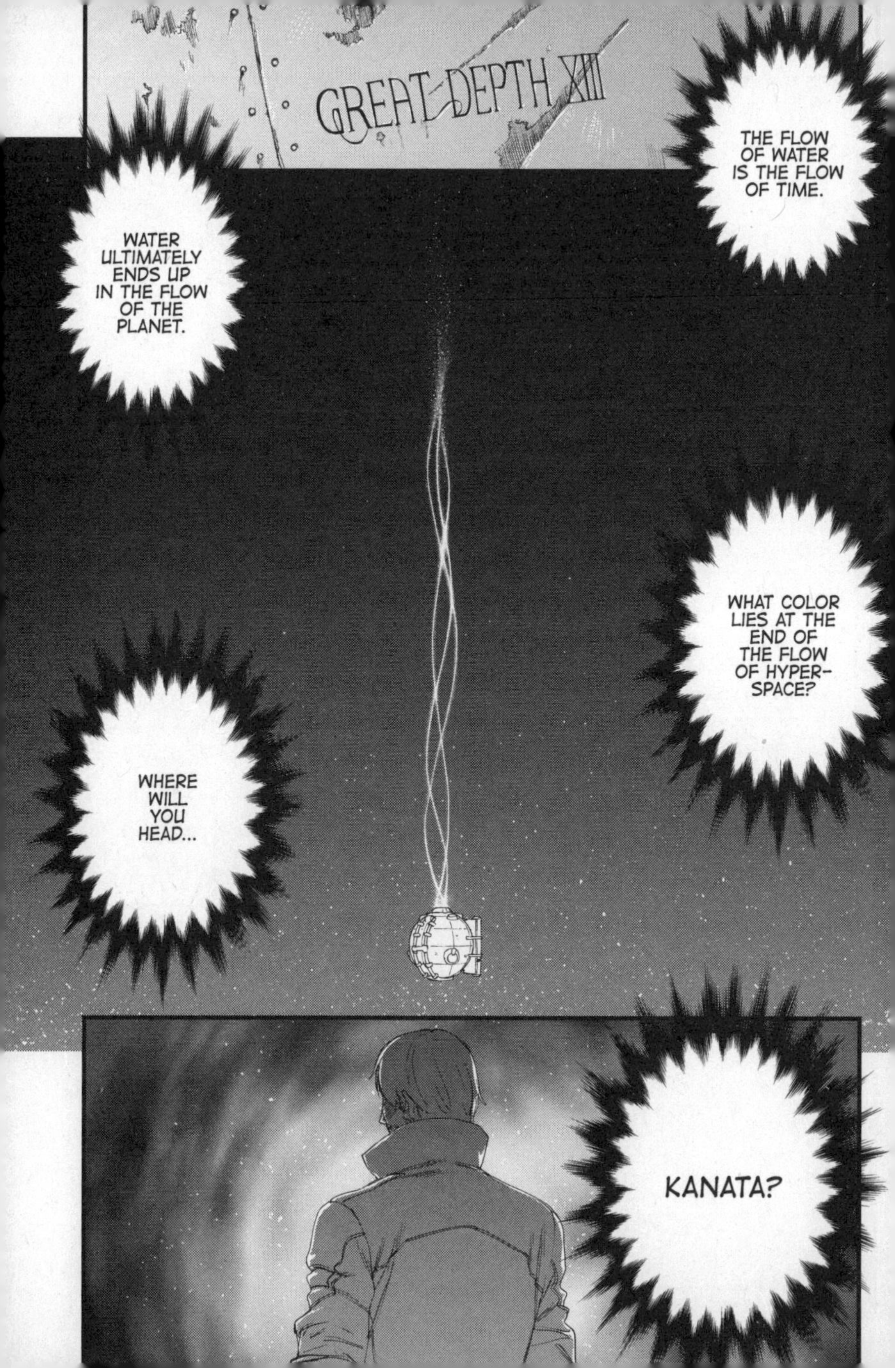
GREAT DEPTH XIII
THE FLOW OF WATER IS THE FLOW OF TIME.
WATER ULTIMATELY ENDS UP IN THE FLOW OF THE PLANET.
WHAT COLOR LIES AT THE END OF THE FLOW OF HYPER-SPACE?
WHERE WILL YOU HEAD...
KANATA?

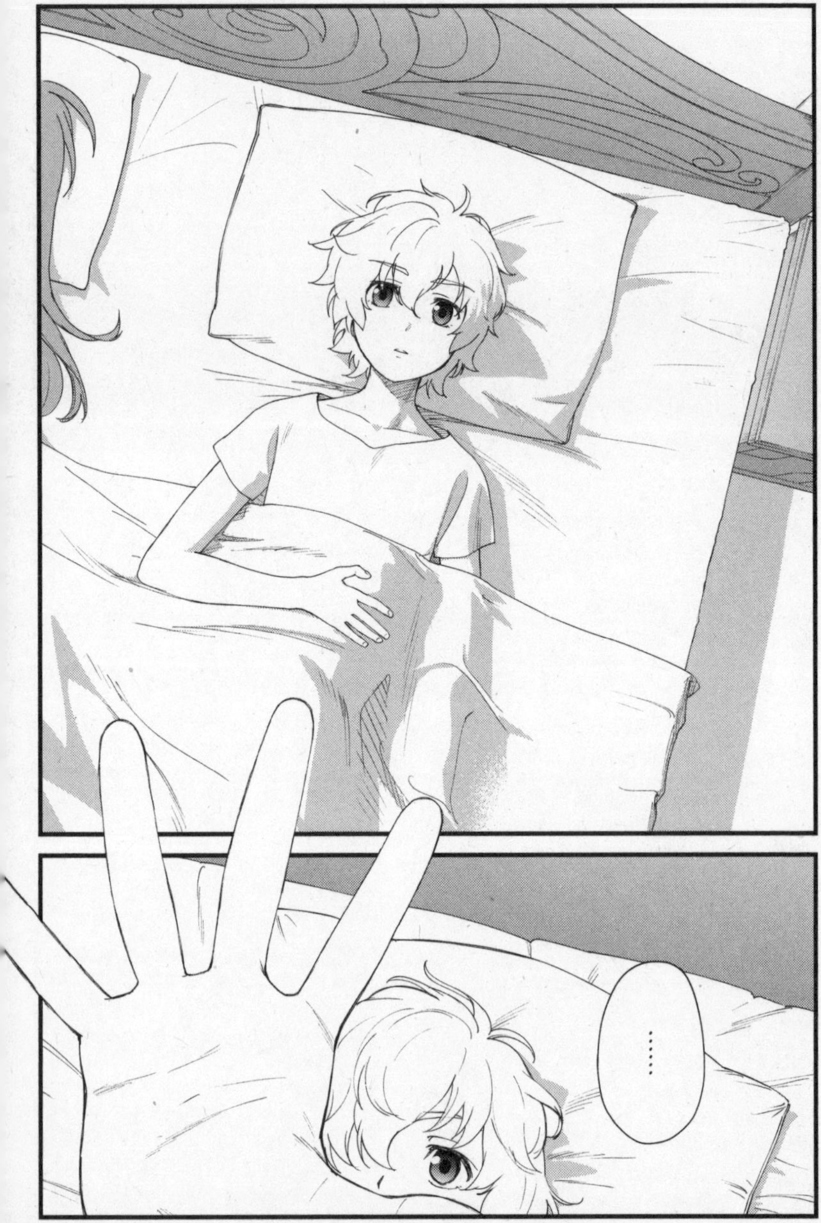
……

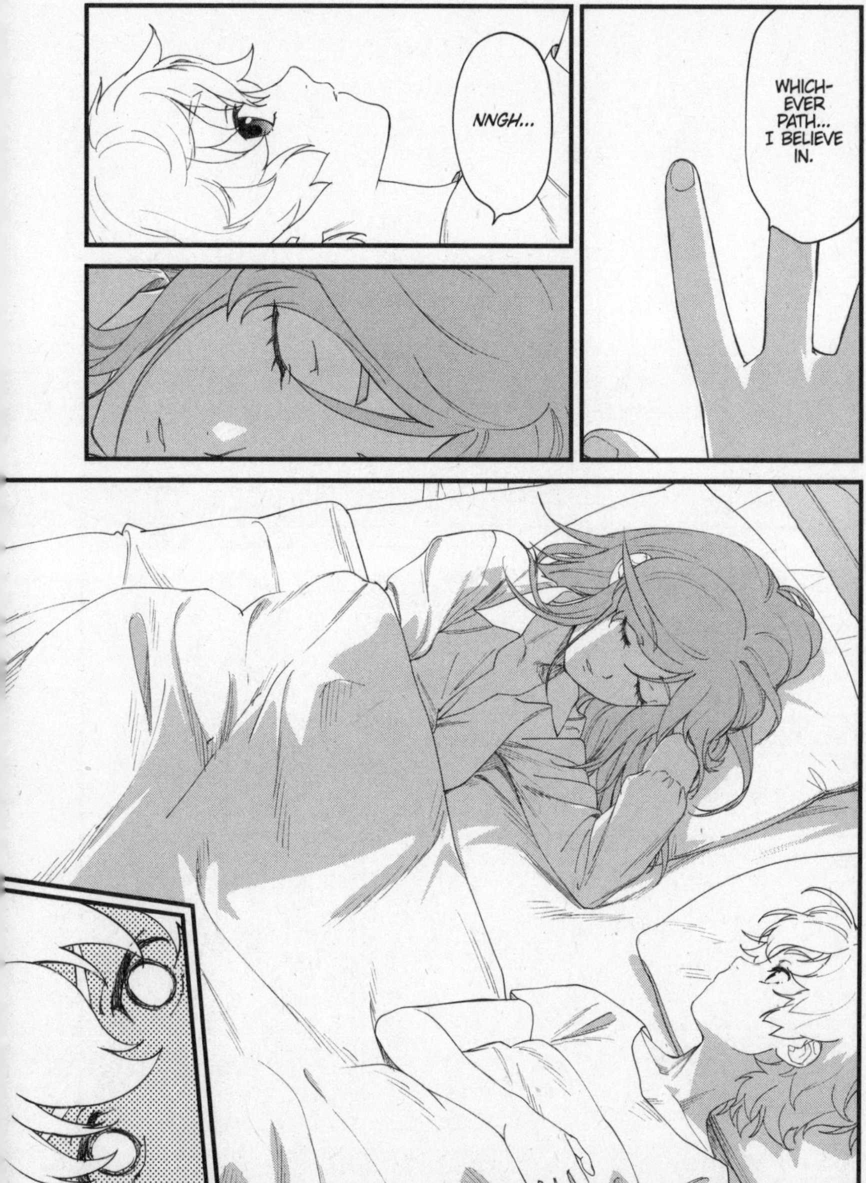
WHICH-EVER PATH... I BELIEVE IN.
NNGH...

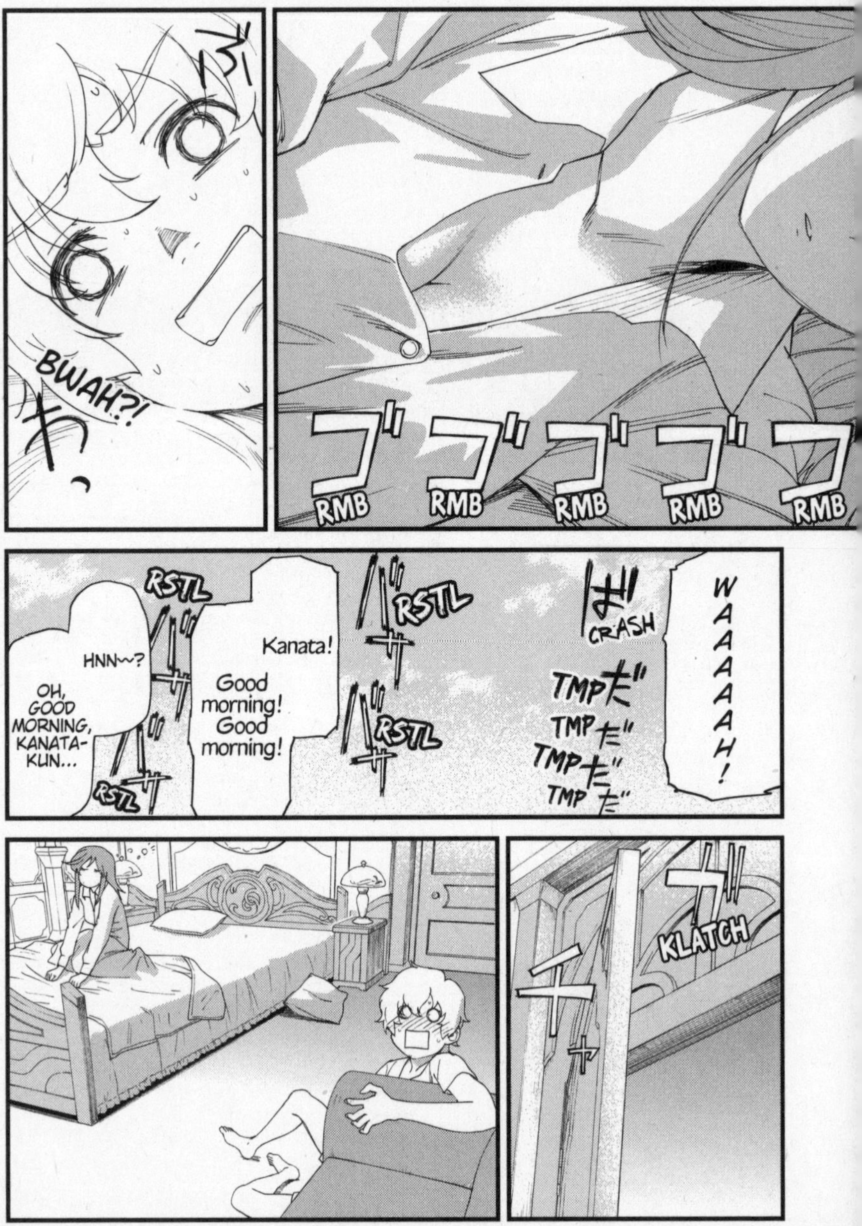

ゴゴゴゴゴ
RMB RMB RMB RMB RMB
ぎ
BWAH?!
わっ
WAAAAAAH!
ば CRASH
TMP だ TMP だ TMP だ TMP だ
RSTL
Kanata! Good morning! Good morning!
RSTL
HNN~? OH, GOOD MORNING, KANATA-KUN...
RSTL
RSTL
ガ KLATCH

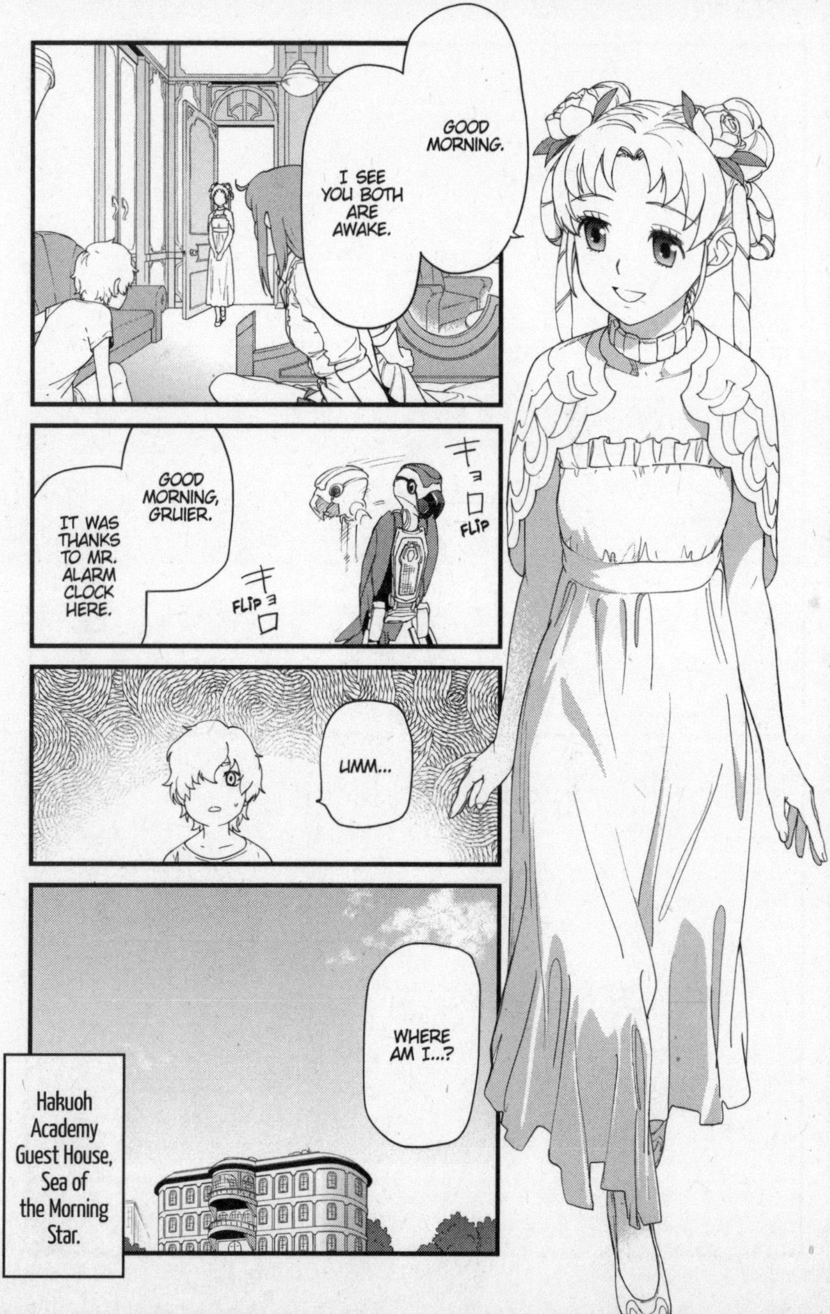
GOOD MORNING.
I SEE YOU BOTH ARE AWAKE.
キョロ FLIP
GOOD MORNING, GRUIER.
IT WAS THANKS TO MR. ALARM CLOCK HERE.
キョロ FLIP
UMM...
WHERE AM I...?
Hakuoh Academy Guest House, Sea of the Morning Star.

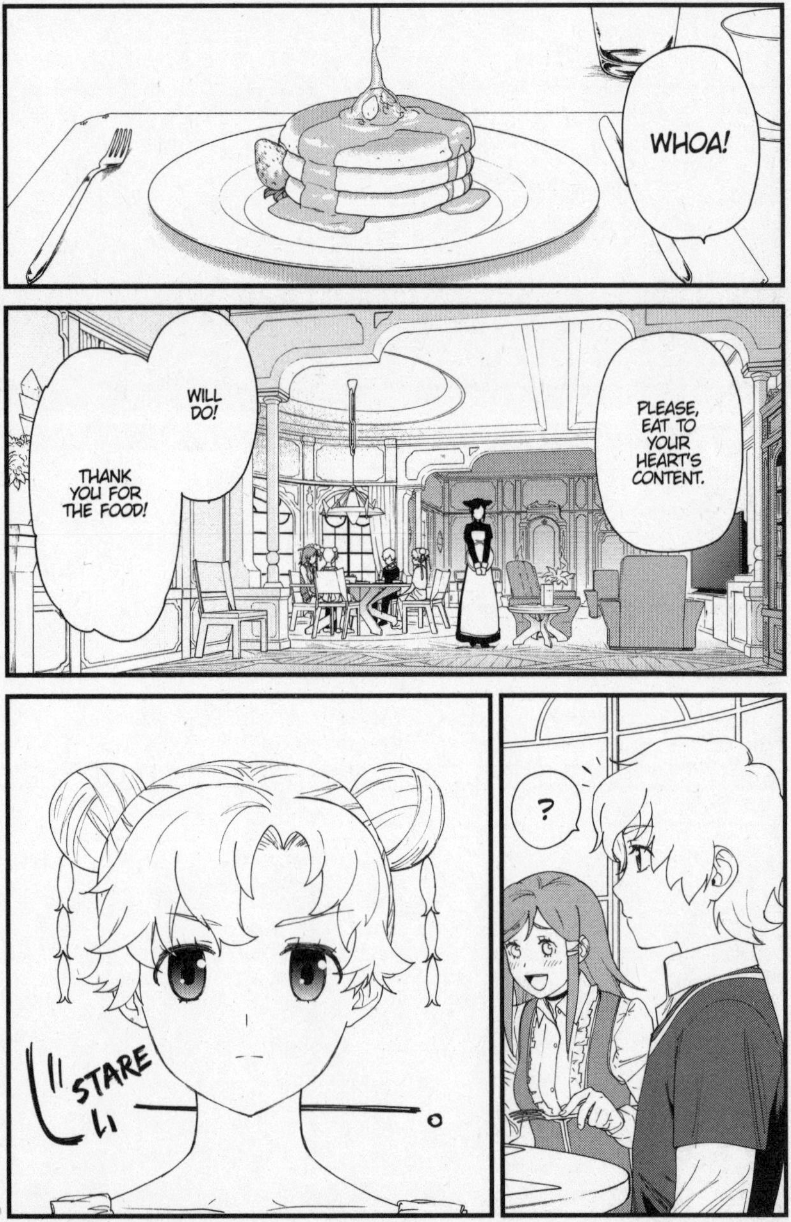
WHOA!
PLEASE, EAT TO YOUR HEART'S CONTENT.
WILL DO!
THANK YOU FOR THE FOOD!
?
STARE

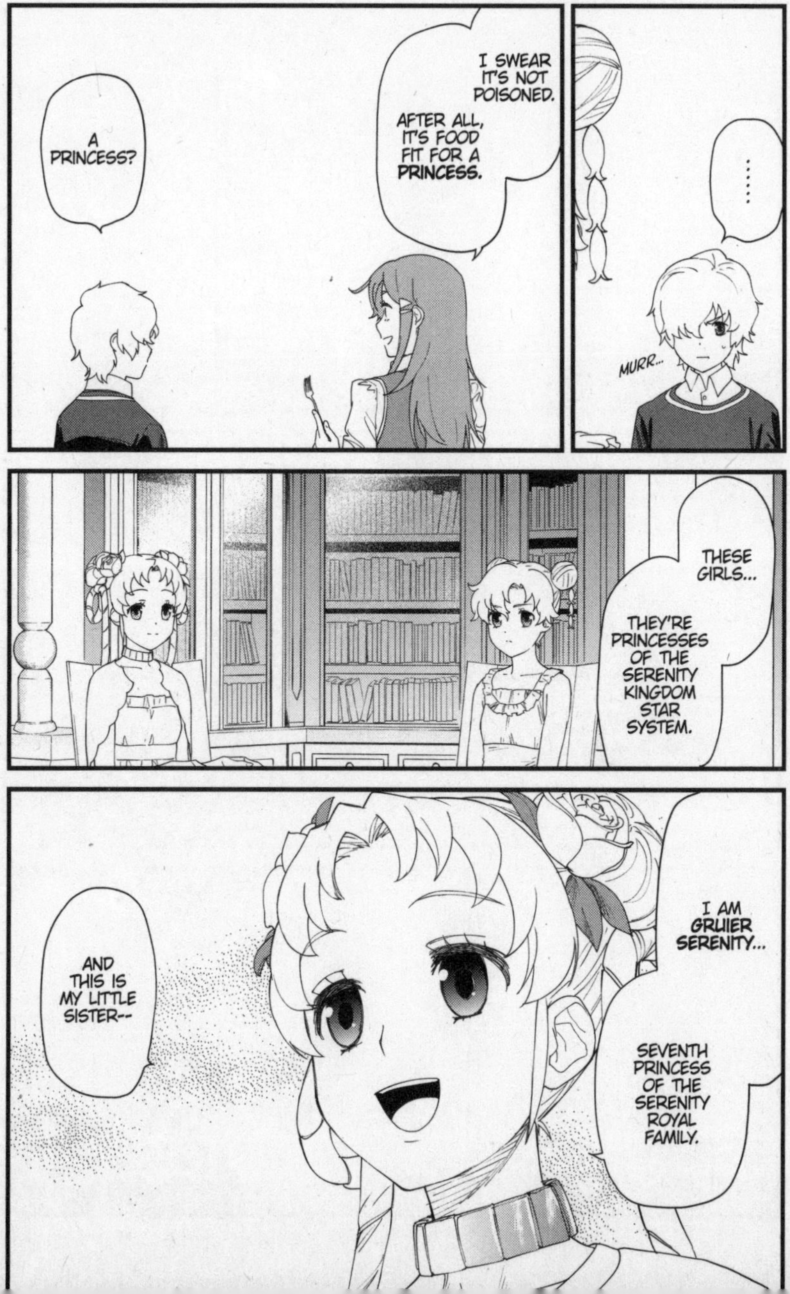
......
MURR...
I SWEAR IT'S NOT POISONED.
AFTER ALL, IT'S FOOD FIT FOR A PRINCESS.
A PRINCESS?
THESE GIRLS...
THEY'RE PRINCESSES OF THE SERENITY KINGDOM STAR SYSTEM.
I AM GRUIER SERENITY...
SEVENTH PRINCESS OF THE SERENITY ROYAL FAMILY.
AND THIS IS MY LITTLE SISTER--

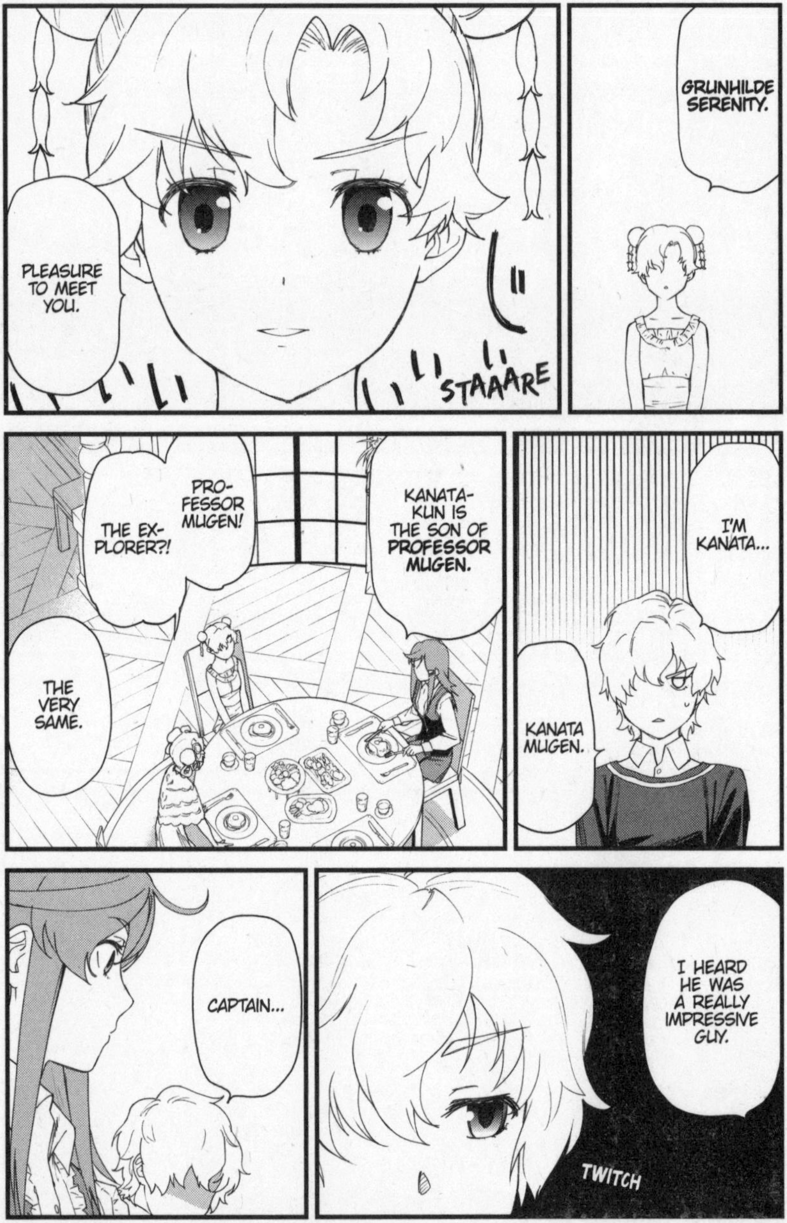
GRUNHILDE SERENITY.
PLEASURE TO MEET YOU.
STAAARE
I'M KANATA...
KANATA MUGEN.
KANATA-KUN IS THE SON OF PROFESSOR MUGEN.
PRO-FESSOR MUGEN!
THE EX-PLORER?!
THE VERY SAME.
I HEARD HE WAS A REALLY IMPRESSIVE GUY.
TWITCH
CAPTAIN...

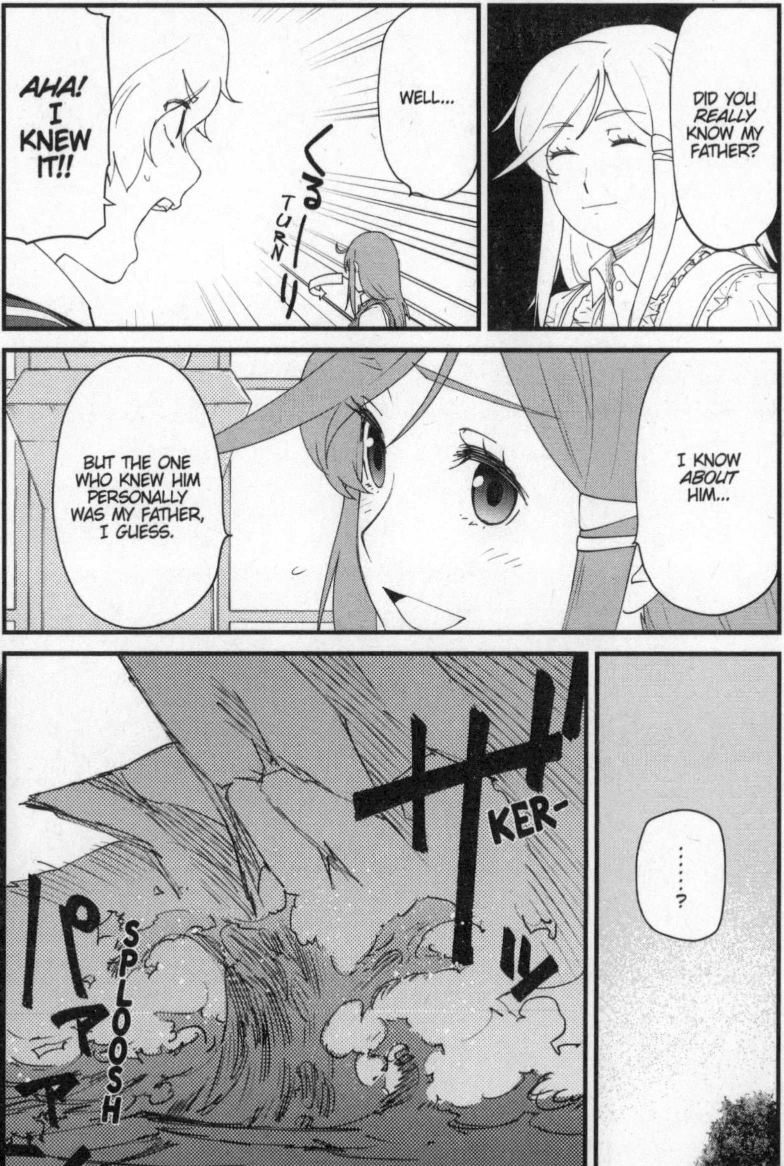
DID YOU REALLY KNOW MY FATHER?
WELL...
TURN
AHA! I KNEW IT!!
I KNOW ABOUT HIM...
BUT THE ONE WHO KNEW HIM PERSONALLY WAS MY FATHER, I GUESS.
......?
KER-
SPLOOSH

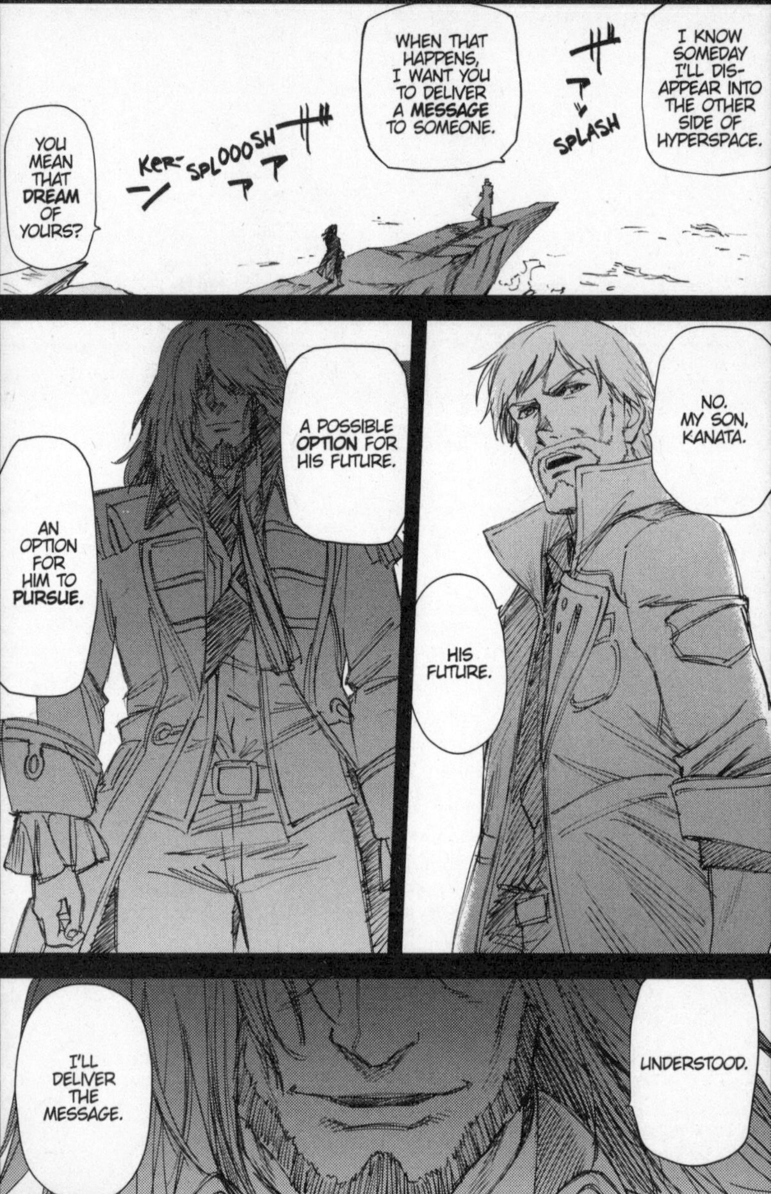
I KNOW SOMEDAY I'LL DIS-APPEAR INTO THE OTHER SIDE OF HYPERSPACE.
SPLASH
WHEN THAT HAPPENS, I WANT YOU TO DELIVER A MESSAGE TO SOMEONE.
KER-SPLOOOSH
YOU MEAN THAT DREAM OF YOURS?
NO. MY SON, KANATA.
HIS FUTURE.
A POSSIBLE OPTION FOR HIS FUTURE.
AN OPTION FOR HIM TO PURSUE.
UNDERSTOOD.
I'LL DELIVER THE MESSAGE.

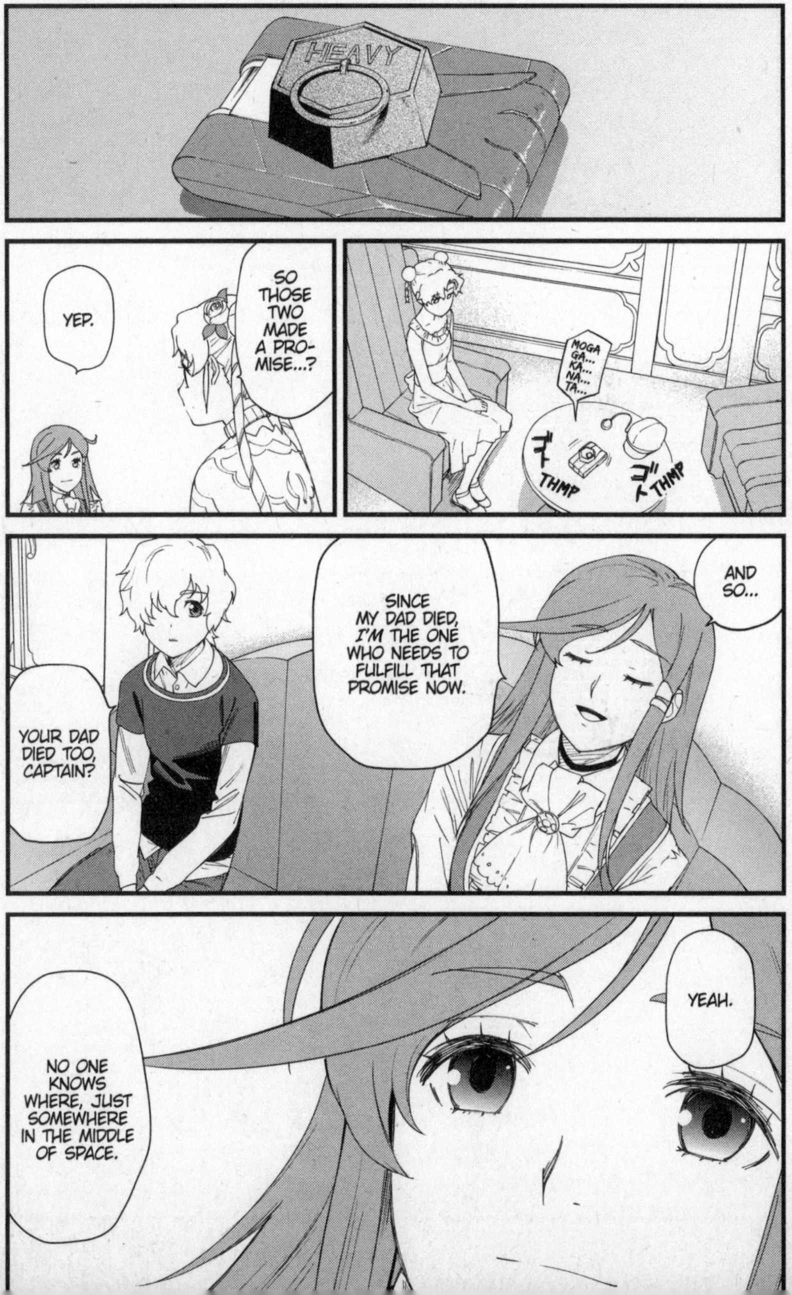
HEAVY
MOGA GA... KA... NA... TA...
THMP
THMP
SO THOSE TWO MADE A PRO-MISE...?
YEP.
AND SO...
SINCE MY DAD DIED, *I'M* THE ONE WHO NEEDS TO FULFILL THAT PROMISE NOW.
YOUR DAD DIED TOO, CAPTAIN?
YEAH.
NO ONE KNOWS WHERE, JUST SOMEWHERE IN THE MIDDLE OF SPACE.

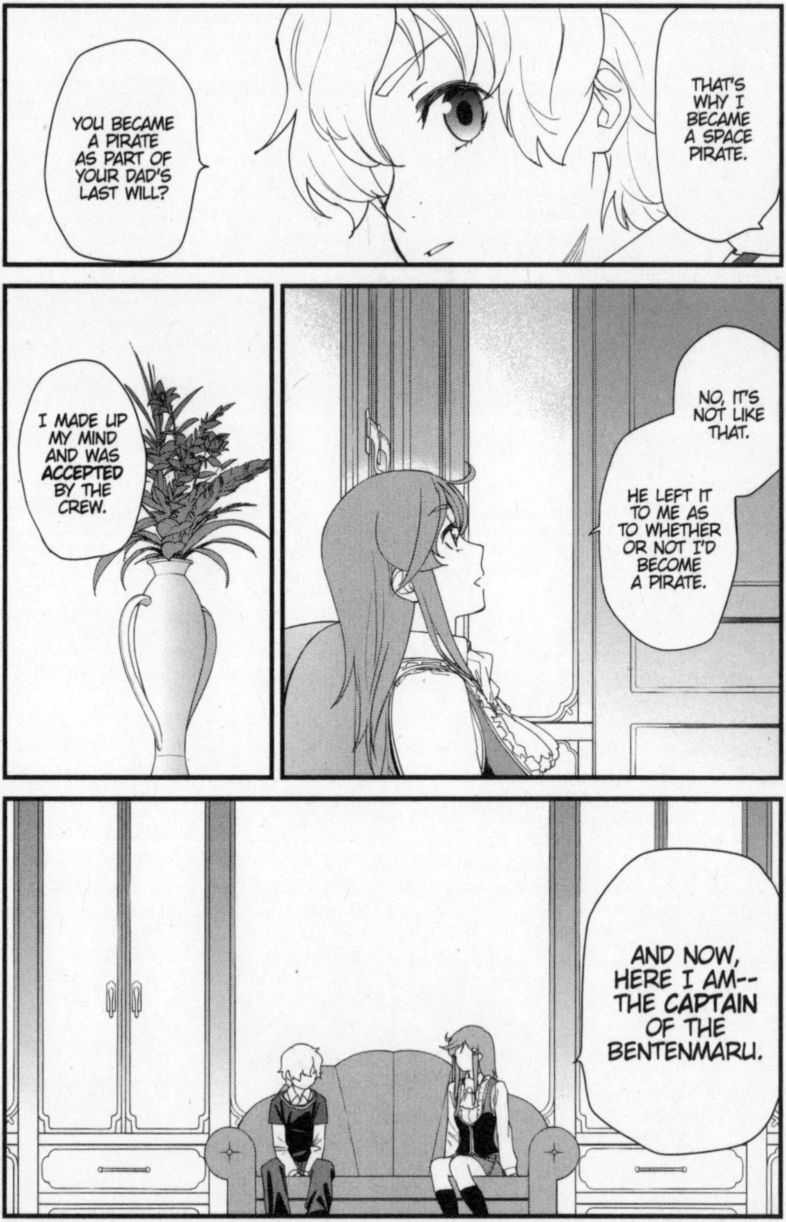
THAT'S WHY I BECAME A SPACE PIRATE.
YOU BECAME A PIRATE AS PART OF YOUR DAD'S LAST WILL?
NO, IT'S NOT LIKE THAT.
HE LEFT IT TO ME AS TO WHETHER OR NOT I'D BECOME A PIRATE.
I MADE UP MY MIND AND WAS ACCEPTED BY THE CREW.
AND NOW, HERE I AM-- THE CAPTAIN OF THE BENTENMARU.

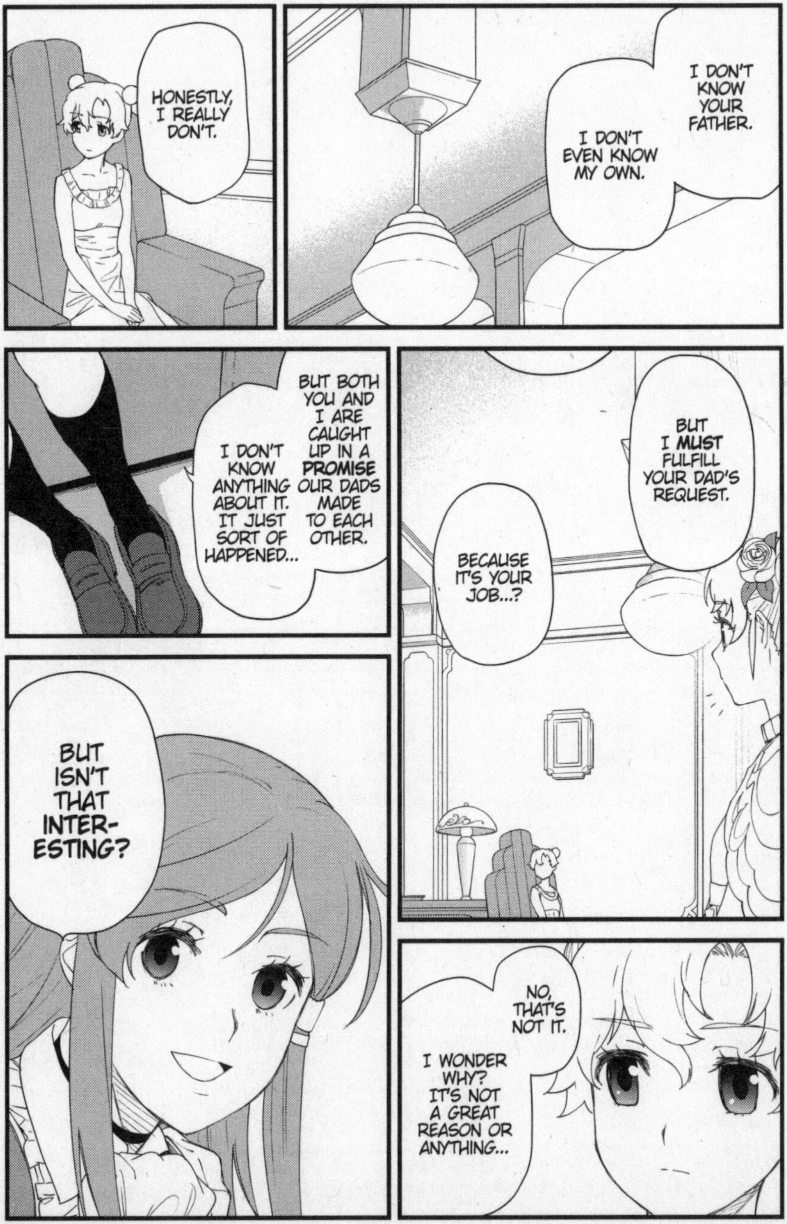
I DON'T KNOW YOUR FATHER.
I DON'T EVEN KNOW MY OWN.
HONESTLY, I REALLY DON'T.
BUT I **MUST** FULFILL YOUR DAD'S REQUEST.
BECAUSE IT'S YOUR JOB...?
NO, THAT'S NOT IT.
I WONDER WHY? IT'S NOT A GREAT REASON OR ANYTHING...
BUT BOTH YOU AND I ARE CAUGHT UP IN A **PROMISE** OUR DADS MADE TO EACH OTHER.
I DON'T KNOW ANYTHING ABOUT IT. IT JUST SORT OF HAPPENED...
BUT ISN'T THAT INTER-ESTING?

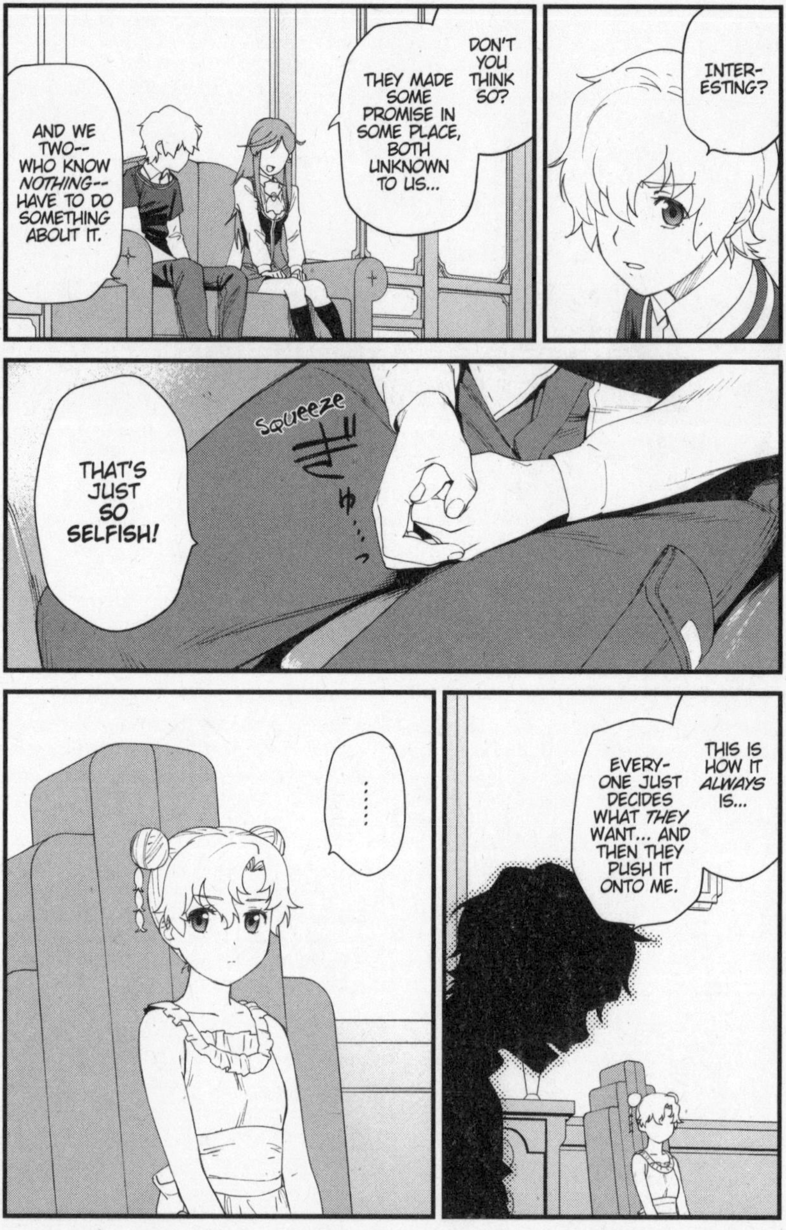
INTER-ESTING?
DON'T YOU THINK SO?
THEY MADE SOME PROMISE IN SOME PLACE, BOTH UNKNOWN TO US...
AND WE TWO-- WHO KNOW *NOTHING*-- HAVE TO DO SOMETHING ABOUT IT.
Squeeze
ぎゅ…っ
THAT'S JUST SO SELFISH!
THIS IS HOW IT *ALWAYS* IS...
EVERY-ONE JUST DECIDES WHAT *THEY* WANT... AND THEN THEY PUSH IT ONTO ME.
......

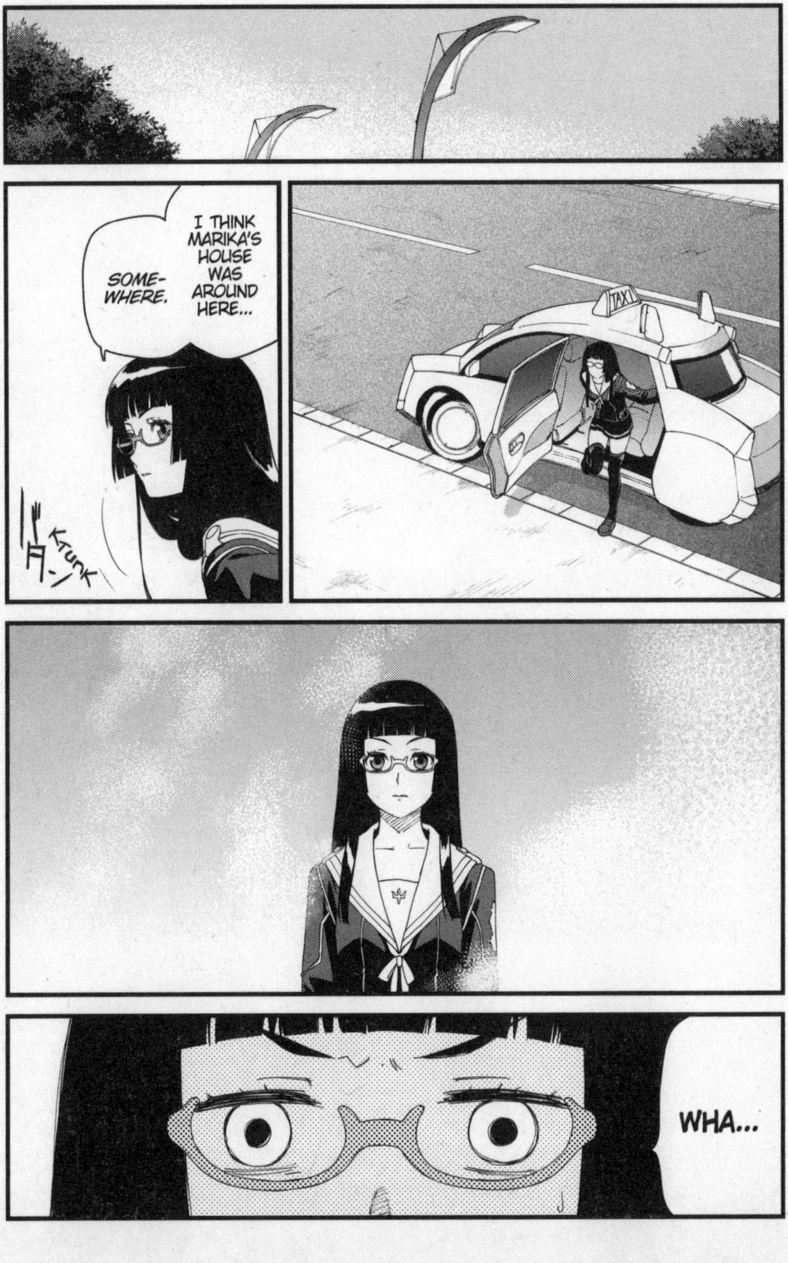
I THINK MARIKA'S HOUSE WAS AROUND HERE... SOME-WHERE.
バタン
Ktunk
WHA...

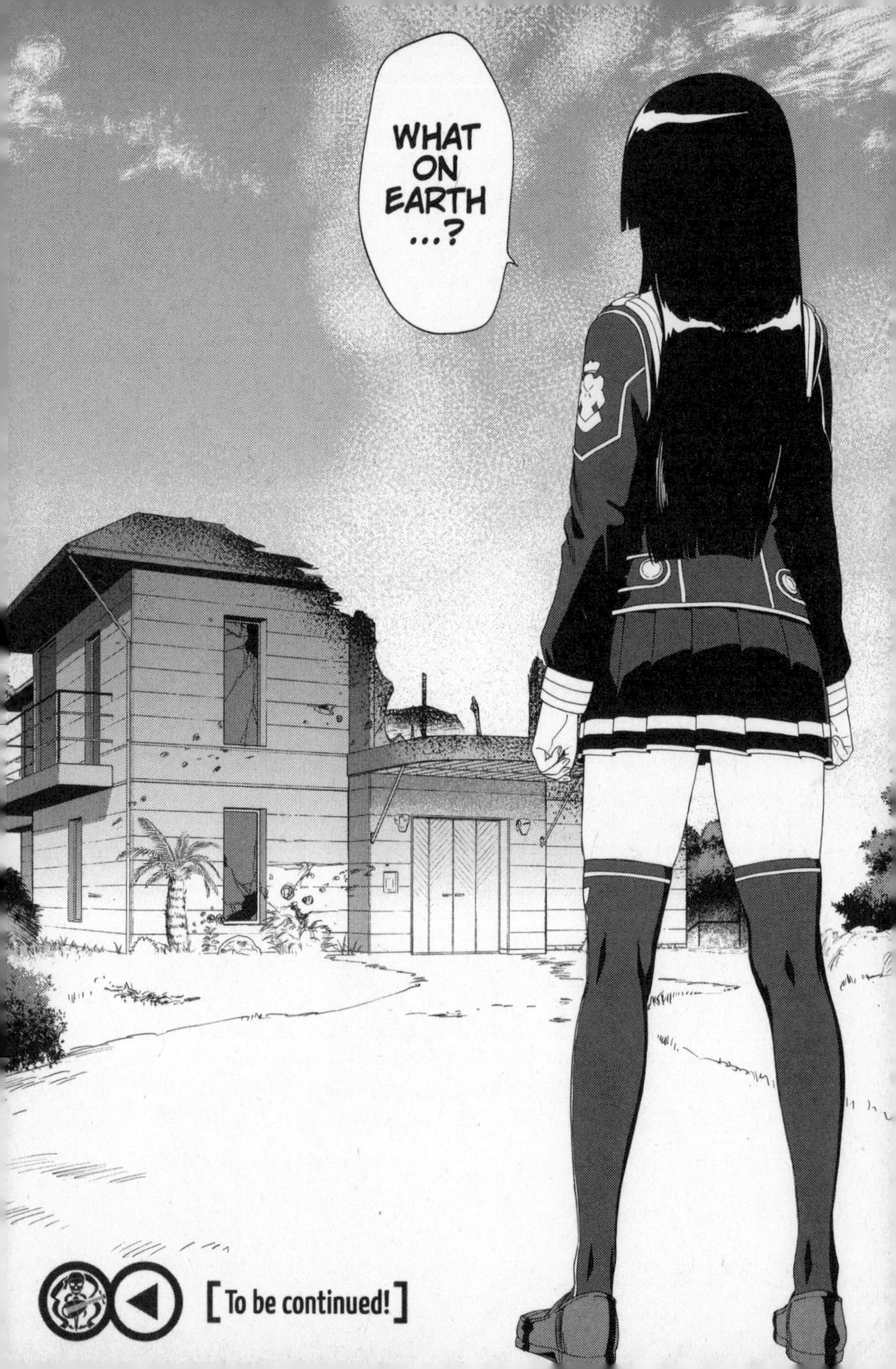
WHAT ON EARTH ...?
[To be continued!]

BODACIOUS
SPACE
PIRATES
[THE MOVIE]
ABYSS OF HYPERSPACE

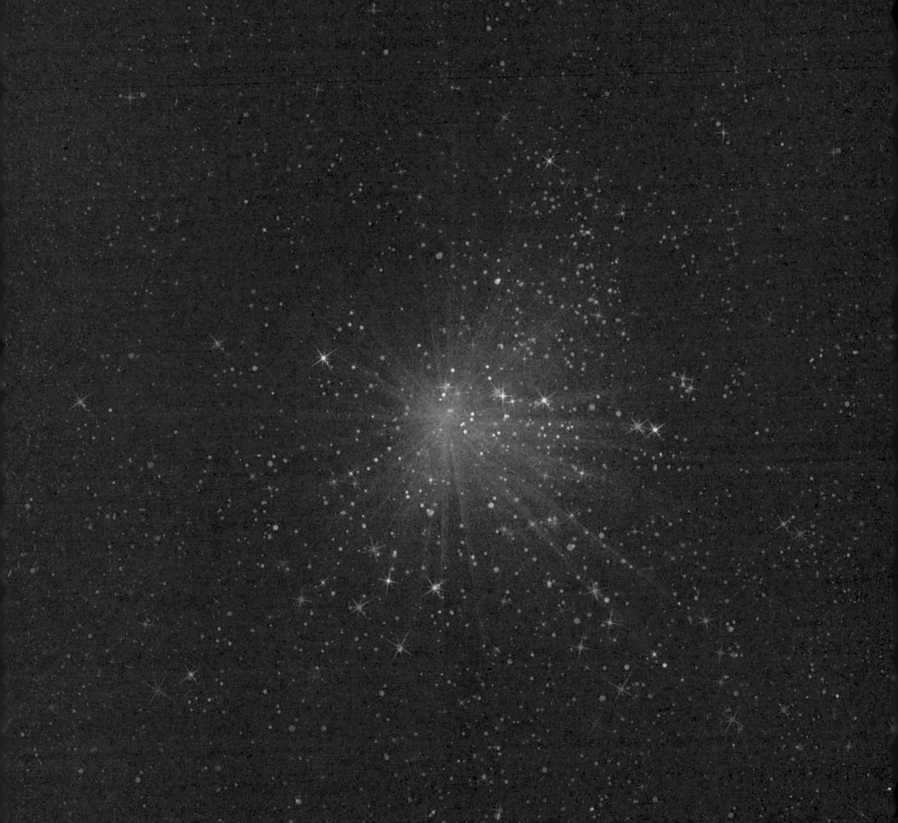

モーレツ★宇宙海賊
ABYSS OF HYPERSPACE —亜空の深淵—

VOLUME 01 Chapter 04 end

BODACIOUS SPACE PIRATES

[THE MOVIE]

ABYSS OF HYPERSPACE

VOLUME **01**

[▼ NEXT ▼]

VOLUME **02**

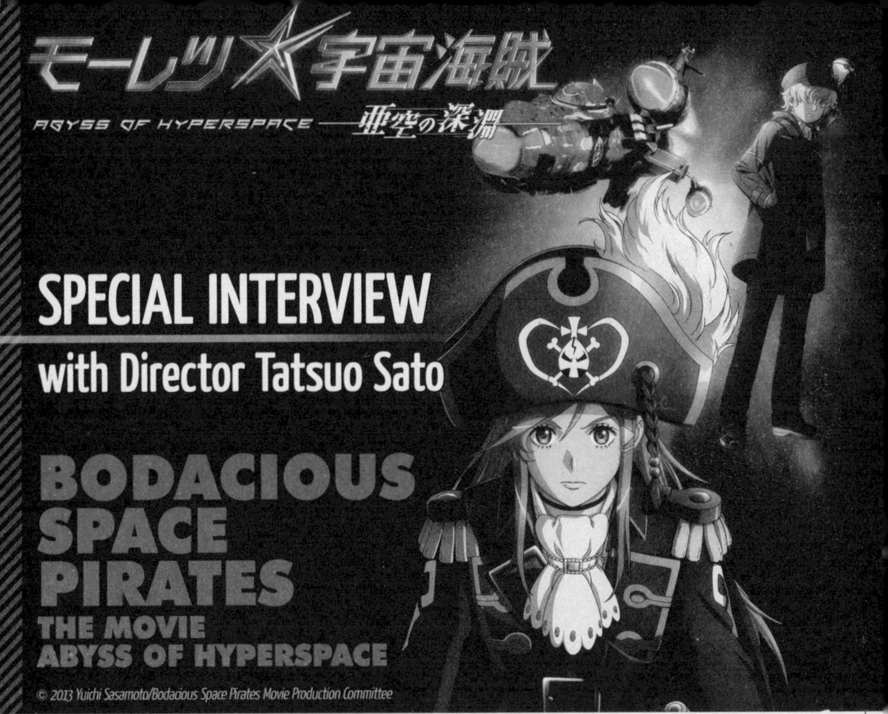
モーレツ宇宙海賊
ABYSS OF HYPERSPACE——亜空の深淵

SPECIAL INTERVIEW

with Director Tatsuo Sato

BODACIOUS SPACE PIRATES THE MOVIE ABYSS OF HYPERSPACE

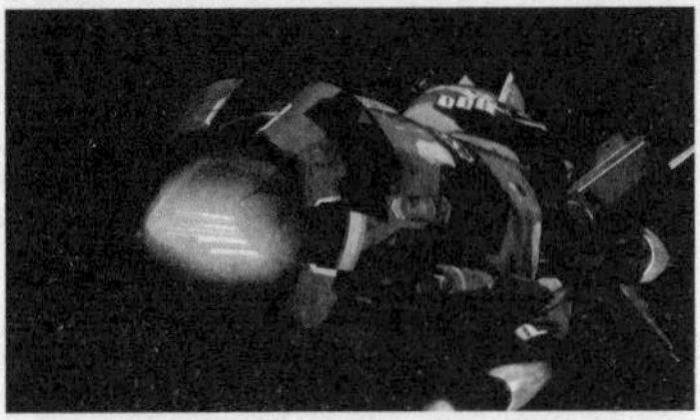

To start off, please tell us the circumstances that led you to be involved in *Bodacious Space Pirates*.

Director Tatsuo Sato: I think it was around the end of 2008, when the first volume of *Miniskirt Space Pirates* was released. Ootsuki-san from King Records brought up the subject of whether I'd like to be involved, since he was planning the project. That's when I first started reading *Miniskirt Space Pirates*.

What was your first impression of the original novel? Please tell us what you thought after reading it.

Sato: I found Sasamoto-sensei's story appealing of course, but I especially liked the sci-fi elements and the thought experiments. I was also truly impressed by the abundance of foreshadowing and historical references in *Miniskirt Space Pirates*. I got a sense of Sasamoto-sensei's style of building up tension step-by-step until a breakthrough at the end.

I think a lot of people have been put off by recent sci-fi novels due to having an impression of them being one clichéd space opera after another. I think something resonated within Ootsuki-san when he saw someone trying to challenge this image. A lot of recent novels have focused on the daily lives of their characters, so perhaps he felt that it might actually feel "new" to do a space opera now.

That being said, once we started animating *BSP*, it had a fair amount of daily life being portrayed (lol). At the time the anime was starting up, the novels were at the stage where I was reading a draft of the second volume, and I thought I'd make the anime about Marika Kato's story up until she becomes a pirate. I thought, "From here on out, she'll be a Bodacious Space Pirate."

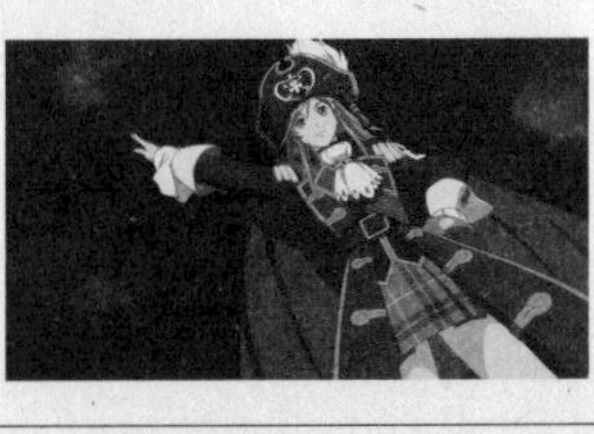

You announced that there would be a movie at the end of the TV series. At what stage of the TV series' production did you know there would be a feature film?

Sato: It was decided in a hurry while we were editing the video of the final episode. If the TV series is the story of Marika until she becomes a Bodacious Space Pirate, then I thought it might be bodacious if the movie was set after she became a Bodacious Space Pirate. After all, she had finally become a pirate, so from here on out, it would be a story about pirates.

In other words, the series will be turning into a full-fledged space opera story.

Sato: I suppose so. To tell the truth, I had the option to either make a second TV series or a film. I thought a movie would be better in the sense that it could bring out the epic scale of becoming a Bodacious Space Pirate, so I opted for a film.

For this movie, what parts did you choose to consciously change or be particularly selective about, when compared to the TV series?

Sato: We wanted to depict *Bodacious Space Pirates* from a new perspective, so we went back to the drawing board for quite a lot, including character designs. The TV series told the story from Marika's point of view. But for the movie, the story is of Marika Kato, as seen from the eyes of the young boy Kanata Mugen, instead of from Marika's perspective. That means it's from the point of view of Kanata-kun, with eyes transfixed on the mysterious pirate Marika.

You said before that you decided to redesign the characters for the movie. Could you elaborate?

Sato: Since the story develops through the eyes of Kanata-kun, the boy's design was very important. The TV series characters were ultimately designed with a focus on female high school students like Marika. We did have the characters of Gruier and Grunhilde Serenity, who were younger and in the position of being princesses, so there were exceptions.

That being said, if we placed the relatively normal boy Kanata-kun next to the Marika design from the TV series without adjusting her height, it would almost certainly just look like two children goofing around. As a result, we ultimately became conscious of "Marika, as seen through the eyes of Kanata-kun" and we redesigned Marika by trying to strike a balance between an adult woman and a teenage girl. We made her nearly a whole head taller, and as a result, I feel like she has a rather different, more mature image.

So if you look at the new Marika design by itself, she looks a little hardier, but when you place Kanata-kun next to her, they fit together perfectly. We redesigned the characters with this kind of detail in mind.

Bodacious Space Pirates features a wide variety of characters. Which one was your favorite?

Sato: Good question... There's Marika of course, but Chiaki's also cute (lol). It was worth it to tool around with her design. In the movie, Chiaki has a particularly juicy role. If we were to equate Marika to the godfather, then Chiaki would be her most trusted confidant. I frequently make comparisons to *Shimizu no Jirochō**, so if Marika were Jirochō, Chiaki would be Ōmasa. Lately there have been a lot of people who don't know about Jirochō, so I don't know if people will really get my comparison (lol).

[***Note:** *Shimizu no Jirochō was a prominent figure and underworld boss in Shizuoka in the 1800s. Ōmasa was one of his underlings, and in film, he is frequently depicted as his right-hand man.*]

A large number of characters also means a large cast. We'd love to hear any secret stories you may be able to share from the dubbing studio.

Sato: We managed to do all of the recording for the film in a single day. It took about twelve hours, and I sat there for nearly the entire time, save for one trip to the bathroom. Afterwards, I was talking with the cast members, and it seems they were doing radio calisthenics in the lobby to prevent blood clots. We had about as many cast members for the movie as we did for the TV series, but since some of the voice actors for the girls in the yacht club had become popular voice actors, we didn't have them all assembled from the beginning to record, and it was something of a strange phenomenon to see people chasing them as they came and went (lol).

You announced the movie immediately after the TV series. Do you have any future plans for *Bodacious Space Pirates*?

Sato: That really depends on how well it sells (lol). There's still plenty of story left from the original novels, so there might be a second season at some point. That said, first and foremost, it's important that fans of the series watch the movie.

Do you have any final words you'd like to say to the fans of *Bodacious Space Pirates* or any suggestions for things to look out for in the movie?

Sato: I'd be extremely happy if you read *Monthly Comic Alive*, buy the compiled volumes of the manga, and go to see the movie while it's in theaters. I'd love it if you become aware of the new Marika Kato, with her simultaneous girlish appeal and mature design. Also, I hope you like the mecha in the movie (lol).

Thank you very much!

PROFILE

Tatsuo Sato
Anime Director and Episode Director

Born July 7, 1964 in Ōiso, Kanagawa. Bloodtype: A. After graduating from Waseda University, he joined Ajia-do Animation Works. He worked his way up from an animator to Assistant Episode Director and finally to Episode Director in 1989. Some of his main works include *Chibi Maruko-chan* and *Lil' Red Riding Hood Cha-Cha*. 1995's *Soar High! Isami* marked his TV series directorial debut. Following this, he directed *Martian Successor Nadesico* (1996) and *Martian Successor Nadesico: The Motion Picture – Prince of Darkness* (1998). Together with Yuasa Masaaki, their film *Cat Soup* won Best Short Film at Montreal's FanTasia Film Festival in 2001 and Excellence Prize (Animation Division) at the 2001 Japan Media Arts Festival. He then went on to create *Shingu: Secret of the Stellar Wars* and to write the script for every episode of the TV series (both in 2001). For *Bodacious Space Pirates: Abyss of Hyperspace*, he reprised the role of scriptwriter and director, the same roles he held for the TV series.

Writer's Afterword ///////////

Thank you so much, whether you are old or new to this franchise. I'm Chibimaru.

When I was first asked to do the manga version of the *Bodacious Space Pirates* movie, I jumped for joy. Not only is it a franchise I like, but I had just been thinking about how I'd like to draw a sci-fi or mecha manga.

So before I started, I was all like "I'm so pumped!" But after I started working on it, I realized it was much more difficult than I had imagined.

I had to draw the ships that were rendered in 3D CG for the anime... by hand. Ugh. There's a bit more to the story and to my work, so I'd really appreciate it if you read the rest.

BODACIOUS
SPACE PIRATES

[THE MOVIE]

ABYSS OF HYPERSPACE

ASSISTANTS

• Black Skull

• Kurobe

• Abara Heiki

• Yuu Tsurusaki

• Taishi

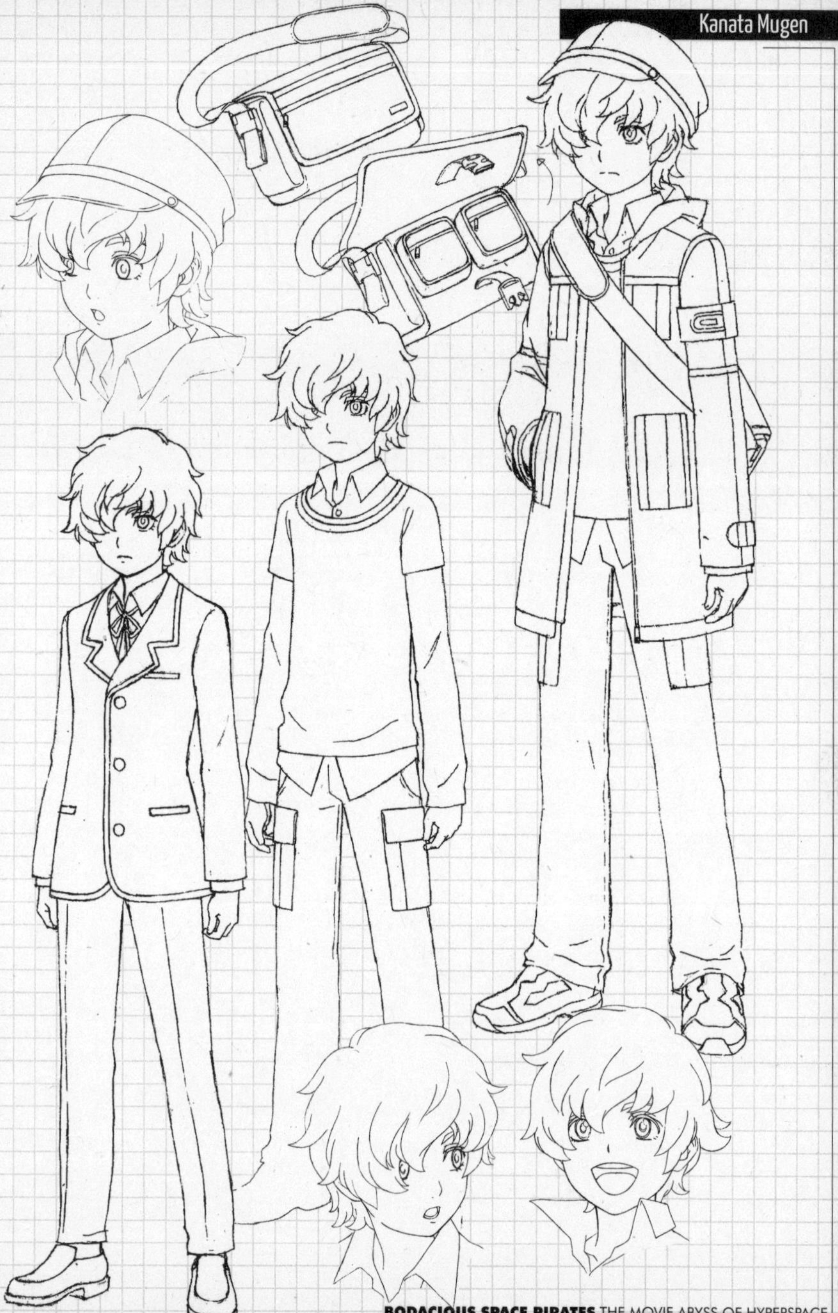

Chiaki Kurihara

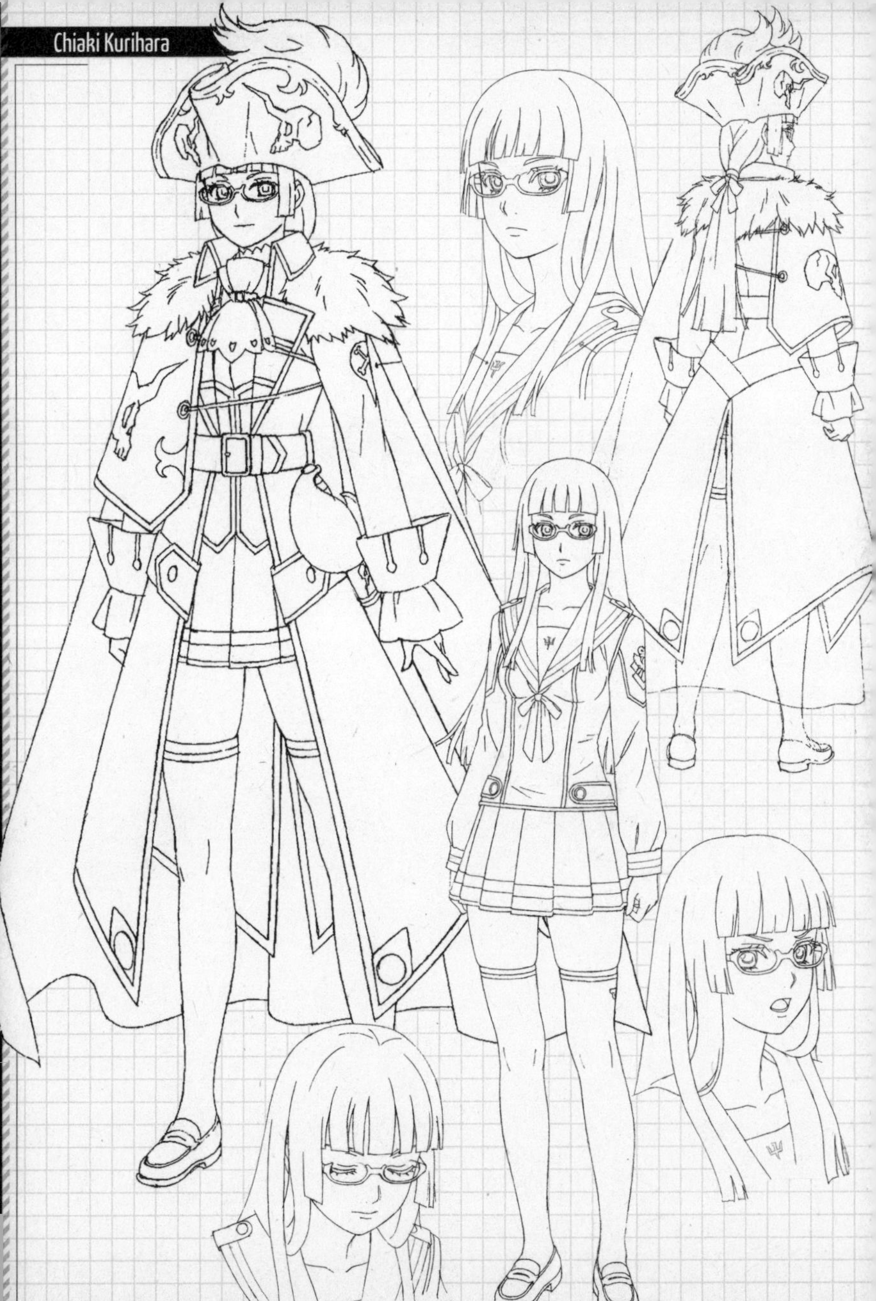

Grunhilde Serenity

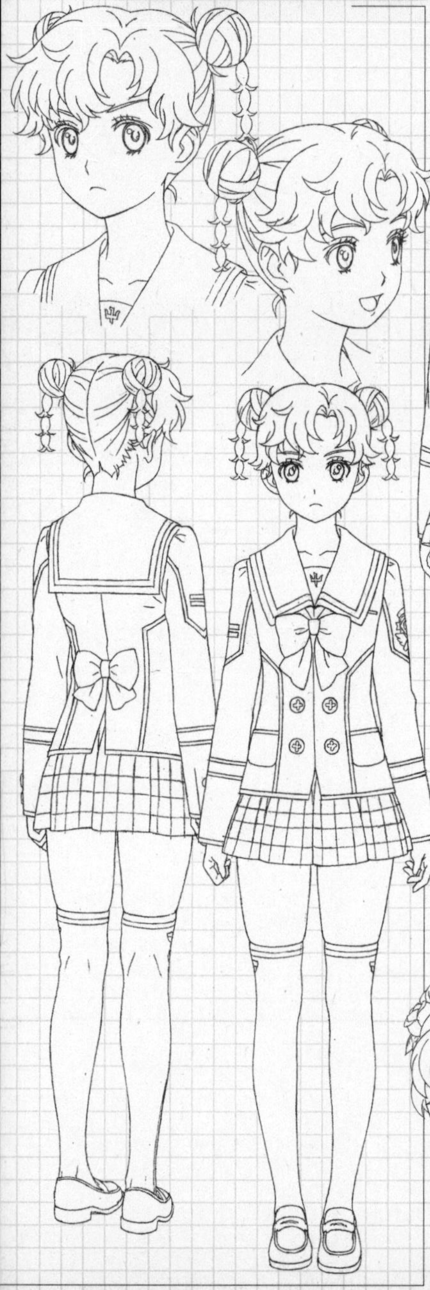

Gruier Serenity

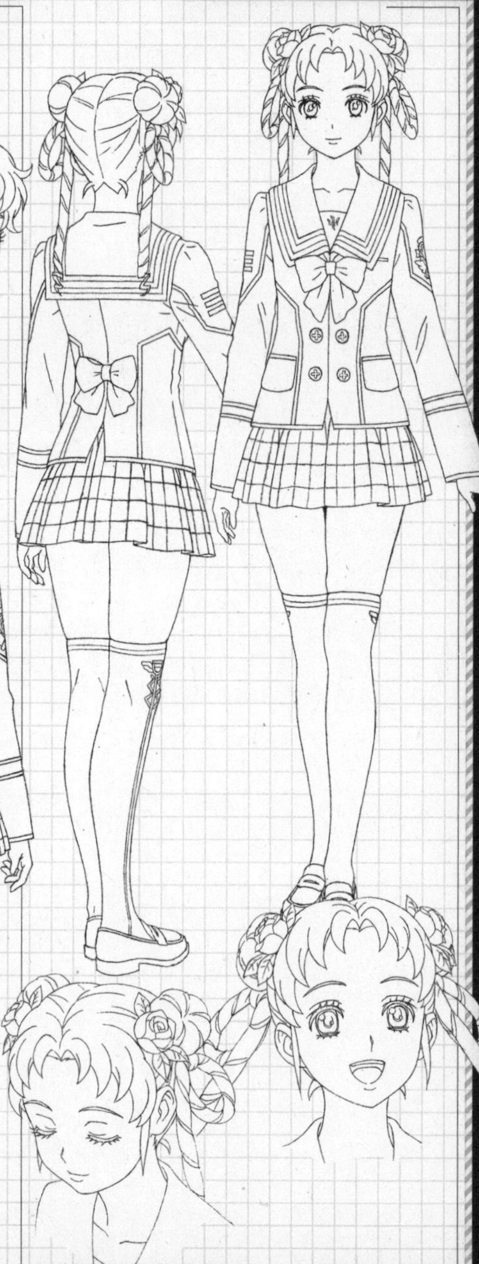

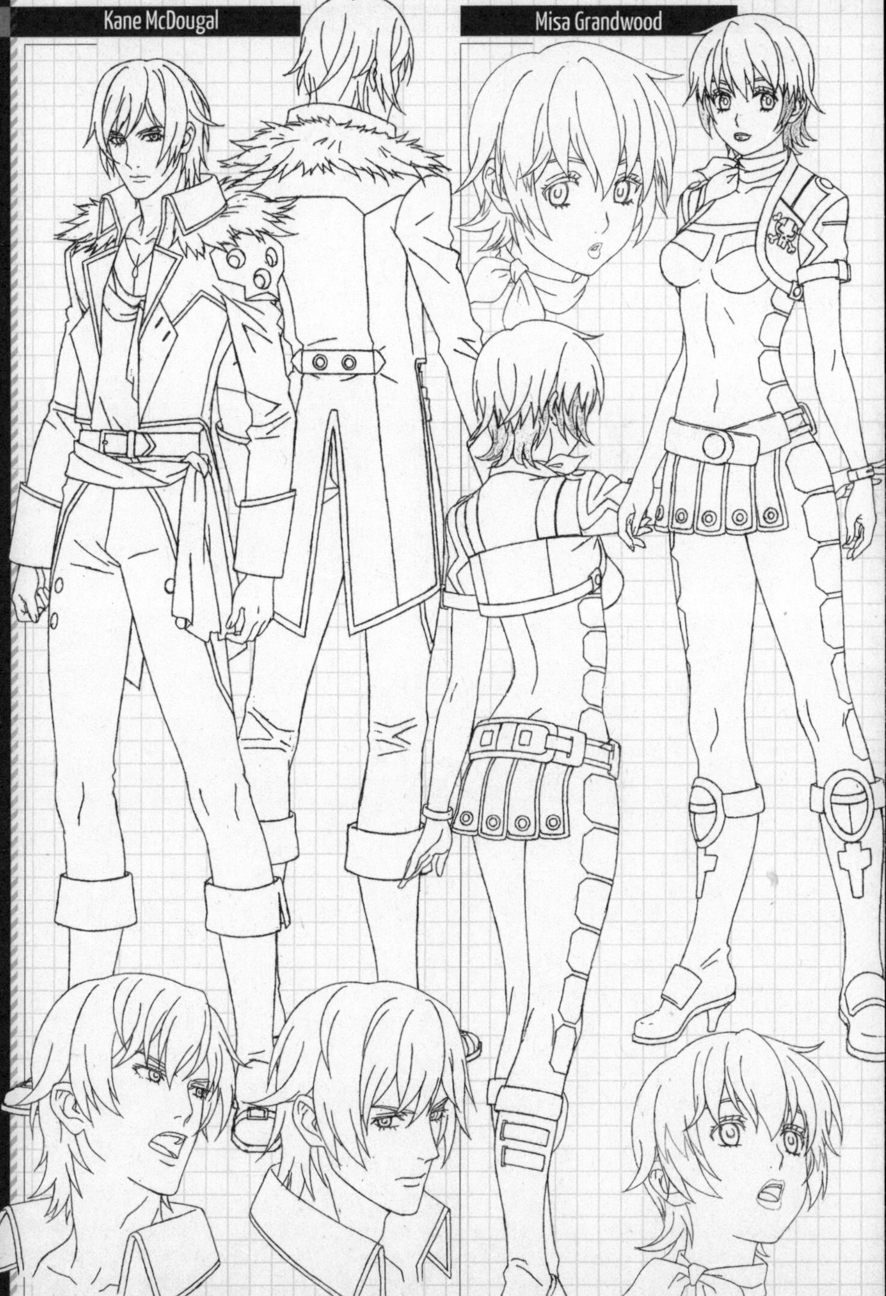
Kane McDougal
Misa Grandwood

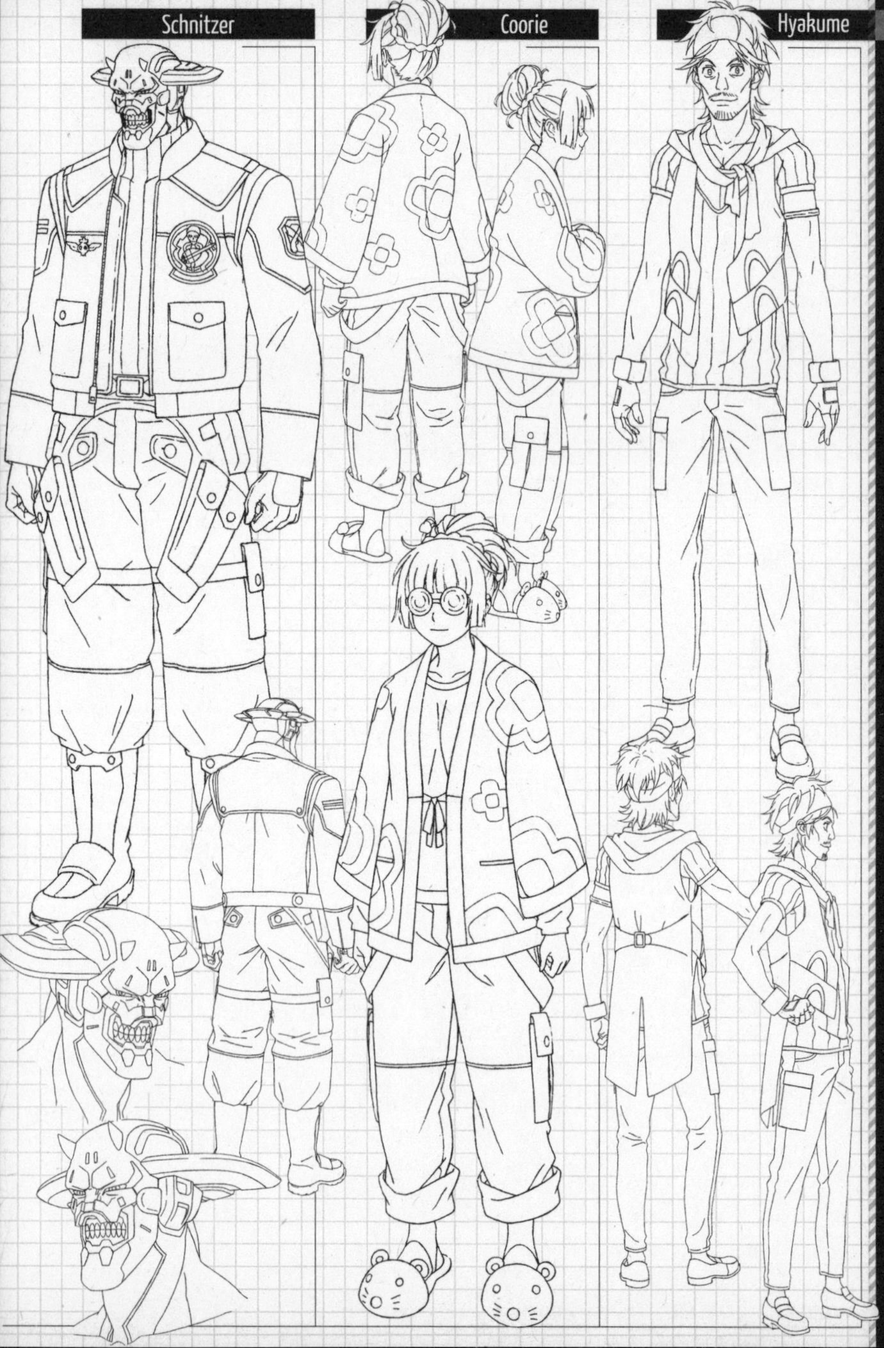
Schnitzer
Coorie
Hyakume

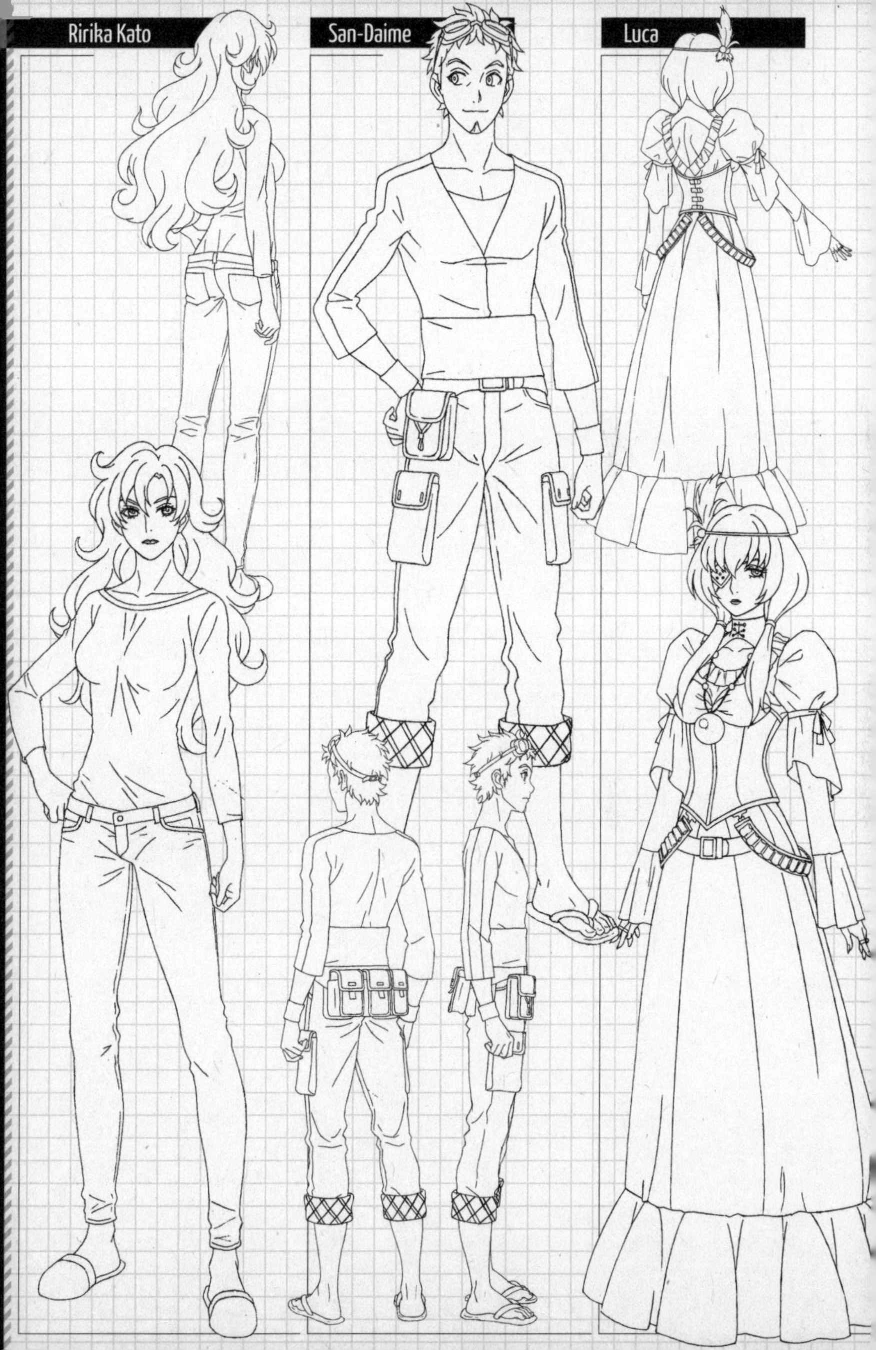
Ririka Kato
San-Daime
Luca

Bentenmaru

Thrusters

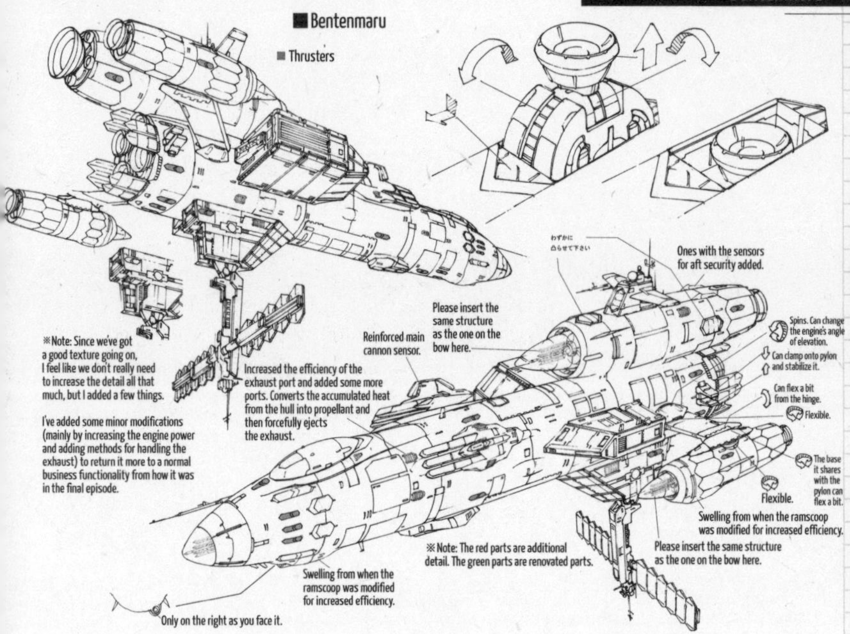
※Note: Since we've got a good texture going on, I feel like we don't really need to increase the detail all that much, but I added a few things.
I've added some minor modifications (mainly by increasing the engine power and adding methods for handling the exhaust) to return it more to a normal business functionality from how it was in the final episode.
Reinforced main cannon sensor.
Please insert the same structure as the one on the bow here.
Increased the efficiency of the exhaust port and added some more ports. Converts the accumulated heat from the hull into propellant and then forcefully ejects the exhaust.
Ones with the sensors for aft security added.
Spins. Can change the engine's angle of elevation.
Can clamp onto pylon and stabilize it.
Can flex a bit from the hinge.
Flexible.
The base it shares with the pylon can flex a bit.
Flexible.
Swelling from when the ramscoop was modified for increased efficiency.
※Note: The red parts are additional detail. The green parts are renovated parts.
Please insert the same structure as the one on the bow here.
Swelling from when the ramscoop was modified for increased efficiency.
Only on the right as you face it.

Bentenmaru

Torpedo

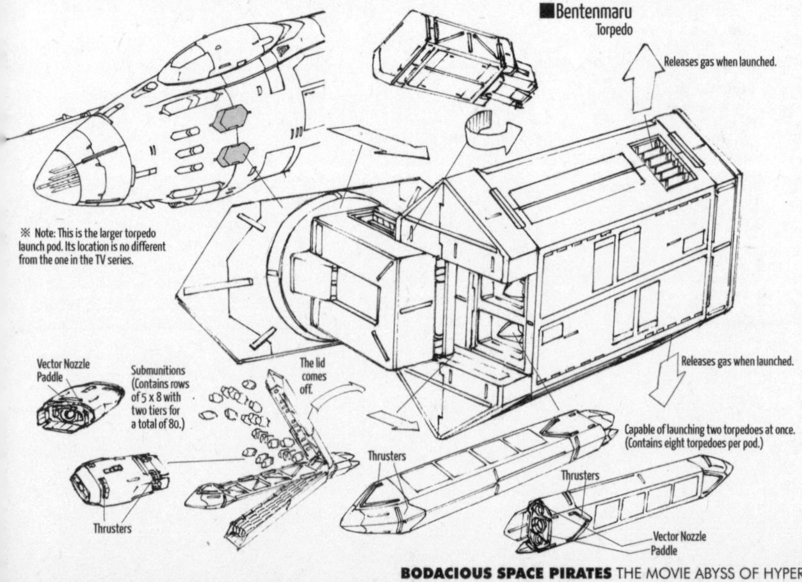
Releases gas when launched.
※ Note: This is the larger torpedo launch pod. Its location is no different from the one in the TV series.
Releases gas when launched.
Vector Nozzle
Paddle
Submunitions (Contains rows of 5 x 8 with two tiers for a total of 80.)
The lid comes off.
Capable of launching two torpedoes at once. (Contains eight torpedoes per pod.)
Thrusters
Thrusters
Thrusters
Vector Nozzle
Paddle

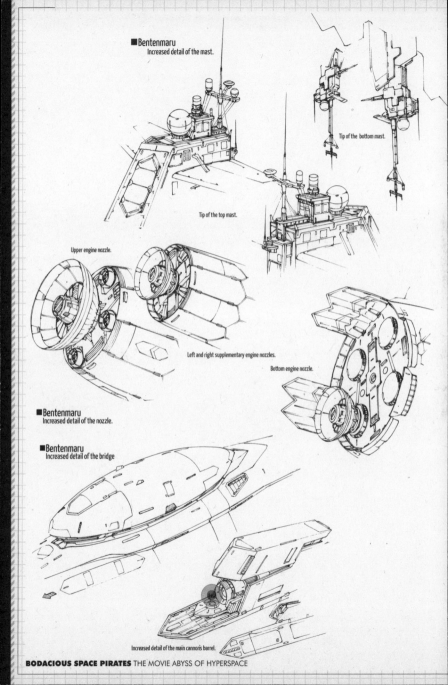

■Bentenmaru
Increased detail of the mast.

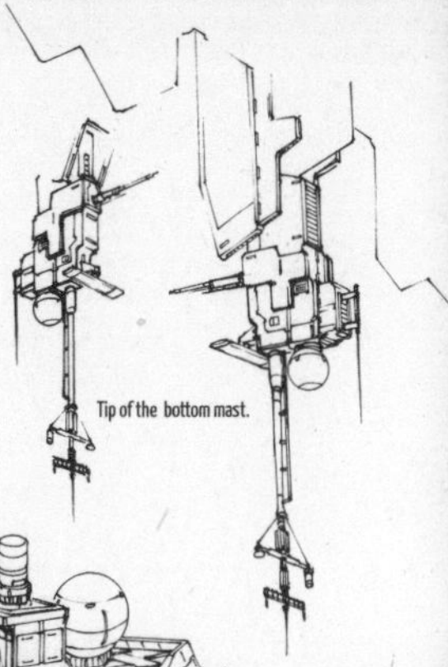

Tip of the bottom mast.

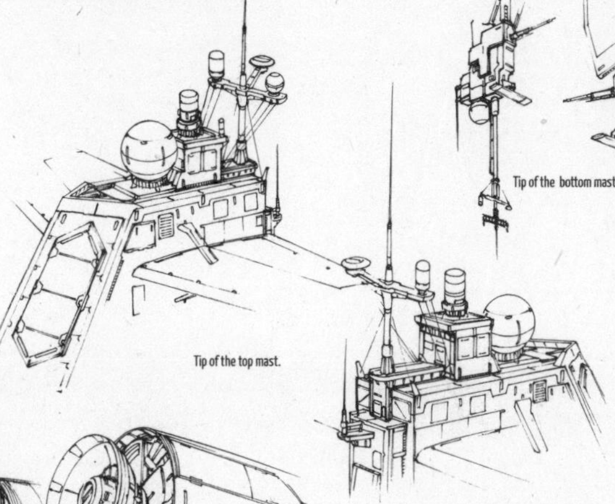

Tip of the top mast.

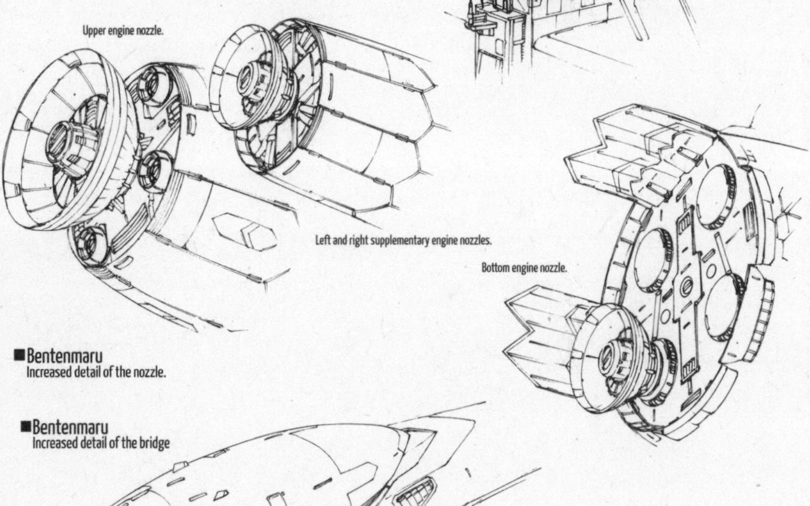

Upper engine nozzle.
Left and right supplementary engine nozzles.
Bottom engine nozzle.

■Bentenmaru
Increased detail of the nozzle.

■Bentenmaru
Increased detail of the bridge

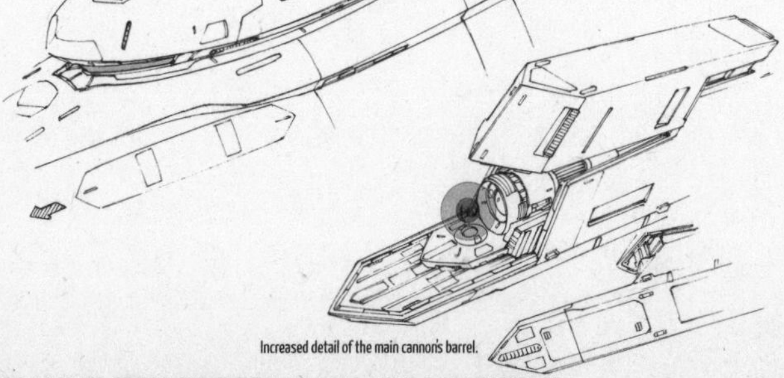

Increased detail of the main cannon's barrel.

Yggdrasil Fleet/Rhincodon-class Battleship Hughroque

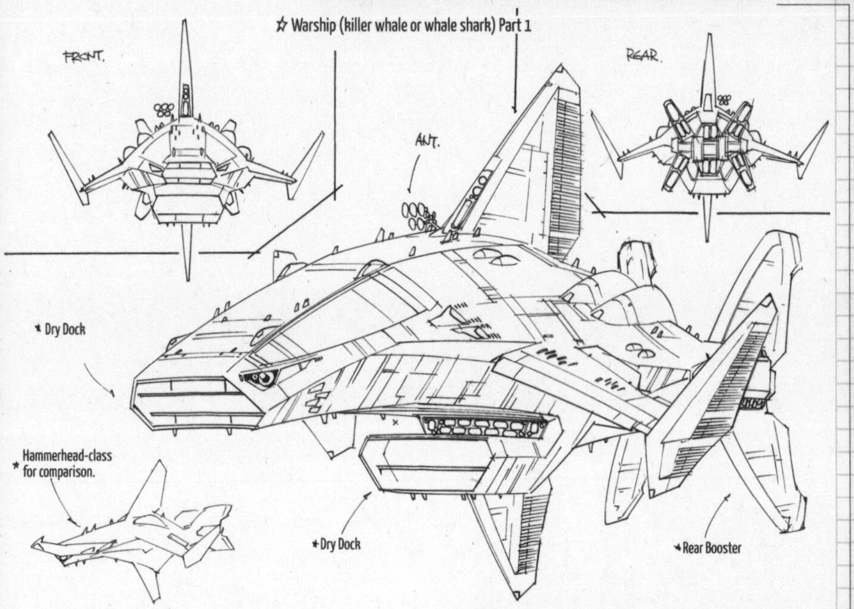
☆ Warship (killer whale or whale shark) Part 1
FRONT.
REAR.
ANT.
* Dry Dock
* Hammerhead-class for comparison.
*Dry Dock
*Rear Booster

Yggdrasil Fleet/HH-class Escort Vessel

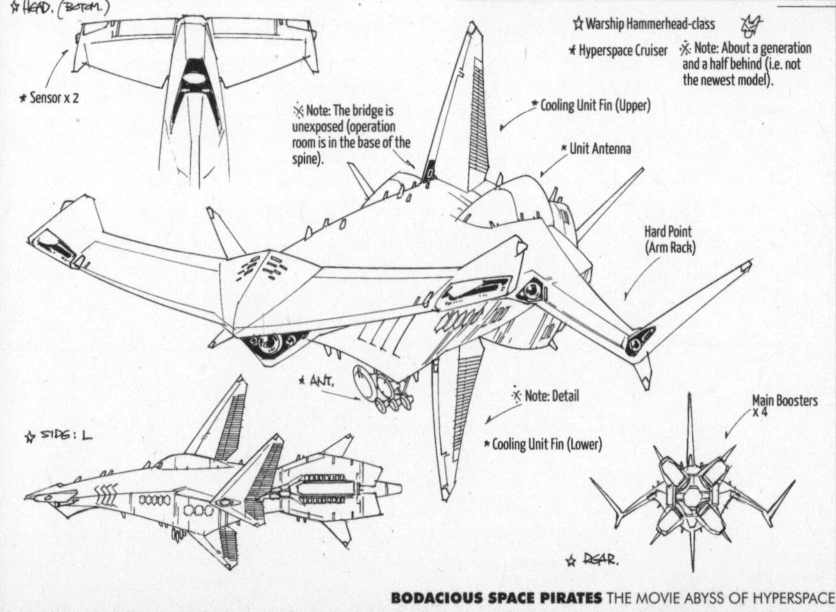
☆ HEAD. (BOTOM.)
* Sensor x 2
☆ Warship Hammerhead-class
* Hyperspace Cruiser
※ Note: About a generation and a half behind (i.e. not the newest model).
※ Note: The bridge is unexposed (operation room is in the base of the spine).
* Cooling Unit Fin (Upper)
* Unit Antenna
Hard Point (Arm Rack)
* ANT.
※ Note: Detail
* Cooling Unit Fin (Lower)
Main Boosters x 4
☆ SIDE : L
☆ REAR.

Yggdrasil Fleet/Assault Ship

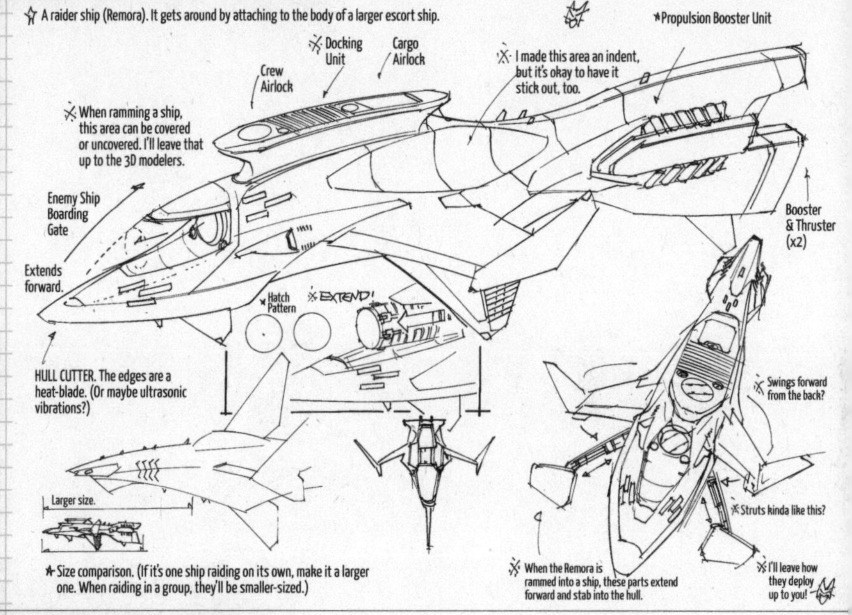
☆ A raider ship (Remora). It gets around by attaching to the body of a larger escort ship.
*Propulsion Booster Unit
※ Docking Unit
Cargo Airlock
Crew Airlock
※ I made this area an indent, but it's okay to have it stick out, too.
※ When ramming a ship, this area can be covered or uncovered. I'll leave that up to the 3D modelers.
Enemy Ship Boarding Gate
Booster & Thruster (x2)
Extends forward.
*Hatch Pattern
※ EXTEND!
HULL CUTTER. The edges are a heat-blade. (Or maybe ultrasonic vibrations?)
※ Swings forward from the back?
Larger size.
※ Struts kinda like this?
*Size comparison. (If it's one ship raiding on its own, make it a larger one. When raiding in a group, they'll be smaller-sized.)
※ When the Remora is rammed into a ship, these parts extend forward and stab into the hull.
※ I'll leave how they deploy up to you!

Great Depth XIII

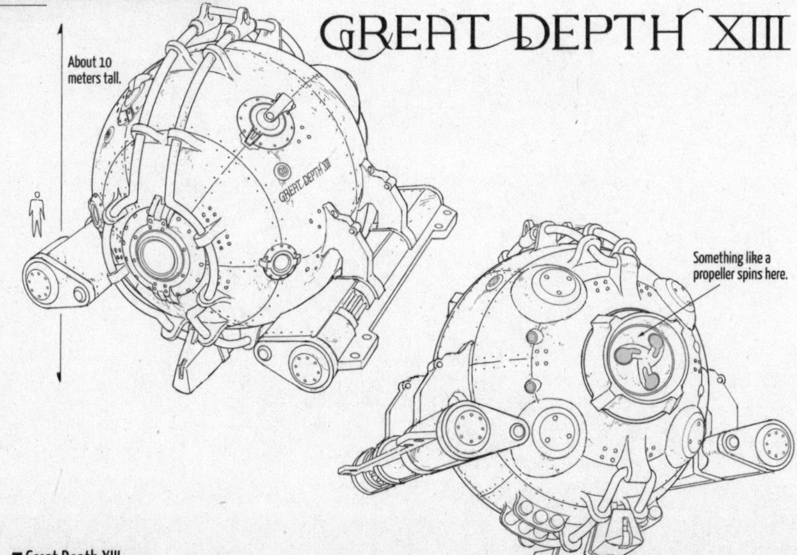
GREAT DEPTH XIII
About 10 meters tall.
GREAT DEPTH XIII
Something like a propeller spins here.

■ Great Depth XIII
Thomas Romain 07/26/2013

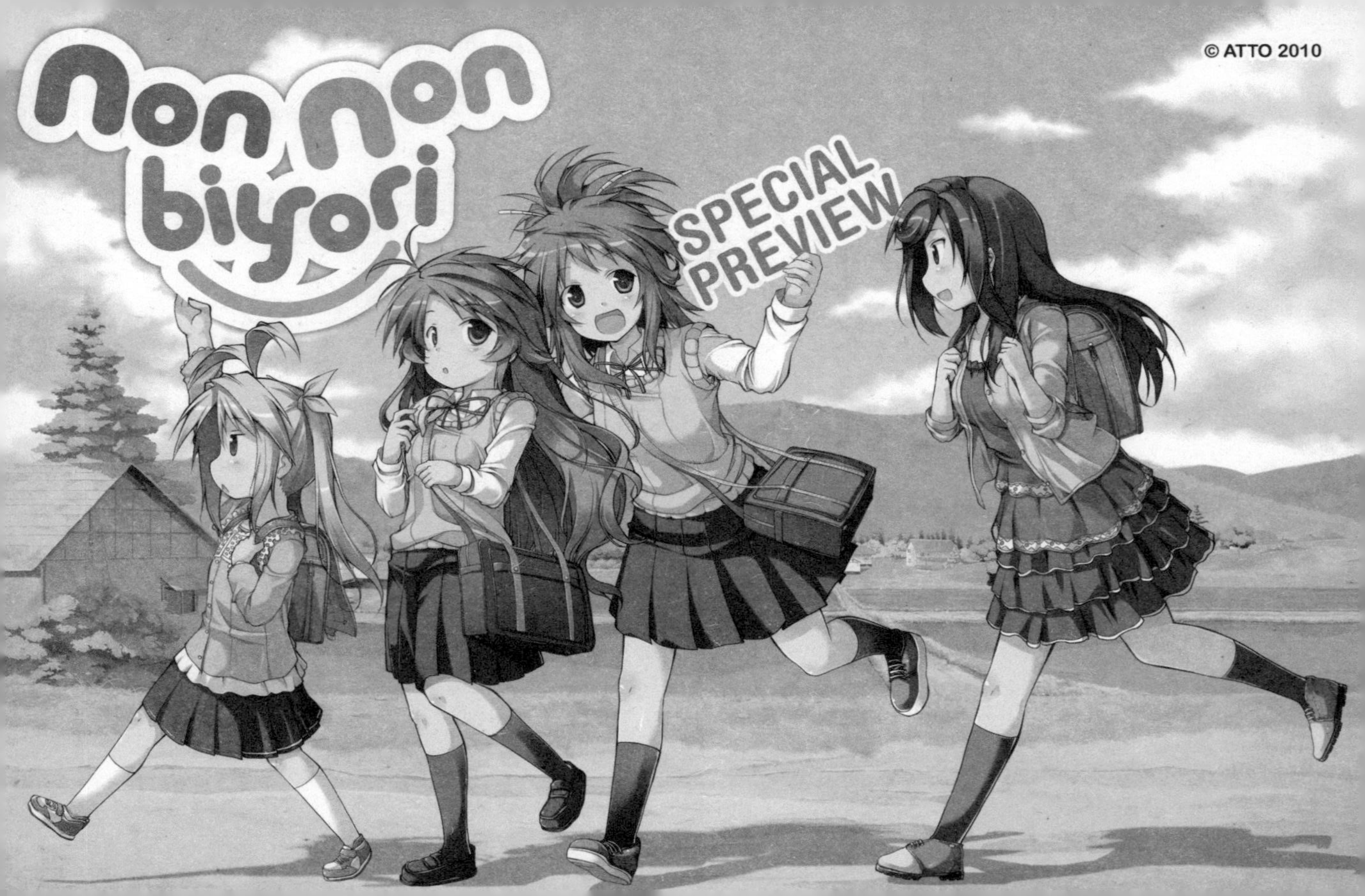
non non biyori
SPECIAL PREVIEW
© ATTO 2010

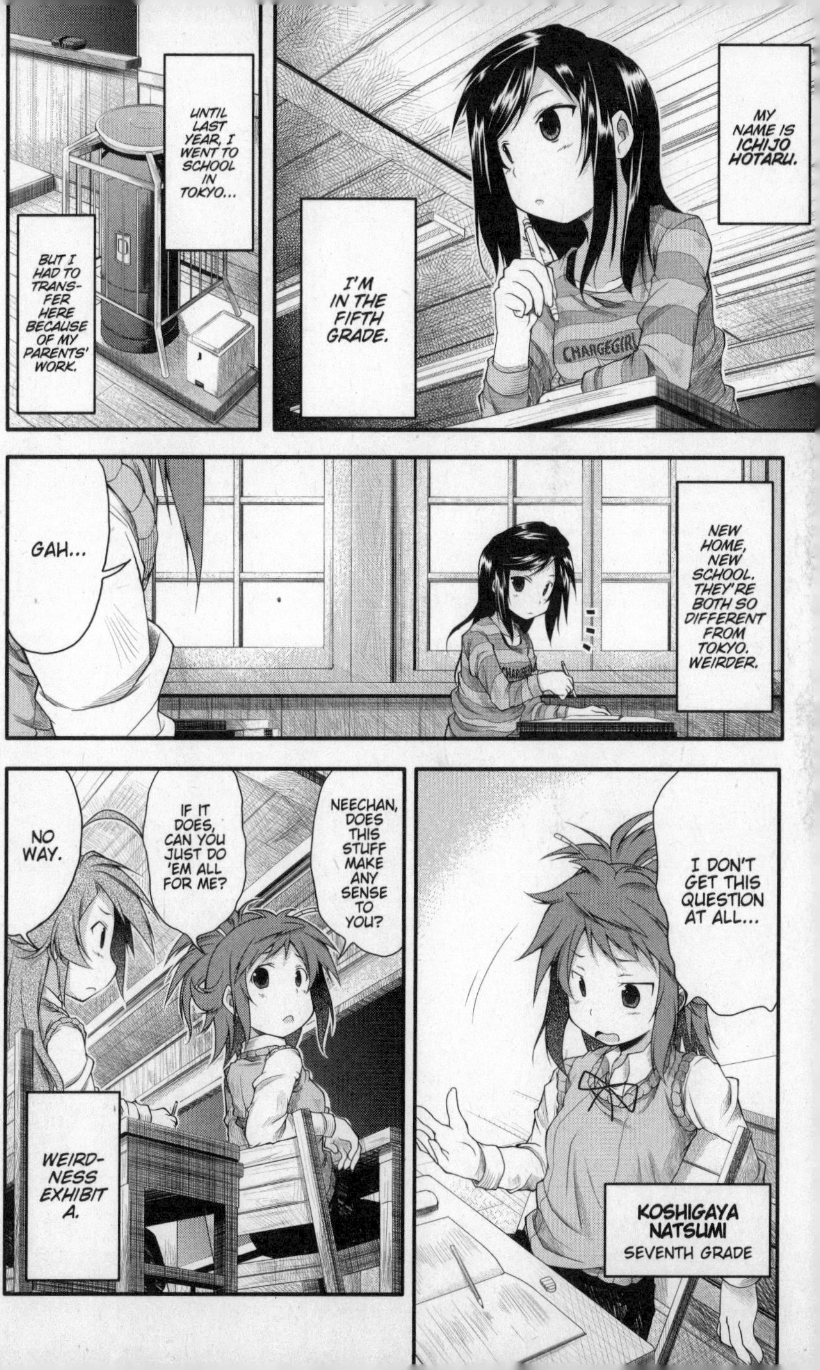
MY NAME IS ICHIJO HOTARU.
I'M IN THE FIFTH GRADE.
CHARGEGIRL
UNTIL LAST YEAR, I WENT TO SCHOOL IN TOKYO...
BUT I HAD TO TRANSFER HERE BECAUSE OF MY PARENTS' WORK.
NEW HOME, NEW SCHOOL. THEY'RE BOTH SO DIFFERENT FROM TOKYO. WEIRDER.
GAH...
I DON'T GET THIS QUESTION AT ALL...
KOSHIGAYA NATSUMI
SEVENTH GRADE
NEECHAN, DOES THIS STUFF MAKE ANY SENSE TO YOU?
IF IT DOES, CAN YOU JUST DO 'EM ALL FOR ME?
NO WAY.
WEIRDNESS EXHIBIT A.

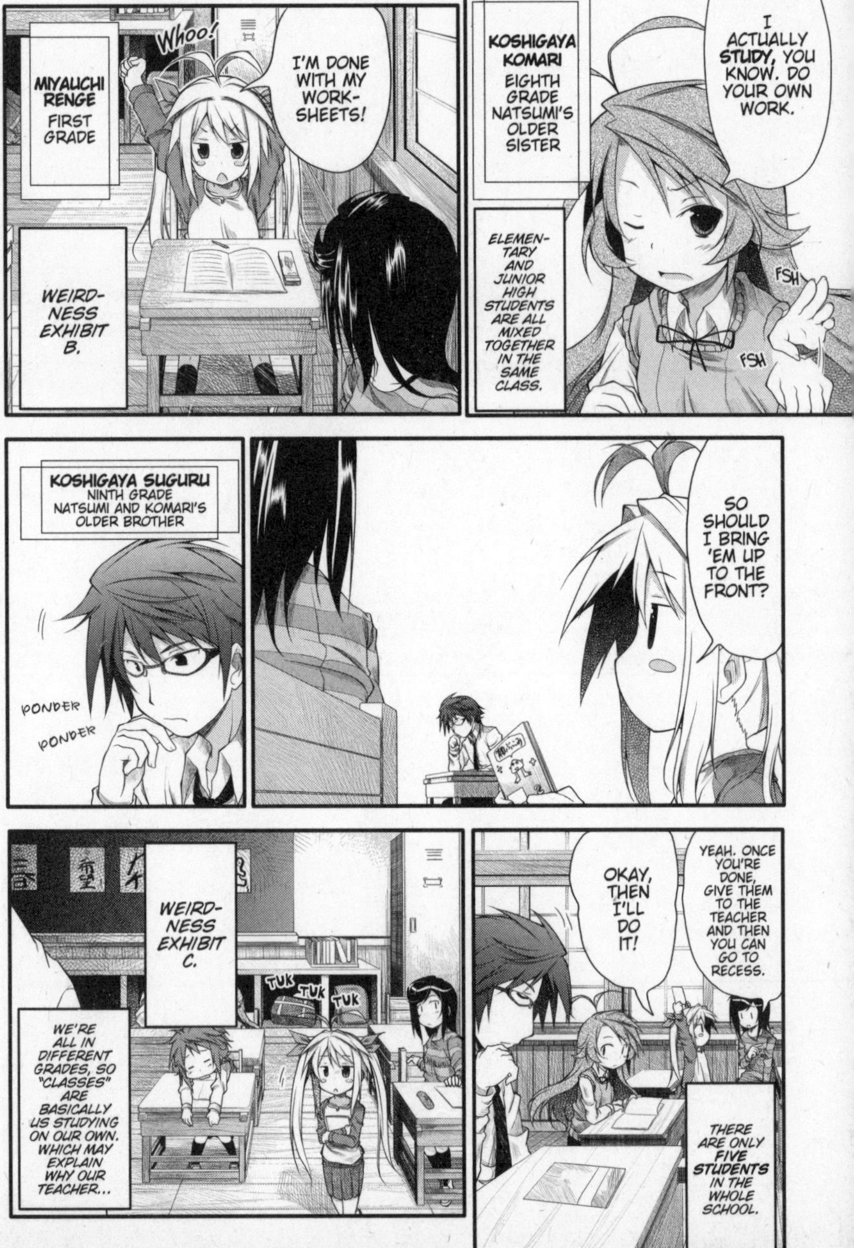
I ACTUALLY STUDY, YOU KNOW. DO YOUR OWN WORK.
KOSHIGAYA KOMARI EIGHTH GRADE NATSUMI'S OLDER SISTER
FSH
FSH
ELEMENTARY AND JUNIOR HIGH STUDENTS ARE ALL MIXED TOGETHER IN THE SAME CLASS.
I'M DONE WITH MY WORKSHEETS!
Whoo!
MIYAUCHI RENGE FIRST GRADE
WEIRDNESS EXHIBIT B.
SO SHOULD I BRING 'EM UP TO THE FRONT?
KOSHIGAYA SUGURU NINTH GRADE NATSUMI AND KOMARI'S OLDER BROTHER
PONDER
PONDER
YEAH. ONCE YOU'RE DONE, GIVE THEM TO THE TEACHER AND THEN YOU CAN GO TO RECESS.
OKAY, THEN I'LL DO IT!
THERE ARE ONLY FIVE STUDENTS IN THE WHOLE SCHOOL.
WEIRDNESS EXHIBIT C.
TUK
TUK
TUK
WE'RE ALL IN DIFFERENT GRADES, SO "CLASSES" ARE BASICALLY US STUDYING ON OUR OWN. WHICH MAY EXPLAIN WHY OUR TEACHER...

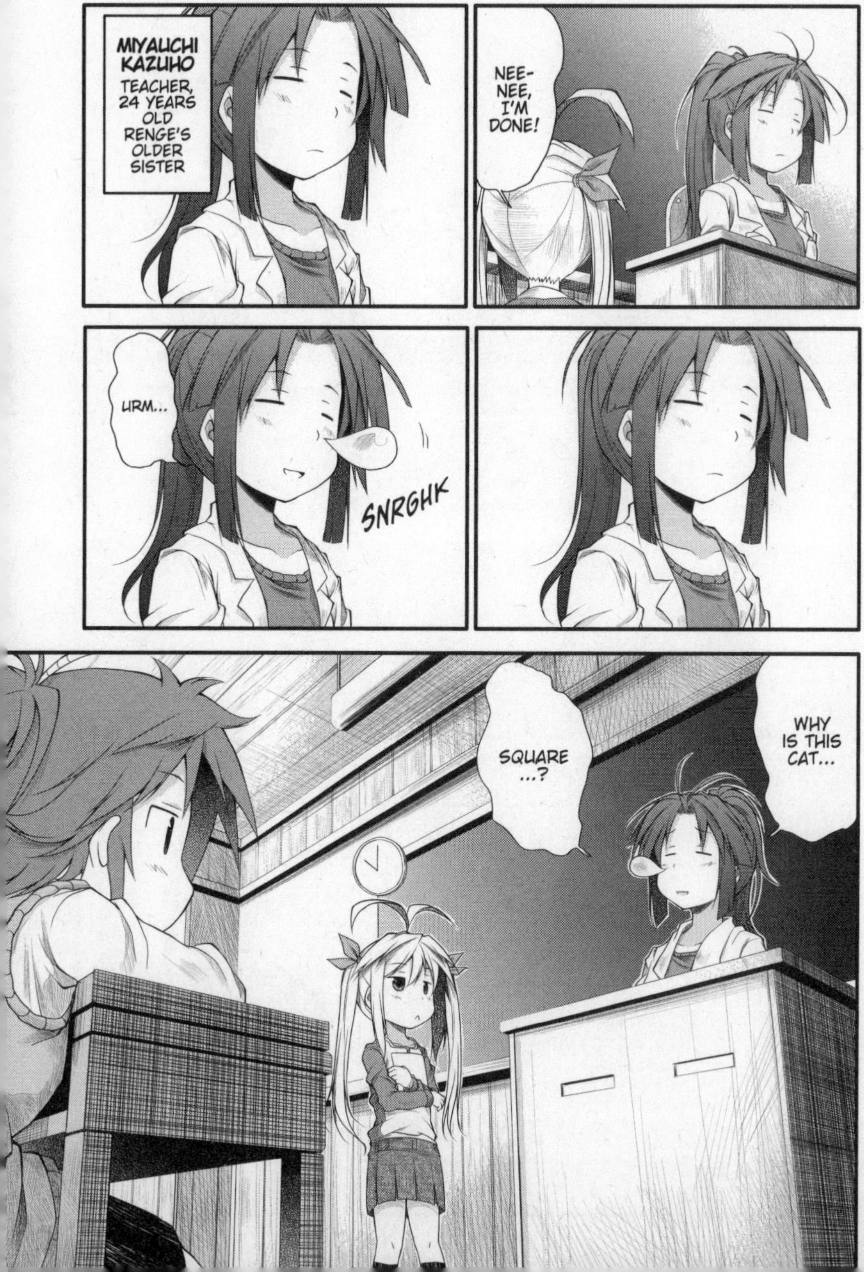
NEE-NEE, I'M DONE!
MIYAUCHI KAZUHO
TEACHER, 24 YEARS OLD
RENGE'S OLDER SISTER
URM...
SNRGHK
WHY IS THIS CAT...
SQUARE ...?

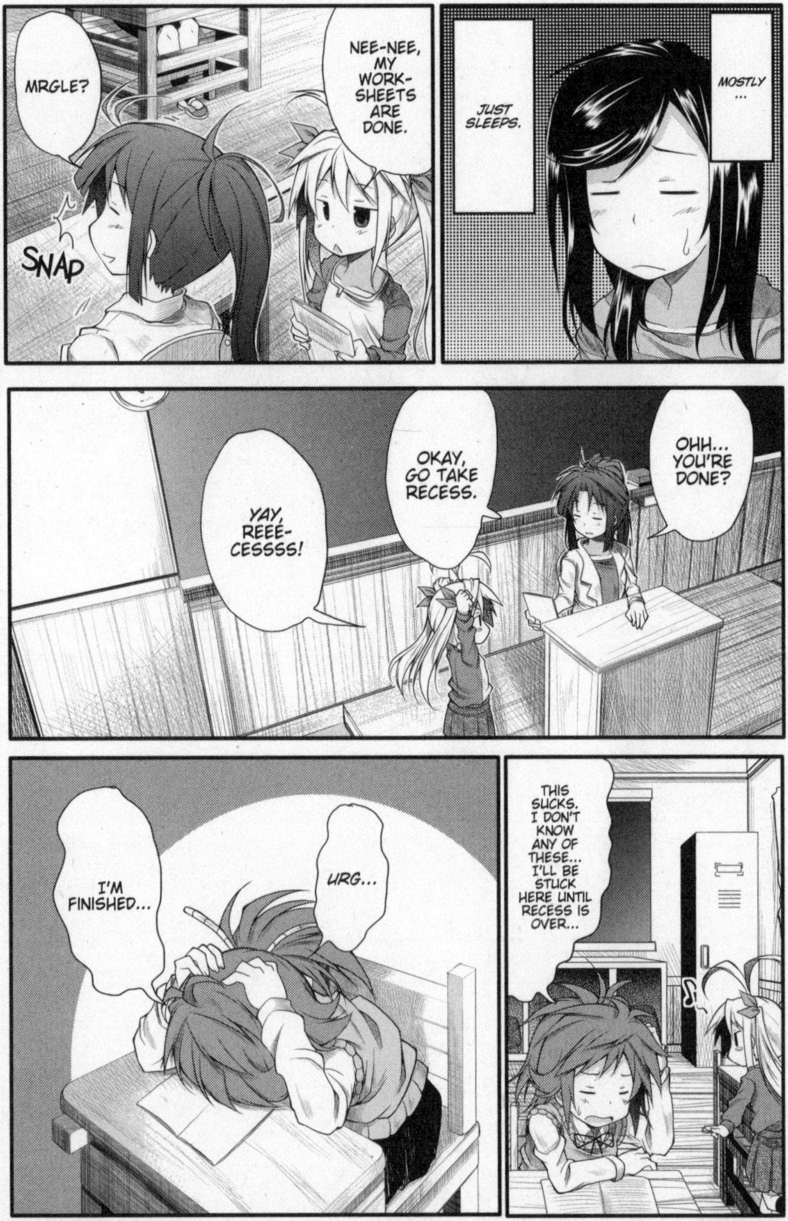
MOSTLY ...
JUST SLEEPS.
NEE-NEE, MY WORK-SHEETS ARE DONE.
MRGLE?
SNAP
OHH... YOU'RE DONE?
OKAY, GO TAKE RECESS.
YAY, REEE-CESSSS!
THIS SUCKS. I DON'T KNOW ANY OF THESE... I'LL BE STUCK HERE UNTIL RECESS IS OVER...
URG...
I'M FINISHED...

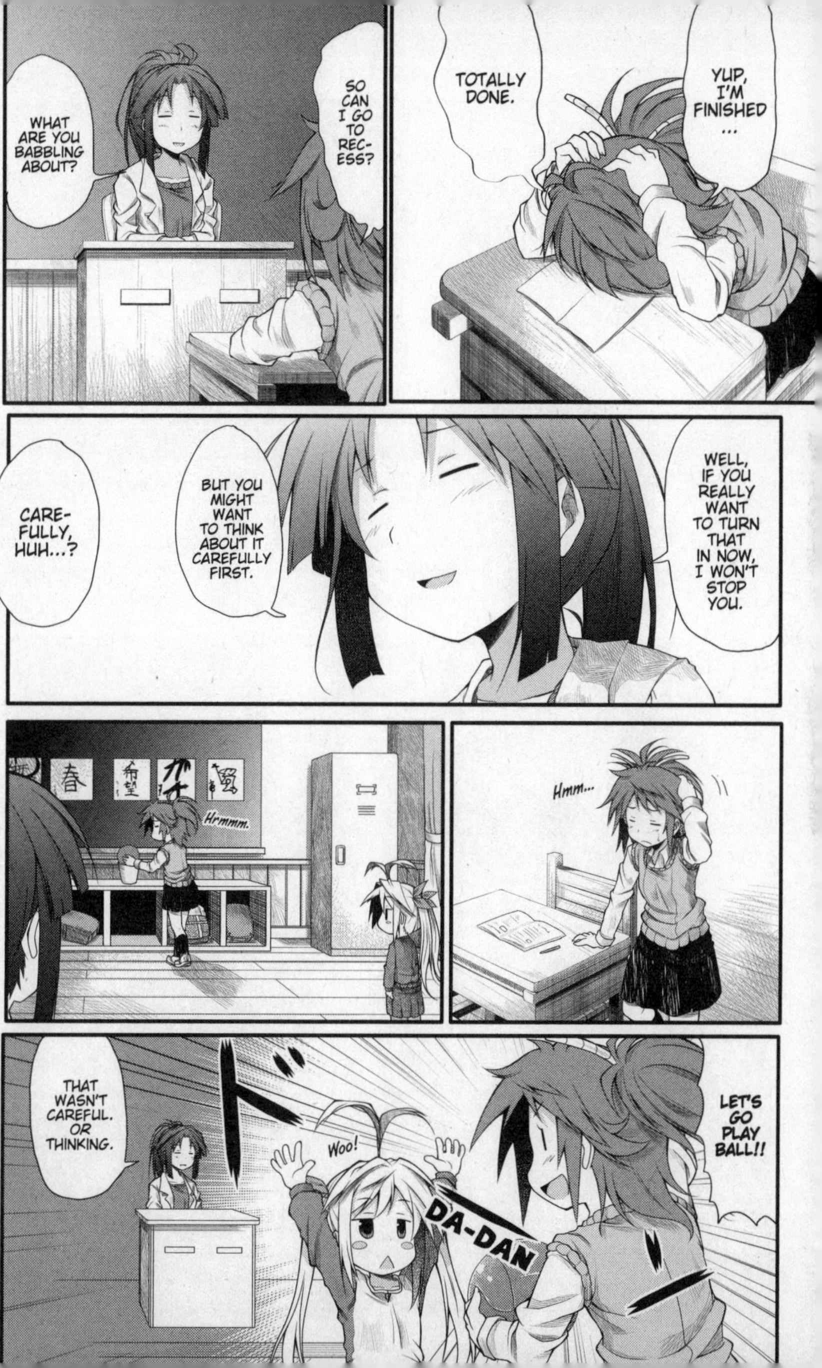
YUP, I'M FINISHED ...
TOTALLY DONE.
SO CAN I GO TO REC-ESS?
WHAT ARE YOU BABBLING ABOUT?
WELL, IF YOU REALLY WANT TO TURN THAT IN NOW, I WON'T STOP YOU.
BUT YOU MIGHT WANT TO THINK ABOUT IT CAREFULLY FIRST.
CARE-FULLY, HUH...?
Hmm...
Hrmmm.
春
LET'S GO PLAY BALL!!
DA-DAN
Woo!
THAT WASN'T CAREFUL. OR THINKING.

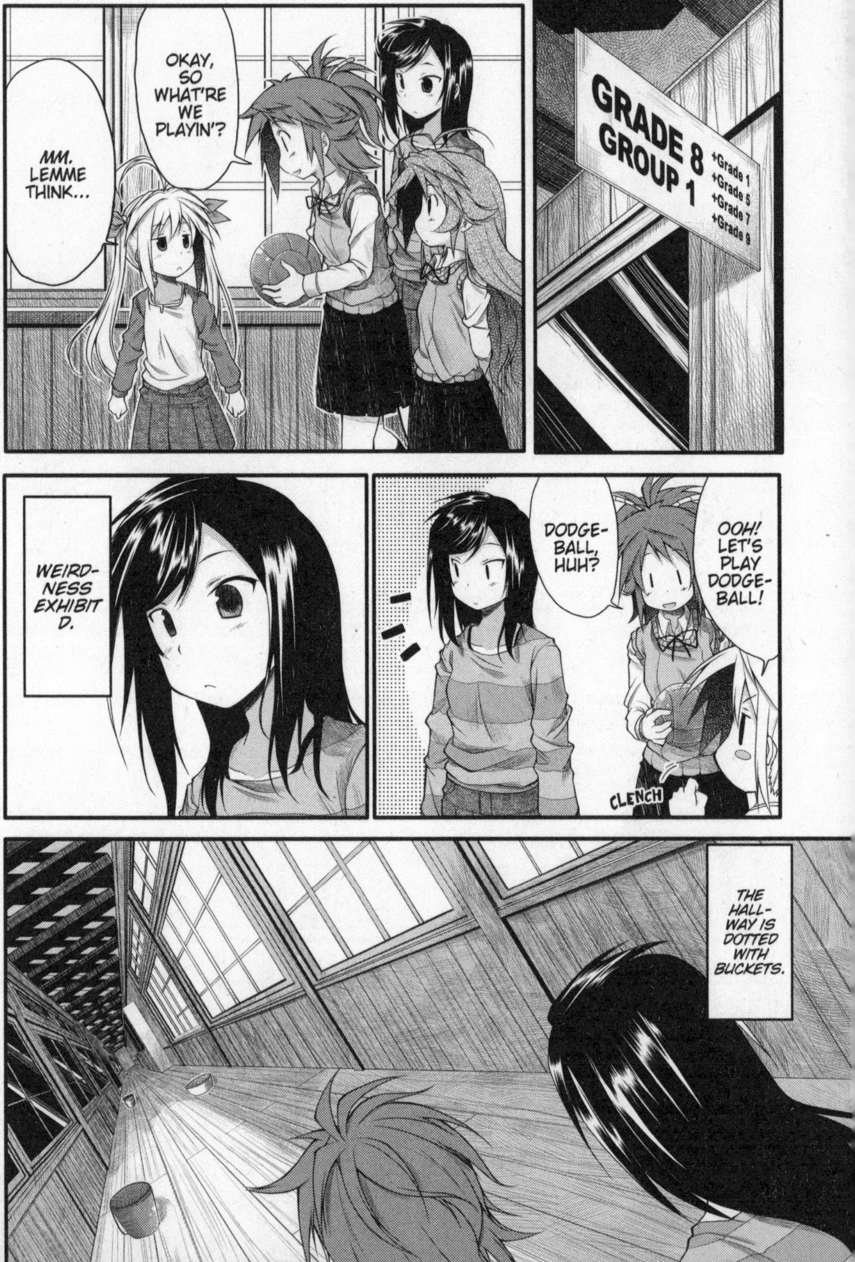
GRADE 8
GROUP 1
+Grade 1
+Grade 5
+Grade 7
+Grade 9
OKAY, SO WHAT'RE WE PLAYIN'?
MM. LEMME THINK...
OOH! LET'S PLAY DODGE-BALL!
DODGE-BALL, HUH?
CLENCH
WEIRD-NESS EXHIBIT D.
THE HALL-WAY IS DOTTED WITH BUCKETS.

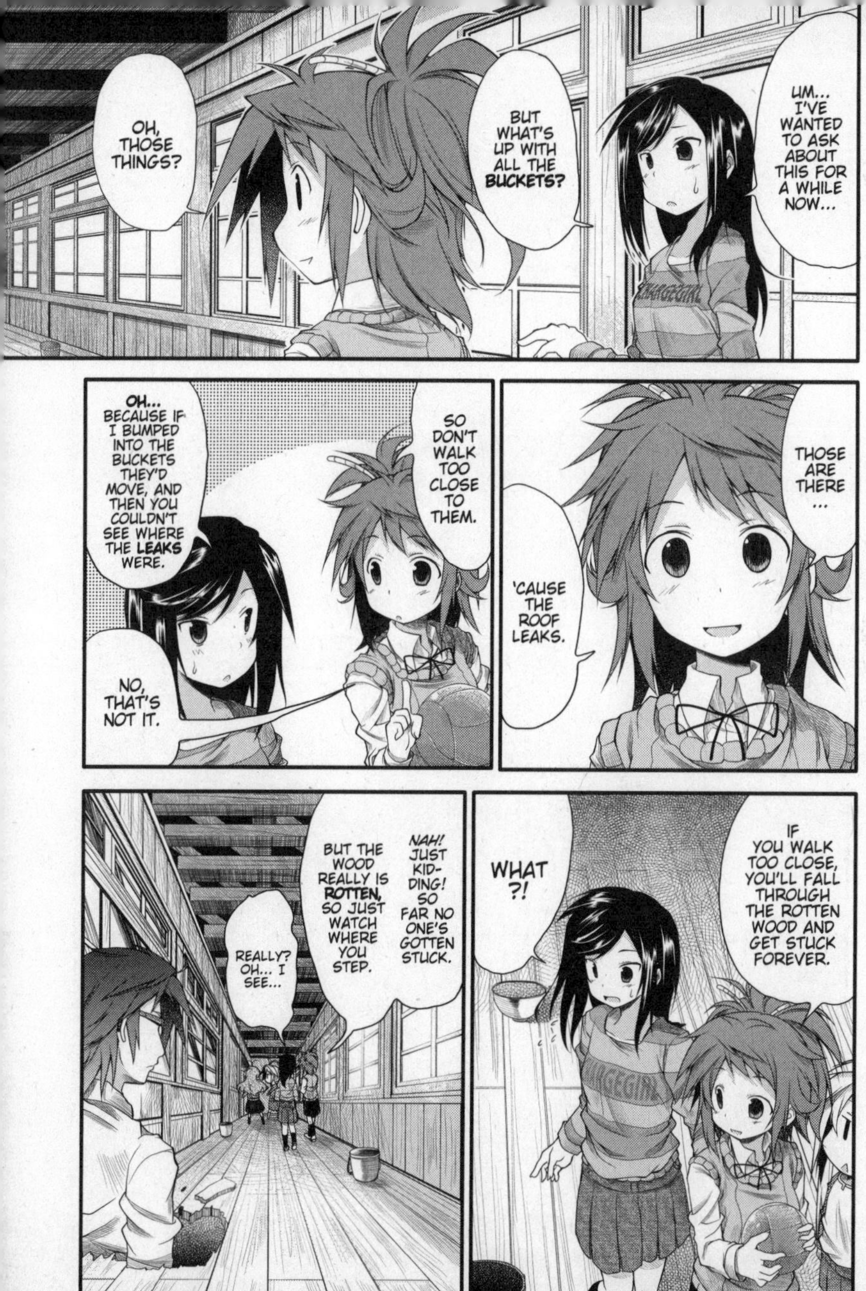
UM... I'VE WANTED TO ASK ABOUT THIS FOR A WHILE NOW...
BUT WHAT'S UP WITH ALL THE **BUCKETS?**
OH, THOSE THINGS?
THOSE ARE THERE...
'CAUSE THE ROOF LEAKS.
SO DON'T WALK TOO CLOSE TO THEM.
OH... BECAUSE IF I BUMPED INTO THE BUCKETS THEY'D MOVE, AND THEN YOU COULDN'T SEE WHERE THE **LEAKS** WERE.
NO, THAT'S NOT IT.
IF YOU WALK TOO CLOSE, YOU'LL FALL THROUGH THE ROTTEN WOOD AND GET STUCK FOREVER.
WHAT?!
NAH! JUST KID-DING! SO FAR NO ONE'S GOTTEN STUCK.
BUT THE WOOD REALLY IS **ROTTEN,** SO JUST WATCH WHERE YOU STEP.
REALLY? OH... I SEE...

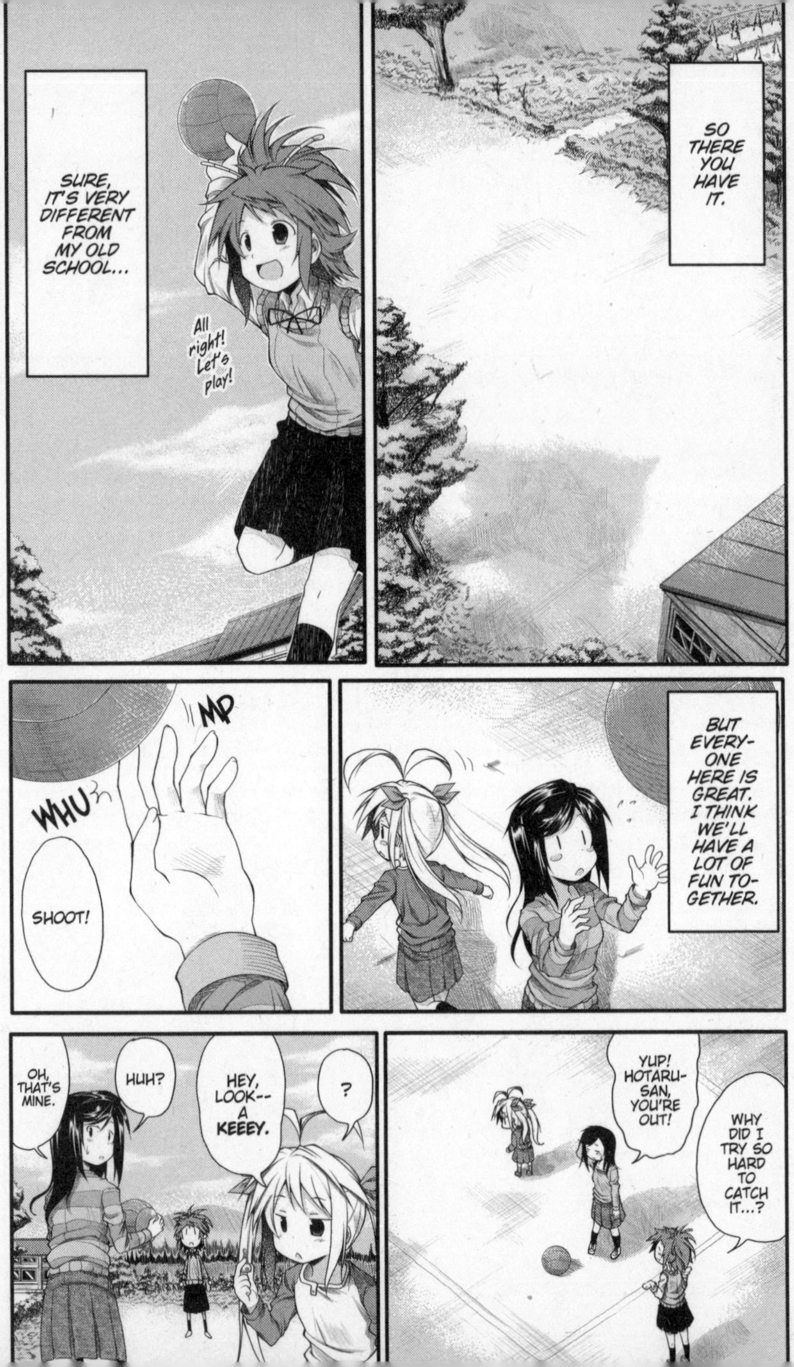
SO THERE YOU HAVE IT.
SURE, IT'S VERY DIFFERENT FROM MY OLD SCHOOL...
All right! Let's play!
BUT EVERY-ONE HERE IS GREAT. I THINK WE'LL HAVE A LOT OF FUN TO-GETHER.
MP
WHU
SHOOT!
YUP! HOTARU-SAN, YOU'RE OUT!
WHY DID I TRY SO HARD TO CATCH IT...?
?
HEY, LOOK-- A KEEEY.
HUH?
OH, THAT'S MINE.

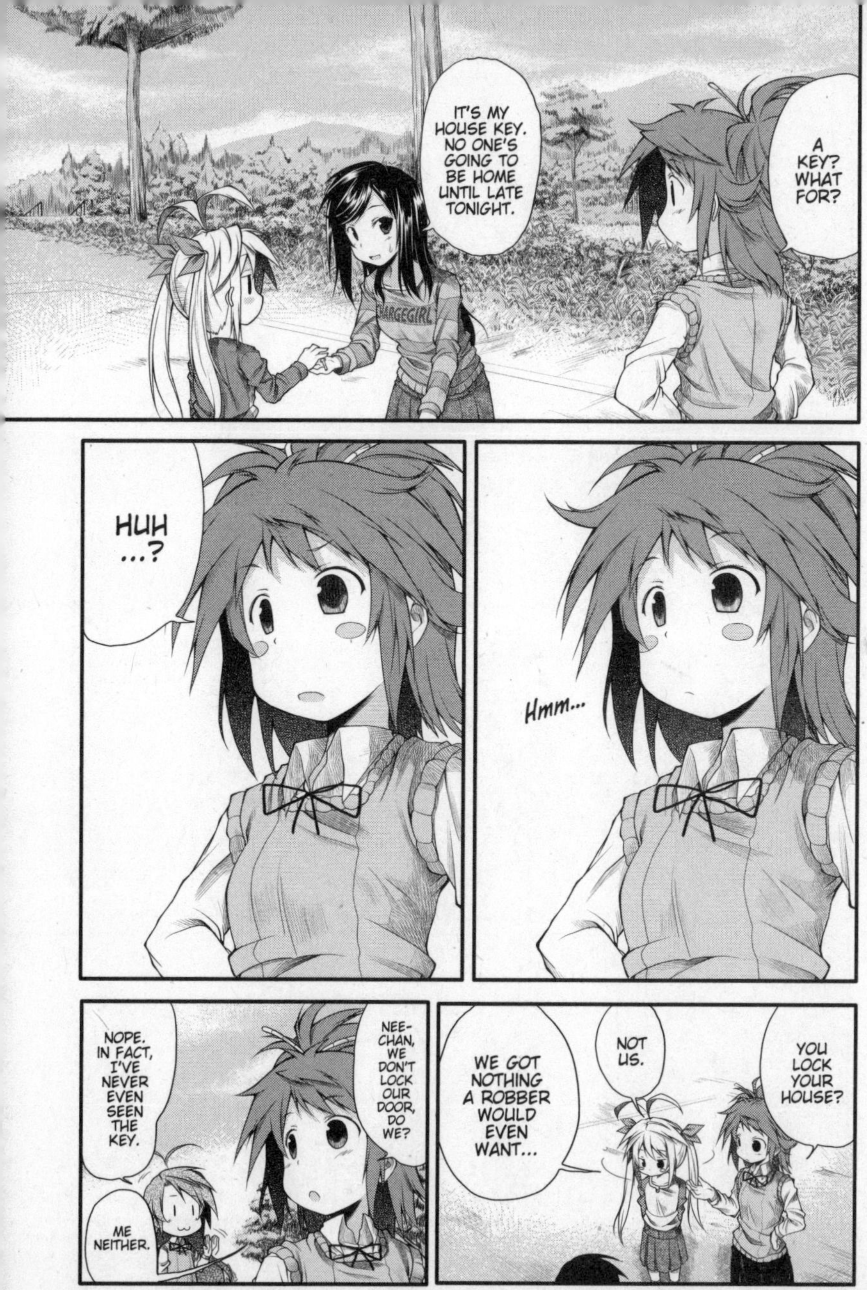
A KEY? WHAT FOR?
IT'S MY HOUSE KEY. NO ONE'S GOING TO BE HOME UNTIL LATE TONIGHT.
Hmm...
HUH ...?
YOU LOCK YOUR HOUSE?
NOT US.
WE GOT NOTHING A ROBBER WOULD EVEN WANT...
NEE-CHAN, WE DON'T LOCK OUR DOOR, DO WE?
NOPE. IN FACT, I'VE NEVER EVEN SEEN THE KEY.
ME NEITHER.

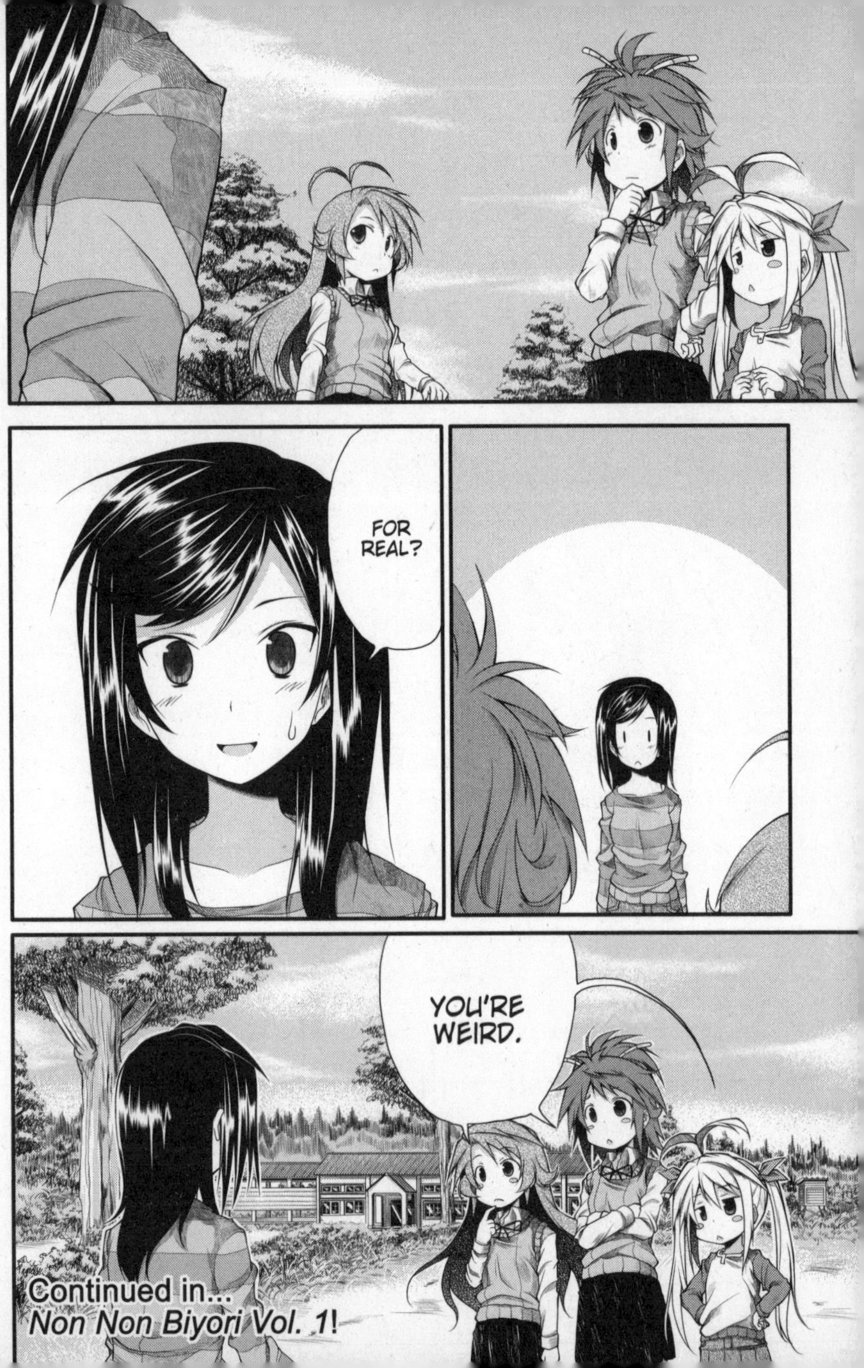
FOR REAL?
YOU'RE WEIRD.
Continued in...
Non Non Biyori Vol. 1!

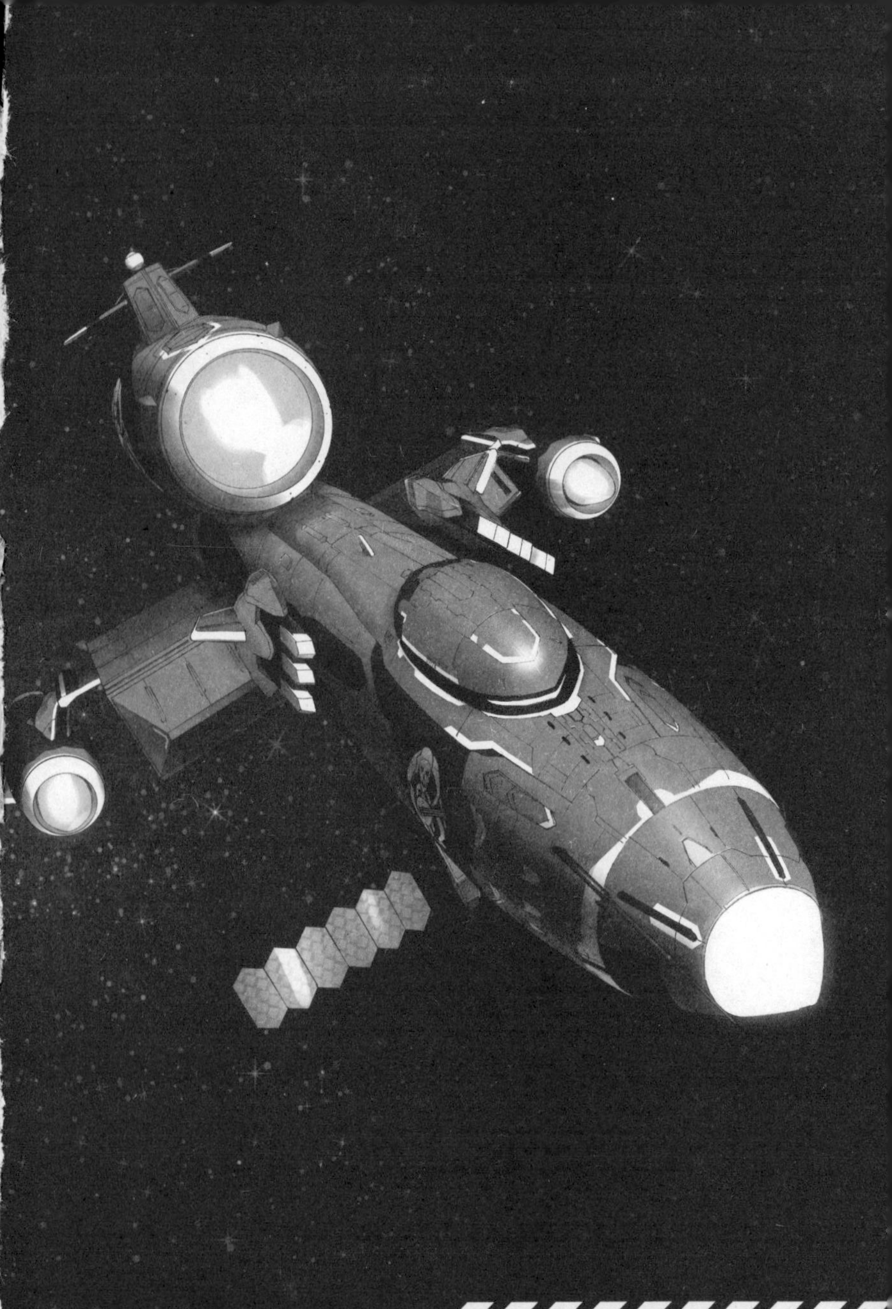

000 BENTENMARU